T0413221

PRAISE FOR

BEYOND
BLOOD QUANTUM

"The tough issues of Native American identity come from within our communities as well as the harmful legacy of oppressive federal Indian policy. From the rise in "pretendians" to the fetishization of Native culture, contributors allow readers to explore the complexities of what it means to belong to a Native Nation, according to their own customs and governance."

—**Karen Diver**, Fond du Lac Band of Lake Superior Chippewa, Senior Advisor to the President for Native American Affairs at the University of Minnesota, Former Chairwoman of Fond du Lac Band of Lake Superior Chippewa, Former Special Assistant to President Obama for Native American Affairs

"Our elders teach us that no man, or government, not even the most powerful nation in the world can take away all that defines who we are as Indigenous people—that the Creator gifted to our foremothers and forefathers at the time of Creation—but ourselves. They say that if we are not mindful of our past experiences of our foremothers and forefathers surviving every conceivable policy and laws imposed upon our people, generation after generation, we can at some point in our journey be capable of becoming our own worst enemy. When we internalize the oppression as exhibited by this nation upon our people, and internalize that oppression, we can become the oppressors. The elders warn and prophesied that when that happens, it will be the beginning of the end of us. It is deviating from our core values as gifted to us by our Creator as the deepest expression of love for us. Blood quantum is the epitome of this departure from the Original Instructions of embracing all sacred beings that our children represent so that our lifeways will continue and thrive. The elders say, they are the sacred beings, gifts from the Creator so that we shall continue as a People. The use of blood, our lifeline, to define our relations and our connections ironically in this time of self determination could be the cause of our end. What the government designed, we shall complete. This cannot be the end of our journey."

—**Regis Pecos**, Regis Pecos, Cochiti, Co-founder and
Co-director of the Leadership Institute at the Santa Fe Indian School,
Former Governor of Cochiti Pueblo, Former Chief of Staff to the Speaker
of the New Mexico House of Representatives

"A testament to the refusal to disappear and inherent Indigenous sovereignty, Beyond Blood Quantum offers profound insights and reflections on the path forward."

—**Wayne Leo Ducheneaux II**, Cheyenne River
Sioux, Chief Advancement Officer, Intertribal Agriculture Council,
Former Vice Chairman of Cheyenne River Sioux Tribe

"Tribal citizens must become informed of where we are and where we are going on the explosive issue of blood quantum. The chapters in this book are a tool for self-education and constitute possible road maps for the future of Indian nations."

—**Henrietta Mann**, Tsetsehestaestse (Cheyenne),
Professor Emerita at Montana State University, Founding President Emerita of the
Cheyenne and Arapaho Tribal College, National Humanities Medal Awardee

"Blood quantum is an issue that all tribes need to be aware of as they exercise their sovereign right to set their membership standards."

—**John Echohawk**, Pawnee, Executive Director,
Native American Rights Fund

BEYOND
BLOOD
QUANTUM

The Great Vanishing Act
Blood Quantum and the Future of Native Nations

by
Kathleen Ratteree and Norbert Hill

greatvanishingact.com

BEYOND BLOOD QUANTUM

REFUSAL TO DISAPPEAR

Edited by
Norbert S. Hill Jr.
Megan Minoka Hill
Desirae Louise Hill

Fulcrum Publishing
Lakewood, Colorado

Copyright © 2025 Norbert Hill

All rights reserved. No part of this book may be reproduced or transmitted in any form or by any means, electronic or mechanical, including photocopying, recording, or by any information storage and retrieval system, without permission in writing from the publisher.

Edited by Norbert S. Hill Jr., Megan Minoka Hill, and Desirae Louise Hill
"Seven Generations," from AN AMERICAN SUNRISE: POEMS by Joy Harjo. Copyright © 2019 by Joy Harjo. Used by permission of W. W. Norton & Company, Inc.
"How to Be a Real Indian." Copyright © 2017 by Kenzie Allen from *Cloud Missives*. Reprinted with permission of Tin House Books, LLC. All rights reserved.
"River" and "How Memory Works" shared with permission of Richard "Lotni" Elm-Hill. Copyright © 2022 by Richard G. Elm-Hill Jr.
Cover Art: *Passing on Traditions*, painting by Daniel Ramirez, depicts the passing on of cultural education. Modified for publication with permission of the artist.

Editor's note:
Authors of essays in this book have individual preferences for treatment of terms, such as capitalization of "tribe/Tribe," "treaty/Treaty," and so on. Wherever possible, we have honored those preferences.

Library of Congress Cataloging-in-Publication Data

Names: Hill, Norbert S., editor. | Hill, Megan Minoka, editor. | Hill, Desirae Louise, editor.
Title: Beyond blood quantum : refusal to disappear / edited by Norbert S. Hill Jr., Megan Minoka Hill, and Desirae Louise Hill.
Description: Lakewood, Colorado : Fulcrum Publishing, 2025. | Includes bibliographical references.
Identifiers: LCCN 2024034374 (print) | LCCN 2024034375 (ebook) | ISBN 9781682754627 (trade paperback) | ISBN 9781682751619 (ebook)
Subjects: LCSH: Indigenous peoples--Legal status, laws, etc.--America. | Indigenous peoples--Kinship--America. | Indigenous peoples--Race identity--America. | Indigenous peoples--America--Ethnic identity. | Citizenship--America.
Classification: LCC KDZ481 .B49 2025 (print) | LCC KDZ481 (ebook) | DDC 342.708/72--dc23/eng/20240731
LC record available at https://lccn.loc.gov/2024034374
LC ebook record available at https://lccn.loc.gov/2024034375

Printed in the United States of America
0 9 8 7 6 5 4 3 2 1

Fulcrum Publishing
7333 W. Jefferson Ave., Suite 225
Lakewood, CO 80235
(800) 992-2908 • (303) 277-1623
www.fulcrumbooks.com

Dedicated to a sense of belonging.
To those who came before us,
and on whose shoulders we stand,
and to those who will come after us.

Contents

xiii   *Acknowledgments*

xv   *Foreword*
       Philip J. Deloria

1   **River**
       Richard "Lotni" Elm-Hill

3   **Moving Past the Flawed Equations of Blood and Property**
       David E. Wilkins

13   **Degree of Indian Blood**
       Amber Starks

21   **The Color of Blood: Race, Power, and the Dangerous Legacy of Racial Purity Laws**
       Doug Kiel

29   **The Federal Indian Blood Quantum Fiction**
       Gabriel S. Galanda

43   **Practicality: Native American Tribal Adoption in Historical Perspective**
       Laurence M. Hauptman

53   **How to Be a Real Indian**
       Kenzie Allen

57 In the Wake of Pretendians
Kanyʌhtakelu (Snow scattered here and there)
Rebecca M. Webster and
Yakoyʌtehtauhi (She is continually going along learning)
Amelia M. Webster

65 The Explosion of the 2020 Census "Indian" Population and Its Implications for Tribal Policymaking
Karl Eschbach and Jonathan Taylor

83 Now What?
Suzan Shown Harjo

93 Saving Seeds
Kenzie Allen

95 "There's More at Stake Than Just My Love Life!" Understanding Tribal Enrollment as a Reproductive Justice Issue
Danielle Lucero

107 Gidoodeminaanig
Kadin Mills

115 Who's Your People? Living with a Multi-tribal Native Identity
Jennifer Hill-Kelley and Sadie Kelley

123 Life at the Intersections: A Black Oneida Perspective on Blood Quantum and Belonging
Marena Bridges

131 Food, Sovereignty, and Belonging
Toni House

139 How Memory Works
Richard "Lotni" Elm-Hill

141 The Long Arc of Time: Who Are You?
Kcheyonkote Burton W. Warrington

149 Learning Our Path into the Future
Artley M. Skenandore

157 Blood Quantum and the Auto-Colonization of the
Michigan Anishinaabek
Matthew L.M. Fletcher

175 Path Forward: Indigenous Place In-Community
Lois Stevens

183 Two Truths
John Danforth

189 Osage Spring
Jim Gray

195 Aanikoobijigan: Intergenerational Connections as the
Foundation of Contemporary Citizenship Requirements
Jill Doerfler

203 Seven Generations
Joy Harjo

205 Afterword
207 Questions for Reflection
209 Notes
241 Contributors
261 Index

Acknowledgments

With full hearts we offer our most sincere gratitude and appreciation to each of the authors who graciously and passionately share their thoughts through the enclosed essays. We recognize each for the time, energy, and life's work that they bring to writing. Their voices, leadership, and courage to delve into these issues brings Indian Country closer to viable solutions. Special mention to Jill Doerfler for her help in naming this volume.

We thank author and poet Joy Harjo for being a light in the dark and allowing us to republish the poem "Seven Generations." We also thank poet Kenzie Allen for writing an original piece for this collection while contemplating new life. To poet Lotni for providing safe passage through his good mind and good words.

We also give thanks to artist Daniel Ramirez, who shared the painting *Passing on Traditions* to adorn the cover.

Many thanks also go to Kathleen Ratteree, whose community involvement and editorial contributions to the first volume were critical in seeding this anthology. Without Kathleen's effort and diligence, neither book would have been made possible.

We thank our friends at Fulcrum Publishing for their help and support in publishing this work. A special thanks to Betty Christiansen for her keen attention to style and detail. And a nod to our colleagues for their efforts to facilitate permissions.

We are humbled by the steadfast friendship of the Endeavor Foundation, whose leaders listen and understand the importance of Indigenous self-determination. The support and belief in our efforts to address citizenship is unparalleled. We are eternally grateful.

We also recognize that none of the work gets done without the support of our nonhuman and human relatives, family, friends, and companions on the path.

With humility, we acknowledge that this collection of essays and poems brings together resonant voices, and there are many more to be heard. In shaping this volume, our intention is that it gives more than it takes. That this work offers something to the heart, the mind, and spirit. That you leave anything that doesn't serve you and forgive any errors that might remain.

Finally, we offer our gratitude to all those before us and those here for engaging these hard yet vital conversations to ensure the future of Indian Country—especially for everyone who will come after.

DESIRAE LOUISE HILL

MEGAN MINOKA HILL

NORBERT S. HILL JR.

Foreword

The Indian Reorganization Act (IRA) of 1934 has nineteen sections, roughly divided into three parts. The first part deals with Indian landholding, ending the disastrous allotment policy and setting out new provisions for trust lands. The second part, sections nine through fifteen, turns to economic development funds, specific cases, and tribal exemptions. Sections sixteen through eighteen set out the mechanics for tribal governance under the act. But there is one final section, nineteen, that a reader might have expected to appear at the beginning of the act rather than the end, for it is a definition:

> The term "Indian" as used in this Act shall include all persons of Indian descent who are members of any recognized Indian tribe now under Federal jurisdiction, and all persons who are descendants of such members who were, on June 1, 1934, residing within the present boundaries of any Indian reservation, and shall further include all other persons of one-half or more Indian blood.

It was not the first time, nor the last, that quantifications of Indian blood appeared in American law and policy, but its location in the Indian Reorganization Act made it a critically important instance, one that reverberates to the present and poses challenges for Native American futures.

The IRA legislation has always been an oddity. Driven by the Indian policy studies and political reform movements of the 1920s and energized by the pace and urgency of the New Deal, it ended the disastrous policy of allotment and encouraged tribal nations to set up governmental structures. At the same time, however, it established conditions for a neoimperial practice of indirect rule and continued familiar traditions of paternalistic oversight. As Vine Deloria Jr. and Clifford Lytle have demonstrated, the original act sought to go much further in undoing the effects of American colonialism, but it was attenuated and transformed as the

legislation passed through the houses of Congress. A deeper question, perhaps, is why the United States was willing to pass such an act in the first
place? After all, by the turn of the twentieth century, the United States had
nearly completed a multiscaled and devastatingly adaptive set of policies
for acquiring Indian land, shrinking Native landholdings, and destroying
Native language and culture among those who survived.

It worked something like this:

English settlers originally imagined a continental vision of Indigenous lands. In their early maps, they drew lines straight west from their
chartered colonies, claiming territory in narrow (or sometimes large)
swaths that ran to the Mississippi River and, in some cases, crossed the
entirety of North America. Treaties and contracts paired together with
colonial charters to create the crucial diplomatic forms through which
land was alienated. This continental sensibility took concrete shape with
the Proclamation Line of 1763, with which England tried unsuccessfully
to use the Appalachian Mountains to divide Indian land from settled land.

After they won independence, Americans tried similar restrictions,
even as they moved to shrink their strategies of Indian land acquisition
from continental to regional scales. Crucially, the Northwest Ordinance
of 1787 laid out the way in which territories could become fully fledged
states: get sixty thousand Americans to settle there. These new states were
regional-sized political entities, and so Americans adopted a regional strategy in acquiring Indian land. Indian people could be removed to someplace
else, emptying the territorial region. Or they could give up most of their
land and see their populations compressed into shrunken spaces—reservations—and contained there, isolated, segregated, and preyed upon.

Over time, the regional strategy also proved insufficient, for
Native people continued to hold their reservation lands, and so a new
generation of Americans figured out how they might acquire those lands
as well. Colonialism shapeshifted again, shrinking its spatial imagi-
nary to that of the local neighborhood. Reservations were allotted into
parcels, and then assigned to individuals, who could then be stripped
of their lands through all manner of scams and manipulations. This
third strategy *disaggregated* Native lands—no longer could those lands
be held collectively—and *desegregated* them: now white settlers intermingled with Indian neighbors on adjoining 160-acre parcels. Those

Indian neighbors were often forced to give their children up to boarding schools while missionaries, agents, boss farmers, and teachers sought to remake Native life on these individualized lands.

The United States adopted other strategies too. They made Indians citizens, charged them taxes, and then seized their lands when they went into arrears. They used eminent domain to confiscate tribal and individual land for "public good," in the form of national parks, reclamation projects, and military bases. But it was the allotment policy that drove the most consistent land loss in the late nineteenth and early twentieth centuries. Highly effective, it might well have been a final mechanism in the centuries-long taking of Native lands.

Instead, the IRA explicitly repudiated the allotment policy. What happened? We usually chalk that policy reversal up to the curious romantic fanaticism of Commissioner of Indian Affairs John Collier and a conjunction of progressive reform and New Deal legislation. If you squint a little, the first part of the IRA looks something like a decolonizing move, and the second part looks something like a restoration of limited sovereignty.

But as many Native commentators have pointed out over the years, the IRA was just as much an expression of yet another form of colonialism, a new strategy of neoimperial indirect rule. The new tribal governments were to be highly beholden to the US government; they were, among other things, to serve as agreement signers and negotiating parties that enabled further attacks on tribal resources. And buried within eighteen articles laden with transformational change, legal language, and a bit of money was section nineteen, which told Indians who was and was not an Indian.

If the IRA itself was an oddity, so too was this article. If your tribe was under federal jurisdiction and you were a member of that tribe, you got to be an Indian. Membership was defined not in the political sense that tribes would later demand, but as a matter of descent. The language of blood was not explicit in that first phrase, but it was present just the same. If you were a descendant of a member and you lived on a recognized reservation, you also got to be an Indian. Thus, in the first two clauses (in one long sentence!) did the idea of the "federally recognized tribe" enter the law, as applied to individual identities. Those tribes not federally recognized—for whatever reasons—would have to struggle for that recognition for their members to be considered Indians. The final phrase, at last, lays down the term "blood" and gives us the quantum: "one half or more Indian blood."

Article nineteen does two things. It points to a tribally situated, descent-based way of determining membership, and it sets a high mark: a quantized, verifiable demand for "blood," as determined by parentage. In the years that followed, the Bureau of Indian Affairs (BIA) would publish its famous charts, modern versions of the old Spanish castas, outlining every possible combination of parentage, down to the sixty-fourth fraction. But the BIA would also apply the second part of the provision—blood quantum—to the first, demanding that tribes adopt blood quantum as the measure of their descent-based determinations of membership. As Jill Doerfler has demonstrated in the essay "Making Ourselves Whole with Words: A Short History of White Earth Anishinaabeg Tribal Citizenship Criteria," for instance, the Department of the Interior rejected the White Earth constitution repeatedly—until they agreed to a blood quantum level for membership.

This distinction—between descent as a *general idea*, applicable in different ways, and quantum—literally *quantifiable* as a fixed number (if not always easily calculated)—has dogged decisions about tribal citizenship ever since. Because Indian people have a long history of outmarriage, it becomes increasingly difficult to maintain a citizenry that meets blood quantum standards; thus, Native people encountered a new great vanishing act, one that echoed the old nineteenth-century version. The old "vanishing" insisted that by a "law of nature" Indian people were destined to melt away into nothingness at the approach of "civilization." That idea was an ideological one, which rendered harmless and natural the violence of American dispossession. White settlers described themselves through "manifest destiny"; they defined Indians as the subjects of a preordained and inevitable disappearing act.

Blood quantum carried ideological freight to be sure—ideas about purity, essence, contamination, mixing, hybridity, and one-drop rules, and that's just for starters. But the quantizing of "blood" proved to be a deeply *materialist* practice as well. It offered "real" criteria, supposedly hard evidence for definitions of Indian identity that led to inclusion or exclusion. And as Native people would soon learn, over time and across generations blood quantum almost always ran toward exclusion. It was the poison pill in the IRA, the secret weapon that made giving up allotment imaginable, the colon that kept things colonial: a new and effective strategy aimed, like all the others, at the acquisition of Indian land and the attenuation of Indian life. From "full blood" to "half" to "quarter" to "eighth" to "sixteenth" and beyond, Indian blood—and with it, Indian populations—were once again destined to vanish.

The initial publication, in 2017, of *The Great Vanishing Act: Blood Quantum and the Future of Native Nations* arose out of a specific case—the Oneida Trust and Enrollment Committee's efforts to deal with a declining population of citizens who met the one-quarter blood quantum enrollment requirement. But as editors Kathleen Ratteree and Norbert Hill insisted, the Oneida case was emblematic of Indian Country as a whole. Blood quantum and enrollment was a shared problem that therefore demanded the sharing of many streams of Native thought and creativity. Accordingly, they convened a robust conversation, one that included personal testimony, fiction and art, technical arguments, and polemics emerging from the worlds of literature, genetic science, history, law, and politics. Adopted in classrooms, passed around as separate essays, engaged by tribal leaders, *The Great Vanishing Act* proved to be a catalyst for a discussion that crossed Indian Country. What was then an edited collection of reflections aiming for accessibility and range has, with this latest effort, assumed the august status of Volume One. The issues have continued to shift and change. And no one ever said a single book was enough to define *any* conversation requiring meaning, depth, and reflection.

And thus, we arrive at Volume Two. Much has happened over the last six years, and the time is right for a new round of discussion, an effort to advance our thinking still further. How have the ongoing revelations of identity fraud in academe and the entertainment industry, the presence of "pretendian" lists and vernacular investigations, and the critiques of those queries changed our sense of blood quantum as a tribal and/or colonial practice? How did the racial and epidemiological reckonings of the pandemic years change the conversation around blood quantum, multiracialism, tribal sovereignty, and the obligations of cross-racial alliance? How might the *McGirt v. Oklahoma* decision and other legal cases cause shifts in practices of identity, not simply in Oklahoma but across

Indian Country? How have tribal nations dealt with new possibilities surrounding language fluency, kinship and citizenship models, disenrollment issues, placemaking, food sovereignty, and multitribalism? How have the intensifying realities of climate change put an exclamation mark on every question we might pose and ponder?

Beyond Blood Quantum: Refusal to Disappear mixes new voices with ones familiar from the first book. Like that effort, this book aims to generate community conversations, to inspire the next generations, and to support Native nations as they take up these issues in the years to come. Appropriately, it makes the same demands of its readers: questioning, listening, thinking, and deep engagement, all cast with the same tolerance, intelligence, courage, and humor always in abundance when Native folks gather to consider a problem—especially one such as this, which cuts so deeply to the heart of Indigenous survivance. May we all learn as much from this book as we did from the first.

PHILIP J. DELORIA

River

They say his tears
Made the rivers
His dreadlocks—the rivers
Her blood—the rivers
The braid down her back
A river

River

They say his tears
Made the rivers

His dreadlocks
The rivers

Her blood
The rivers

The braid down her back
A river

LOTNI

Moving Past the Flawed Equations
of Blood and Property

DAVID E. WILKINS

Native nations are bounded but inclusive communities that pride themselves on maintaining distinctive religious-cultural identities while also incorporating—whether through force, invitation, or acceptance—individuals from other Indigenous, racial, and ethnic groups. Native peoples have always managed to creatively augment their numbers, incorporating new members and ideas that keep their populations healthy. Outsiders, from Natives to Europeans, Africans, or others, were frequently welcomed into Indigenous communities through traditional ceremonies and later through ceremonies sanctioned by governmental action. This openness evidenced an inherent cultural confidence and generosity that were hallmarks of Native nations—qualities that for millennia were bolstered, not threatened, by inclusion.

Native lands, languages, spiritual beliefs and activities, and well-honed, longstanding kinship systems provided sacred boundaries and frameworks. Thus, each nation, and the individuals, clans, and moieties constituting those nations, could generally rest assured in their collective and individual identities.

The advent of European and, later, Euro-American colonialism had dramatic effects on Indigenous lives, properties, liberties, and identities. In fact, as Martin Case points out in *The Relentless Business of Treaties*,[1] a splendid examination of the white men who negotiated treaties with Native nations on behalf of the federal government between 1778 and 1871, the collision of the West with Indigenous peoples was a metaphysical confrontation between two radically different ways of understanding and relating to the natural world.

For Indigenous peoples, the most important organizing principle was *kinship*—"where rivers are relatives and shape the traditional political structures, cultural infrastructure, commerce, and international diplomacy of those societies" and which "defines moral behavior and determines which communally made decisions are politically acceptable."[2] Case continues and notes that for non-Natives, exemplified here by the behavior and institutions of the federal government, the states, and many white Americans, the most important ongoing principle has always been *property*—with white Americans and policymakers viewing their relationship to the natural world as a *property relationship*.

As Case describes it, "the westward growth of the US—the business of treaty making—was essentially the expansion of the system of property."[3] John Locke and others provided much of the intellectual language guiding America's founding fathers and helped the United States in its infancy to become the first nation based on the idea that "private property could be equated with personal Liberty." This way of relating to the natural world is rooted in Judeo-Christian history with its command in the book of Genesis to "fill the earth and subdue it."

These two metaphysical realities—kinship and property—are fundamentally irreconcilable. The property system of the United States that dominates our political, economic, and cultural affairs and has been accepted in many parts of the world is the basis for the climate crisis that threatens our very existence. While the Indigenous system persists in various degrees and patterns throughout Native America, it suffered through a cataclysmic period of social experimentation in which the federal government tried mightily—via boarding schools, the imposition of Western political and legal systems, Christian missionary activity, and especially the dramatic subdivision of Native communal property into private property increments—to "save" Natives from themselves by compelling massive changes in virtually every sphere of life.

Ironically, privatization of property through individual allotments was hailed as a panacea for all the US government-created ills that devastated Native peoples. The bureaucratic process of dividing the lands of Indian Country and the determination of ownership eligibility became dominant concerns for federal officials and, of course, Tribal nations. The calculations were not simple. Complicating land division were the resources appurtenant to the allotment (be they water, coal, oil, or gas). Ownership hinged on who should be entitled to continued trust recognition (that is, wardship or incompetent status, in the US Supreme Court's parlance).

During this period, we also begin to see greater evidence of factionalism or segmentation in many Indigenous communities. Whether driven by education (returned boarding school students versus nonformally educated students), religion (those who adopted Christianity, remained "traditional," or attempted to blend the two together), geographic residence (remained on the reservation or moved away), allotment status (allotted and retained the parcel, allotted and sold or leased the parcel, or never allotted), or blood quantum (full blood, half blood, or mixed race), the result was Native communities internally divided more than ever before.

Blood Matters

While each of these actualizing elements heavily impacted Native communities and their collective identity, it is the last factor—blood quantum—that begs for more attention. Ample literature has been produced in recent decades that focuses on the origin, dispersal, and myriad problems the blood quantum system has generated for those Indigenous peoples who continue to utilize it in some fashion as definitional criteria in determining whether a Native person is or is not a bona fide tribal citizen.[4]

Of course, as much of the previous research has shown, federal lawmakers who initially enacted blood quantum statutes and Bureau of Indian Affairs administrative officials who drafted blood quantum rules and regulations did so, in large part, because of reasons related to *property*. That is to say, the seemingly cut-and-dried math of blood quantum was a cynical, underhanded way to minimize the funds, benefits, and resources expended on behalf of Native nations and their citizens. The formula seemed to always end up as subtraction, magically reducing the actual number of communities and individuals eligible to receive federal financial support. As the population was fractionated and subtracted, the expenses associated with the trust obligation diminished in tandem. These bureaucratically vicious yet bloodless means sought to erase entire peoples and thereby reduce the federal budget allocated under treaties and statutes to Native affairs.[5]

Interestingly, and not surprisingly, federal and state officials creatively applied precisely the opposite social and racial arrangement to African Americans. In that instance, blood quantum was all about addition. By devising the infamous one-drop rule that maintained a single drop of African blood made a person Black, the government sought to increase the number of persons who could legally be held in bondage, thus setting up a maniacal system to maintain slavery as an economic institution in perpetuity. After emancipation, the calculation continued to support patently discriminatory Jim Crow legislation that severely constrained the civil and human rights of African Americans even after the Thirteenth, Fourteenth, and Fifteenth Amendments to the Constitution had been ratified in 1865, 1868, and 1870, respectively, in the wake of the US Civil War.[6]

As Vine Deloria Jr. succinctly put it in 1969 in *Custer Died for Your Sins*, "Because the Negro labored, he was considered a draft animal. Because the Indian occupied large areas of land, he was considered a wild animal."[7] In a society that valued property over virtually everything else, *more* draft animals were required to maintain and grow the economy, but *fewer* wild animals were necessary because they were considered nuisances or threats. Thus, blood quantum was a powerful economic tool created by the US government to control resources and property by simple addition or subtraction, depending on the need. It was never about kinship or humanity.

Where to from Here?

The tension between kinship and property continues unabated. In fact, it has become even more complex as increasing numbers of Native political and economic elites are now embracing the property paradigm, whether through the use of DNA testing or reconfiguring existing blood quantum criteria when making calculations about questions of Native identity and enrollment standards. We see this in the decisions of some Native lawmakers—typically those from Nations with well-to-do gaming enterprises—when they choose to disenroll otherwise bona fide members, claiming, usually with little or no evidence, that those to be disenrolled lacked sufficient or inappropriate blood quantum to remain on the nation's rolls. This is not an uncommon problem for a number of Indigenous communities, including those like the Chukchansi Tribe in California.[8]

The question of how to address the massive problems generated by Tribal nations' ongoing reliance on blood quantum (and now DNA testing) as the primary definitional criteria is a "wicked" problem, as Keith Grint, Warwick University professor emeritus of public leadership, termed it. In other words, it is a problem of great complexity because it "cannot be removed from its environment, solved, and returned without affecting the environment."[9] If it were merely a "tame" problem, it would be easily resolved, because while tame problems may be complicated, they are usually resolvable—for example, how to build a railroad, how to prepare for heart surgery, and so on. But like the effort to create universal health coverage in the United States, figuring out how to solve global warming, or addressing persistent antisocial behavior, dealing with the question of how to decide who belongs in a given Native community has become a "wicked" problem because no single individual has a definitive answer. In other words, "wicked problems require the transfer of authority from individual to collective because only collective engagement can hope to address the problem."[10]

There are, therefore, no elegant or simple solutions to the blood quantum quandary, in part because of the legion of complicating factors discussed earlier that have been thrust upon Native peoples since the early colonial era—Western education, Christianity, capitalism, forced removal, land allotments, and ultimately blood quantum laws and policies, to name but a few. The fact that some federal policymakers continue to insist that Native nations have enrollment policies that factor in blood degree is a hard reality that Indigenous governments have to bear in mind.

Blood quantum is often wrongly conflated with genealogical relations, which have always mattered to Indigenous peoples. Entire sociocultural structures were predicated on kinship ties that, unlike blood quantum, sustained and expanded relations—a calculation based on multiplication, not subtraction. As Ella Deloria, a prominent anthropologist, put it in 1944: "Kinship ties being that important, blood connections were assiduously traced and remembered, no matter how far back, if only they could be definitely established. That was no easy feat either since there were no records. However distant a relative might seem according to the white man's method of reckoning, he would be claimed as Dakota."[11]

Vine Deloria's Suggested Reforms

Of course, unlike some observers, I do not worry about Native nation bloodlines becoming so thinned out by outmarriage that we might become extinct. As an example, the Red Lake Nation of Anishinaabe in Minnesota, which requires one-quarter blood quantum for enrollment purposes, adopted an ordinance in 2019, amending their constitution, and declared that every member who was on the 1958 base roll, regardless of the blood degree at the time, was henceforth to be recognized as a full-blood. This action also increased the blood quantum of the base roll members. As a result, Red Lake's membership increased immediately by more than three thousand.[12] This politically dramatic alteration of facts shows that Natives can be quite creative in maintaining their continuity, even if such actions do nothing more than postpone the need for far more fundamental changes to community identity.

Vine Deloria Jr. was an astute observer of the Indigenous condition, and in the broad corpus of his work had occasion to address national and individual identity. His most detailed assessment appeared in a 1977 special report for the Field Foundation, *A Better Day for Indians*, wherein he offered, with his signature direct practical savvy, some possible strategies that he believed might help Tribes deal with collective and individual recognition of Native peoples, both internally and intergovernmentally: (1) a uniform recognition of Indian communities, (2) a clarification of Tribal membership, and (3) a standard definition of the status of an Indian Tribe. The second is directly on point.[13]

Much as his Aunt Ella had observed thirty years earlier, he noted: "Prior to the establishment of formal legal relationships with the United States, tribal membership was a function of clans and families, and adoption ceremonies many times brought new members into a tribe, often to replace people killed in war. *No tribe is genetically pure, now or at any time in the historical past*"[14] (emphasis added). He also warned those Native leaders who were acting more from an economic orientation that membership was much more than that: "Some, no doubt, will complain," he said, "that establishing an accurate roll interferes with the established right of an Indian tribe to determine its membership. In recent years this doctrine has been breaking down. The application of the 1968 Indian Civil Rights Act to tribal governments has increased the pressure to open membership to Indians on the basis of more reasonable criteria, as tribal membership is seen more and more as a *property right rather than a citizenship status. But continued deprivation of the rights of individual Indians by tribal governments using the shield of tribal sovereignty is much more destructive of Indian communities in the long run than revision of the rolls"*[15] (emphasis added).

After nearly half a century, Deloria's views on membership conditions still resonate, as do his criticisms of both Native politicians and federal officials. He acknowledged the reality of Indigenous inclusivity rather than exclusivity of members/citizens; stressed that blood quantum was problematic, inadequate, and unjust as the central criteria for enrollment; and noted the long-term benefits of having a more flexible, sensible, and historically grounded approach to deciding who belongs in a Native nation.

While Deloria was a visionary, he was also a pragmatist, fully understanding that it would be challenging for Native nations to undertake the kind of detailed enrollment changes he knew were necessary. Unfortunately, too many Native governments are presently entrusting their enrollment policies and practices to outside non-Native-controlled organizations like Creating Stronger Nations, Inc., Automated Election Services, Falmouth Institute, J. Dalton Institute, and others, rather than relying on their own citizens working with their own members and, when required, federal officials.

There is more than sufficient knowledge within Indian Country to tackle the critical task of creating authentic and verifiable rolls. To hire high-priced outside organizations or consultants, even those who claim to be Native allied or owned, diminishes Tribal governments and disrespects the power and agency of their citizens. As paid consultants, their commitment is to find a quick, efficient solution to a problem that has no easy fix. That external business approach means their expensive answers will be tidy and written with an air of authoritative finality, much like any other mainstream legal matter dealing with property and ownership. It does not mean those answers will be the right ones. Nor does it mean they will be humane and ethical, and certainly there is no alignment with traditional ways that are still pervasive in many Indigenous communities.

These third-party entities will never have the same core values, historical understanding, or fundamental commitment that a group of competent, dedicated, and fully trained Native members possess. All they would need are the necessary historical data, including Tribal records, family accounts, and federal records that are often incomplete, at best. With this information, solid and consistent ethical guidelines, and a willingness to engage respectfully and meaningfully with their own citizens, they could use member-given authority to make authentic determinations.

Conclusion

Native citizens must provide the authority needed to move beyond the dangerous, antitraditional, and insidious math of blood quantum. By demanding that their leaders develop and employ sensible, transparent policies that offer a realistic pathway to gain or retain citizenship, as well as a fair process to question and appeal decisions, we can reject an equation designed to erase Native peoples from their own lands and traditions. No Native nation should invest in any venture that chooses profit over people or pits sovereignty against human and civil rights. Instead, we can choose to multiply and enhance who we are, as we have always done. This means a commitment to the longer path following traditional values of inclusion and community survival, leaving behind efficient, property-based business models.

Ultimately, such a detailed, compassionate *Native* solution is the only realistic way to eliminate the subtractive calculations of blood quantum.

*What is our responsibility to our ancestors, ourselves,
and our descendants?*

Degree of Indian Blood

AMBER STARKS

Blood quantum—the colonial metric of how "Indian" one is by attempting to calculate one's "degree of Indian blood"—is ultimately about settler colonial violence and domination. It is a colonial policy that seeks to dispossess Native peoples of our lands, cultures, identities, political sovereignty, and self-determination. It is essentially genocide. Therefore, it is vital to understand how blood quantum as a tool of erasure was and continues to be weaponized against Native peoples and nations, and to recognize the secondary intent, which is the nullification of the settler state's responsibility to Native nations via its treaty obligations.

It is crucial to acknowledge blood quantum for what it is: an ongoing insidious settler colonial project of termination. A project designed to exacerbate and accelerate the attempted extermination of Native peoples through the redefining of who is and who is not Native on colonial terms, and by extension through the limiting of belonging and citizenship within our nations. And ultimately through the fracturing of relationships between and among one another. I believe settler architects intended for this specific strategy to accomplish thoroughly and with precision what smallpox blankets, warfare, removal and relocation, rations and starvation, treaty breaking, land privatization, boarding schools, urbanization, and what every other settler campaign ultimately could not (independently or in concert) achieve—that is, to persuade Native peoples to agree to our own demise.

After all the unsuccessful attempts at addressing the "Indian problem" quickly, definitively, and without resistance, colonizers and their budding settler nation must have realized that genocide was impossible if the Natives they sought to destroy refused to willingly submit. They must

13

have then concluded that Indigenous people must become co-conspirators who would accept, internalize, and cooperate with the process if it was to be successful. Finally, they must have determined that if they could not overtly force our surrender (and by extension force us to forfeit our autonomy and stewardship of our ancestral lands) through acute violence, brutality, and the threat of death, they then would have to design a tool of destruction masquerading as an instrument of Native authenticity. One disguised as a means of verifying and validating belonging, functioning as an apparatus of demography and census taking, and acting as an official means of rationing out treaty funds and the distribution of land allotments to "real" Natives.

They must have also eventually understood that requiring Native peoples to be compliant and administer such a policy was necessary in order for it to take root and become formally integrated into our nations. Thus, they consequently constructed a reductionist, narrow, and racist concept of identity unique to Native peoples with their invention of blood quantum. I assert that through blood quantum—a novel yet depreciating means by which to measure Native identity—the settler state desired to normalize genocide among Native peoples and give it credibility by employing Native nations to authorize and execute the agenda. Also, by requiring our nations to opt in or to otherwise face material and tangible ramifications, they sought to extort Native peoples through manipulation and coercion, to believe in and cosign the eradication of our own peoples.

I'd like to further suggest that blood quantum was and continues to be the colonizer's attempt to both compel and influence Native peoples to adopt their confining and limiting colonial parameters of indigeneity as a means of identifying and claiming, or rejecting, our peoples. Rather than acknowledge and esteem our diverse metrics of belonging and our various understandings of inclusion that have existed pre- and post-contact (whether by blood or through other kinship modalities), colonizers have required and coerced us through blood quantum to surveille one another's indigeneity. Blood quantum also necessitates that we demand proof of one another's pedigree, quantify one another's authenticity based on proximity to being "full-blood," and question one another's legitimacy based on phenotype, featurism, colorism, and race. Additionally, blood quantum has uniquely sought to prime us to understand ourselves and one another through the lens of genocide based on the colonial fabrication of our "degree of Indian blood."

Blood quantum has also asked us to submit to the notion that our ancestors, our cultures, and our futures are reducible and even diminishable based solely on whom we choose to build community with, whom we choose to be in relationship with, and specifically whom we choose to procreate with. Colonizers have endeavored to cement the notion that blood quantum is intrinsic to being Native and is thus the singular, most important metric of how Native one is. Also, by asserting their illegitimate and counterfeit authority to determine who our relatives are or are not, they are attempting to negate individual Indigenous nations' sovereignty by deemphasizing our autonomy and disregarding our inherent right to self-determination, thereby devaluing our traditions and ways of being. For these reasons, many Natives are urging our nations and NDN country to insistently, frequently, and without apprehension interrogate blood quantum (and all settler colonial) policies. It is why many of us are asking our peoples to instead revive our traditional ways of belonging or consider alternative ways of relating to one another. And it is why we are asking one another to remain vigilant and cognizant of the fact that it was (and continues to be) this settler nation's hope that per blood quantum we'd eventually accept and implement our own erasure to finality until we no longer have any claims to our lands, to our peoples, and ultimately of sovereignty.

However, for some, blood quantum is like other protectionist policies. It is understood to be an innocuous means to defend our peoples, maintain our traditions, and guard our cultures by limiting who is considered authentically Native and, thus, who belongs. However, blood quantum should not be excused so easily. Rather, it should be equally understood to be at its core a means of erasure and termination, as well as a tool of eugenics. Blood quantum has from its inception sought to transform so many of us into "not Native enough," and sometimes under the guise of "maintaining" or "protecting" bloodlines. And this process, by which many have been transformed into "not Native," has sometimes happened in a single generation or at the amending of enrollment criteria. This has consequently led to so many of us being rejected from communities and distanced from our cultures and peoples, whom we rightfully belong to or are descended from.

Furthermore, for some of us, this settler nation has constructed and implemented additional barriers rooted in racism, which function to require us to navigate our identity and belonging to indigeneity to no end. Particularly for Afro-Indigenous/Black Native and Freedmen kin, we have had to simultaneously endure both the settler colonial policy of blood quantum and the white-supremacist, racial-capitalist policy of the "one-drop rule," the legal principle that asserts that any person with even one Black/African ancestor was/is considered and racialized as Black, not as a mechanism of ancestral or cultural maintenance, but as an instrument of subjugation and marginalization. This specific policy, which has been weaponized against Afro-descended peoples, has not only sought to enshrine anti-Black racism into Black bodies indefinitely, but into the very foundation of this settler nation. Thus, this framework has been engineered to ensure that Black folks are relegated to the lowest ranks of a racialized caste in an attempt to perpetually dehumanize us and transform us into an exploitable class. It has also sought to guarantee that there would be no escape from this status even if one holds multiple racial or national identities.

Afro-Indigenous/Black Native kin and Freedmen relatives, therefore, have been and are regularly reminded that under this settler-colonial-anti-Black plantation project, no person can exist as both Black and Native. That the two are mutually exclusive. That Blackness invalidates any other identity (nationality, race, and/or culture) for the sake of first converting Black persons into subjugated bodies, then into property of the state, and finally into commodity of racial capitalism. All of this seeks to uphold and perpetuate the logics and institutions of settler colonialism and white supremacy. During the Dawes Act era and allotment period, many Afro-Indigenous/Black Native kin and Freedmen relatives were dispossessed of identity, culture, peoples, and connection to community. We were ultimately disenfranchised from our nations often based solely on the one-drop rule and/or what we looked like, even if we held legitimate claims of indigeneity. Many Afro-Indigenous/Black Native kin and Freedmen relatives found (and still find) that we are ineligible for belonging based simply on being Black or of African descent.

These targeted policies demanded that if a Native person also descended from African peoples, presented as Black/African, or was a Freedmen, even if confirmed to be Native by blood, they could instead be determined to be "negro," "mulatto," and/or "colored" and thus deemed too Black to be Native! And if an entire tribal nation was deemed too Black presenting, they could have their nation dissolved and land/reservation acquired by settlers or the settler nation. This was the case for some Virginian and northeastern US tribes under colonial policies such as the Racial Integrity Act, which enshrined white supremacy via antimiscegenation statutes into laws as initiated by the likes of Walter Plecker and Thomas Jefferson. This is just another example of settler colonial policies and settler overseers who sought to ensure that no Afro-Indigenous/Black Native person could actualize their Native identity and culture, while also planting a wedge among family, kin, and community—a wedge that was also planted between Black and non-Black Native peoples.

This imagined and constructed notion of hypodescent has therefore intended to genocide Afro-Indigenous/Black Native kin's indigeneity and relegate us to commodifiable and enslavable chattel even before we are born, thereby ensuring that we could never exist as Indigenous or belong to our Native cultures or nations. These two policies—blood quantum and the one-drop rule—have worked simultaneously to the detriment of Afro-Indigenous/Black Native kin and Freedmen relatives, as they have demanded that we compartmentalize our identities, relinquish any claims of belonging and/or citizenship in our nations, and ultimately necessitate that we deny parts of ourselves that we have every right to fully realize. In addition, this has been and remains an effort to further marginalize us within indigeneity and within our families, communities, and nations. These policies in tandem also work to insinuate that Afro-Indigenous/Black Native kin and Freedmen relatives are simply "not Native enough." They often go further and assert that we are not, nor can we ever be, Native at all. This of course is false! Black Natives exist, and we belong!

While recognizing the many ways our oppressors have sought to intentionally distort our perspectives on identity, to disrupt our understandings of belonging, and to shape the future of our communities and nations, my hope is that we can remind ourselves of what is true—that we are inherently sovereign peoples that have existed and will exist outside of settler colonialism, white supremacy, and racial capitalism. That blood quantum (or any other means of Native genocide) is not our inheritance! That our peoples, our nations, our traditions and cultures, and our genealogical relationship to and stewardship of the land are our birthright. We therefore are not required to uphold blood quantum, nor do we have to hold sacred any policies or ideologies of the settler state. We instead have permission to ultimately decide against our own erasure and to practice Black Liberation and Indigenous Sovereignty until we actualize them simultaneously. We have the capacity to be more genius and empathetic than our oppressors. And we absolutely have the potential and creativity to imagine multiple futures more brilliant than what our oppressors have planned for us. We are not limited to nor restricted by their narcissistic and brute ideologies, and ultimately, we do not owe their policies loyalty, devotion, allegiance, or reverence. Finally, we are in no way indebted to them. Decentering our oppressors and their destruction is necessary should we choose to want something different than what they have planned for us.

As Native peoples, we have had to continuously navigate, endure, and resist under settler colonialism. We have also had to survive many attempts to genocide us. Blood quantum is no exception. It has added immensely to our struggle for sovereignty and has made our work around identity and belonging exponentially harder. However, I want to encourage and celebrate us because we have survived and found ways to retain, reclaim, and cultivate our cultures and our relationships to land and place in spite of the violence of settler colonialism, not because of it. We are still here, aren't we? We can therefore continue to choose to assert our inherent and political sovereignty on our own terms, or we can succumb to the colonizer's warped and distorted ideas of relationality and belonging. We can choose to see blood quantum for what it really is—genocide—or we can fan its flame, continue to legitimize it, and weaponize it against kin (and the one-drop rule against Black Native kin and Freedmen). We can either choose to resuscitate and breathe new life into our traditional ways of belonging, or we can proceed to escort our peoples and nations to destruction. We can also choose to be dynamic and imagine and develop new metrics of belonging, or we can decide to forfeit our blood and/or kinship ties because blood quantum is convenient and accessible. How we exercise our sovereignty ultimately is up to us—our nations and our peoples—not the settler state!

Finally, I challenge us to ask ourselves, "What is our responsibility to address blood quantum—the policy and the ideology?" Also, to ask ourselves as it relates to blood quantum, "What is our responsibility to our ancestors, ourselves, and our descendants?" I also want to reassure us that we have permission to wrestle with and exchange ideas about how we reconcile our desire to dismantle blood quantum policies while also upholding, honoring, and respecting tribal sovereignty (as some tribal nations still use blood quantum for enrollment criteria). In addition, I want to encourage us to interrogate and reckon with the marginalization of Afro-Indigenous/Black Native kin and Freedmen relatives within indigeneity, with the understanding that this specific erasure and dispossession is rooted in both blood quantum and the "one-drop" rule, synchronously.

Ultimately, it is right, brave, and an act of resistance to agitate the question of how we press forward—imagining, fashioning, and implementing an Indigenous future outside the parameters of blood quantum, racism (specifically anti-Blackness), capitalism, and settler colonialism. As we move forward, let us be certain that we are not who our oppressors say we are; nor are we who they believe us to be. We are instead the hopes and dreams of our ancestors personified. It is now our time to prepare a place for the ones who will come after us. And it is our responsibility to be intentional about not binding our descendants up in colonial constructs, settler logics, and genocidal policies. We can and should instead choose to be the ones to set them up to be free and to live as sovereign and self-determined peoples, on their own terms. The ones who will never be forced to present a Certificate of Degree of Indian Blood.

The Color of Blood:
Race, Power, and the Dangerous Legacy
of Racial Purity Laws

DOUG KIEL

To fully understand the complex origins and enduring impacts of Native American blood quantum laws, it is necessary to examine the wider context of racial purity laws that have been implemented globally. While earlier versions of these laws existed, it was their modern iterations—based on flawed biological classifications and the principles of social Darwinism and eugenics—that caused significant harm to marginalized communities worldwide. These laws were not confined to North America but have left lasting scars globally, serving as stark reminders of manipulated histories, grave injustices, and the ongoing struggles faced by marginalized communities.

Racial purity laws demonstrate how pseudoscientific racism and biopolitical population control have been used by nation-states to categorize citizens, enforce systemic marginalization, and deprive Indigenous and minority groups of their fundamental rights. Through a comparison of the origins, enforcement mechanisms, and impacts of these policies, this essay briefly highlights the shared ideological foundations and violent consequences that have left a troubled legacy still felt by affected populations today. This comparative analysis highlights the urgent need to reject biopolitical social control.

The racial purity laws and policies examined beyond the United States—in apartheid South Africa, Nazi Germany, and Australia—expose striking similarities in their ideological foundations, enforcement mechanisms, and effects on marginalized populations. At an ideological level, these policies universally rely on now-discredited pseudoscientific theories of racial hierarchies and eugenics. By categorizing human beings into constructed racial groups, states weaponized false scientific racism to label certain groups as inherently superior or inferior. This provided a purported intellectual justification for denying fundamental human rights and implementing systemic social control. The impacts of racial purity laws extend beyond the specific regions and communities directly affected. These laws and their associated ideologies have shaped global perceptions of race and continue to perpetuate systemic racism and inequality on a broader scale. The legacy of colonialism, the horrors of eugenics, and the enduring effects of these policies demand recognition and redress.

To fully understand the evolution of racial purity laws, we must examine their ideological origins in racial hierarchies. The hierarchical categorization of constructed racial groups, ranked by supposedly inherent superiority or inferiority, laid the foundations for later purity laws and policies. These racial hierarchies emerged from fifteenth-century European colonial expansion. As Europeans conquered Indigenous peoples, they developed ethnocentric worldviews positioning white Europeans as civilizationally supreme. Indigenous populations were often derided as "savages" and ranked below Europeans.

The developing transatlantic slave trade also engrained pernicious racial ideologies. As millions of Africans were enslaved and transported to the Americas, racist attitudes equating Blackness with inferiority and servility became entrenched. Pseudoscientific racism classified and ranked racial groups to justify slavery and oppression. Over time, racial hierarchies intermingled with nationalism and social Darwinism.

As European nations vied for global power, they increasingly defined white Europeans as superior, contrasting them against "weaker" or "lesser" races. Darwin's theories were co-opted to portray nonwhite races as less evolved. This fusion of racism, racial hierarchies, nationalism, and social Darwinism fueled exclusionary policies and the myth of racial purity, supporting beliefs that racial mixing would "degrade" white national identities. Maintaining "pure blood" became synonymous with preserving national strength and dominance.

The concept of limpieza de sangre ("purity of blood") was not unique to Spain. Other European powers adopted similar exclusionary policies within their territories and colonies. However, these policies gained rapid momentum in the late nineteenth and early twentieth centuries, propelled by developments like Darwin's theory of evolution. While revolutionary, Darwin's theory was misinterpreted to hierarchically categorize human races. This birthed social Darwinism, propagating the supremacy of select races (mainly white Europeans) and unjustly labeling others as "primitive" or "inferior." These distortions amplified racial disparities and influenced legal systems globally.

One example of the impact of social Darwinism in action is the White Australia policy, a series of racial purity laws and practices implemented from 1901 to 1973 that aimed to restrict nonwhite immigration to Australia and to preserve its British character. The policy employed various methods to exclude or limit the entry of Asians, Pacific Islanders, Africans, and other nonwhite groups into Australia. It also discriminated against Indigenous Australians, who were considered "flora and fauna" until 1967. The policy had detrimental effects on diversity, economy, culture, and international relations for Australia. Inaugurated when Australia became a federated nation, the Immigration Restriction Act of 1901, which allowed the government to deny entry to any individual unable to pass a dictation test in a European language, was intentionally challenging for nonwhite individuals. Passed the same year, the Pacific Island Labourers Act facilitated the deportation of Pacific Islanders working in Australia. Despite opposition from some Australians and government members, the policy persisted, bolstered by influential groups such as the Australian Labor Party and the Returned & Services League. However, the policy began to lose favor in the 1960s as Australian society became more multicultural. In 1973, the Australian government finally abolished the policy.

The influence of social Darwinism is evident throughout the British Empire and the United States. Armed with this distorted ideology, Britain justified its colonization of India and parts of Africa, depicting it as a "civilizing mission" to uplift and educate the "backward" Natives. In reality, this mission was fueled by economic and political interests, resulting in the exploitation and oppression of millions of people under British rule. The colonized peoples were subjected to harsh laws, taxes, policies, and practices that violated their human rights, dignity, and sovereignty. Social Darwinism also influenced the institution of the Jim

Crow laws in the United States, systematically oppressing African Americans from the late nineteenth century until the mid-twentieth century. These laws enforced racial segregation and discrimination in all aspects of public and private life, including education, employment, housing, transportation, voting, and marriage. They denied African Americans equal protection under the law and subjected them to lynching, mob violence, intimidation, and humiliation. These laws were supported by pseudoscientific theories that claimed African Americans were biologically and intellectually inferior to whites.

Eugenics, which emerged between the late nineteenth and early twentieth centuries, aimed to "improve" humanity through controlled breeding and the elimination of "undesirable" traits. Advocates of this movement endorsed shocking practices such as forced sterilizations, abortions, euthanasia, segregation, and immigration restrictions to prevent or reduce the reproduction of those they perceived as "unfit" or "defective." These practices had a significant adverse impact on marginalized groups, including the poor, disabled, and racial minorities. By the mid-twentieth century, the United States alone had authorized over sixty thousand coerced sterilizations based on eugenic beliefs. This movement also shaped immigration protocols, excluding those considered "lesser." However, the most horrifying manifestation of these ideologies was observed in Nazi Germany's Nuremberg Laws of 1935. These laws not only stripped Jews of their citizenship but also forbade intermarriage with non-Jews and defined Jews based on their bloodlines. These laws paved the way for the Holocaust, culminating in the genocide of six million Jews and other marginalized communities, such as the Roma, Slavs, disabled people, and homosexuals. This dark era was the culmination of eugenic and social Darwinist principles, centered on exterminating non-Aryan populations.

In his book *Hitler's American Model: The United States and the Making of Nazi Race Law*, James Q. Whitman explores the connection between American race law and Nazi race laws in Germany. Whitman examines how American immigration policies, miscegenation laws, and racial segregation practices shaped the Nazis' development of their own race policies. He argues that the Nazis drew inspiration from the American eugenics movement and used American race laws as a blueprint for their own discriminatory legislation. Whitman's research challenges previous academic debates about the extent of American influence on Nazi race laws. He contends that Hitler's admiration for American immigration policies, expressed in *Mein Kampf*, was not merely a passing thought but a significant element of Nazi theory and practice. The American government, like the Nazis, legally defined populations using racial categories based on blood percentage. This provided a model that Nazi lawyers referenced when crafting their racist legislation. The Nazi obsession with "racial purity" mirrored America's preoccupation with blood as a means of marginalizing Native and Black populations deemed undesirable and unfit to fully participate in the white-dominant social order. Understanding this troubling history and context is critical to comprehend the harm and lasting impacts of blood quantum policies on Native nations.

The atrocities committed under the banner of racial purity laws did not end with World War II. The system of apartheid in South Africa from 1948 to the early 1990s was heavily influenced by the racist pseudoscience of social Darwinism and eugenics. Under apartheid, the South African government propagated the notion that the white minority was superior to the Black majority. It created a stratified system of racial classification, with whites at the top and Black people at the bottom. Apartheid proponents justified this as a "natural" racial hierarchy, in line with social Darwinist thinking.

The apartheid system was designed to "protect" the white race and prevent racial mixing, which adherents believed would lead to "degeneration" of the white population. Laws were passed to forcibly segregate housing, health care, education, and other public services by race. Interracial marriages were banned. Black South Africans' movements were severely restricted, and they were stripped of voting rights and citizenship. The apartheid regime even tried to establish disconnected Bantustans or "homelands" for different Black ethnic groups to "return to their natural state." Apartheid South Africa represented an extreme case of scientifically racist theories being enacted on a nationwide scale through coercive laws aimed at racial segregation, control, and suppression. The idea that whites were superior was used to justify denying basic human rights to the Black majority population. Apartheid was enabled by the false social Darwinist narrative of intrinsic racial hierarchies and the eugenic goal of cultivating a "superior" white citizenry through state-sanctioned discrimination. The legacy of apartheid demonstrates the catastrophic human impact that can result when pseudoscience is used to classify humans and justify prejudice.

Blood quantum is a relic of the ideologies that underpin global white supremacy. They are part of a larger scheme of weaponizing racial categories against the oppressed. Their continued existence signifies more than an outdated policy; it represents the enduring pernicious reach of racial laws that span both time and space. Blood quantum, however, is not the only mechanism used in North America's quest for white racial purity. The history of forced sterilizations of Indigenous women in both the United States and Canada exemplifies the multiple strategies employed to oppress communities under the guise of racial purity.

The forced sterilization of Indigenous women in both countries is a dark and disturbing chapter in North America's history. This practice, which lasted from the late 1800s to the 1970s, was a grievous violation of human rights and had lasting impacts on Indigenous communities. In the United States, the eugenics movement of the early twentieth century provided ideological justification for the forced sterilization of marginalized groups, including Indigenous peoples, who were deemed "unfit" for reproduction. Thousands of Native American women underwent coercive sterilization procedures at federally funded Indian Health Service facilities during the 1960s and 1970s, often without their informed consent. It is estimated that between 25 percent and 50 percent of Native women of childbearing age were sterilized during this period. In Canada, provincial laws allowed the forced sterilization of those classified as mentally disabled or morally "defective." While such laws were repealed by the 1970s, Indigenous women continued to be disproportionately targeted, especially in state-run Indian hospitals. Procedures were often conducted without proper consent during or after childbirth. It is estimated that thousands of First Nations, Métis, and Inuit women underwent forced sterilizations. These policies had devastating intergenerational impacts on Indigenous communities, violating women's reproductive autonomy and rights.

When understood in a wider context, blood quantum laws and policies in North America symbolize the dangerous tools of a past era, urging a united effort to both understand their origins and work toward their dismantling. The global history of racial purity laws reveals disturbing common roots. These laws stemmed from scientifically flawed attempts to classify human beings into racial categories and justify discrimination against those deemed inferior. As European colonialism expanded world-wide, racial hierarchies and pseudoscientific theories like social Darwinism fueled racial purity laws aimed at preserving white dominance. Manifestations like the White Australia policy, Jim Crow laws, apartheid in South Africa, and the Nuremberg Laws caused egregious harm by legally enforcing the racist belief that racial mixing threatens white purity and national identity. Connections between American and Nazi race laws highlight the global spread of these dangerous ideologies.

While differing in scope and implementation, racial purity laws universally relied on now-discredited biological classifications to deny the humanity of those considered racial or ethnic "others." The resulting marginalization, cultural destruction, and violence emphasize the urgent need to eliminate remaining policies rooted in this painful history of racism, colonialism, and state-sponsored eugenics. Native American blood quantum policies are inextricably tied to this past. The pervasive effects of flawed biological racial theories demand that we confront this history and its contemporary manifestations. The shadows cast by social Darwinism and pseudoscientific racism remain long, but exposing their faulty logic dispels their power to divide and oppress.

Who belongs?
Who should have political recognition?

The Federal Indian Blood Quantum Fiction

GABRIEL S. GALANDA

"Indian tribal membership today is a fiction created by the federal
government, not a creation of the Indian people themselves."
—Vine Deloria Jr., *God Is Red*[1]

Indian blood quantum is a fiction. It is made up. It is fake. It is pretend.[2]

It began as colonial racial fiction.[3] It morphed into federal legal fiction.[4]
It now exists as widespread tribal political fiction.[5]

It is and always has been fictional that certain percentages of "Indian" or
other racial blood run through Indigenous people's veins. Human blood
simply cannot be reduced to fractions or decimal points based on racial
categorization.[6] That idea lacks "intellectual credibility."[7]

The Indian blood quantum fiction is nevertheless enshrined and codified in
US law, as it has been for centuries.[8] That fiction did not begin in 1887 with
the passage of the Dawes Act. Nor did it begin in 1934 with the passage of
the Indian Reorganization Act. That fiction arose in federal law—in fact,
supreme law—within the first fifty years of the United States' existence. That
fiction permeates numerous nineteenth-century Treaties and twentieth-
century federal statutes intended to decimate Indigenous kinship systems, if
not eradicate Indigenous peoples from the United States.

 Federal Indian "blood" jargon and laws remain on the books today,
subjugating Indigenous "customary governance practices or epistemolo-
gies of belonging, affiliation, and kinship" and replacing those traditional

norms with "racialized criteria" in furtherance of "federal objectives for Native government dissolution and land dispossession."[9] Despite *that* truth, Native nations have adopted fictional Indian blood quantum as their own norm, in their own laws. As Lisa Poupart explains, Indigenous peoples "learned and internalized the discursive practices of the West—the very codes that created, reflected, and reproduced our oppression."

Today, Native nations "participate in, create, and reproduce Western cultural forms, [and] internalize Western meanings of difference and abject Otherness, viewing ourselves within and through the constructs that defined us as racially and culturally subhuman."[10] The Indian blood quantum fiction now exists in the enrollment laws of at least 70 percent of the Native nations recognized by the United States.[11] To perpetuate that racial fiction jeopardizes Native nationhood writ large. Tribal blood quantum norms are increasingly cited by those who want to terminate Native nations or curtail tribal sovereignty, including several sitting US Supreme Court justices.[12] While certain Native nations are beginning to confront and resolve the existential threats posed by Indian blood quantum fiction, a great many more should urgently follow suit.

This essay is intended to explain the continuing imperialist, assimilationist, and terminationist aim of federal Indian blood quantum laws so that Native nations might reevaluate tribal blood quantum laws and adopt alternative citizenship criteria.[13] At a minimum, any metric for Indigenous national belonging should be rooted in kinship, not race—and in truth, not fiction.[14]

Indian Assimilation by Racial "Blood" Began with the Treaties

Starting with Treaties in the early 1800s, the nascent United States began to identify individual Indigenous persons according to Indian "blood" and blood quantum.[15] In the Treaty with the Wyandot, Seneca, Delaware, Shawnee, Potawatomie, Ottawa, and Chippewa Tribes of 1817, for example, the United States pledged to allot treaty-reserved lands, in fee simple, to "all of whom are connected with the said Indians, by blood or adoption."[16] The Wyandot Treaty also included a promise of a 640-acre allotment to those children of deceased settler William M'Collock, "who are quarter-blood Wyandot Indians."[17] While recognizing the Indigenous kinship tradition of adoption, the Wyandot Treaty reflects the United States' early superimposition of European blood symbolism and racism upon Indigenous kinship societies and nations.[18]

Dating back at least five hundred years, "blood" connoted lineage, descent, and ancestry to Europeans in connection with royal claims to property and power; it "presage[d] modern conceptions of 'race.'"[19] "Race" did not exist until colonization of the New World.[20] Race "originally denoted a lineage, such as a noble family or a domesticated breed," with "concerns over purity of blood" emerging among eighteenth-century European peoples.[21] Nobility was and "has always been an unconscious but all-consuming goal for the European Immigrant," as Vine Deloria Jr. observed.[22] Concepts of race and blood did not exist within Indigenous kinship societies; those concepts were assigned to Indigenous peoples by European colonizers.[23]

In early eighteenth-century colonial America, it was "blood" that connoted racial difference and inferiority.[24] According to Dr. Kim TallBear, "Blood signified moral and physical purity and social solidarity" among European settlers.[25] By the nineteenth century, the United States began in earnest to identify Indians by bloodline as a "principal tool of genocidal extermination," as explained by Dean Rennard Strickland.[26] Federal officials first categorized Indians by blood degree, as in "full blood" or "mixed blood," and then by blood percentages.[27]

By the mid-nineteenth century, the science of ethnology, which involved the study of racial characteristics, emerged and infiltrated federal Indian affairs.[28] European and European-American scientists believed that each race had a unique blood type, and blood carried a wide range of hereditary traits.[29] That belief morphed into eugenics genealogy by the late nineteenth century, which included a theory of fractional inheritance.[30] Eugenics has since come to be viewed as "intellectually veiled racism."[31] Fractional inheritance has also been dubbed fiction.[32] Jill Doerfler explains that, according to that fiction, "each person received one-half of their hereditary endowment from each parent, one-fourth of which was from each grandparent, one-eighth of which was from each great-grandparent, and so on."[33] The theory held that the admixture of blood in people who had parents of different races resulted in an amalgamation of behaviors and traits.[34] As such, "blood" Indians were considered "biologically inferior to and different from native-born, white Protestant Americans."[35] However, it is "fiction that one inherits 'blood' equally from the male and female side."[36] As Dr. David Wilkins explains, so-called Indian blood has also never been "the carrier of . . . cultural traits."[37] Nevertheless, as settlers bore children with Indigenous people, fictional degrees of Indian blood came to define—and self-define—who belonged to Native nations.[38]

According to Paul Spruhan, "mixed-blood" terminology reflected thinking that "white blood" might uplift "darker 'blood.'"[39] Although a "stain of degeneracy" attached to Indigenous persons of mixed descent,[40] settlers also believed that those of mixed descent—or uplifted blood— might serve as a "'civilizing' force."[41] "Mixed bloods" were thus defined in a category of their own, the thought being that they would more rapidly assimilate into American society.[42] Federal negotiators imported "mixed blood" identifiers into several mid-nineteenth-century Treaties.[43] While most Treaty references to Indian "blood" did not go so far as to dictate who belonged to a Native nation, they marked a racist, assimilative practice that gave rise to fictional blood quantum percentages in many other federal laws.[44]

Over the last two centuries, Native nations have adopted and wielded their own racist Indian "blood" laws to exclude Indigenous peoples as citizens. For example, by the mid- to late-nineteenth century, there was "a very strong prejudice" between the so-called "Indian blood of the Cherokee Nation" and Cherokee emancipated slaves—the Freedmen—which contributed to the racist denial of Cherokee citizenship to the Freedmen and their descendants for more than 150 years.[45] In 2017, a US federal court ruled that Cherokee Freedmen descendants belonged as citizens of the Cherokee Nation.[46] Four years later, the Cherokee Nation eliminated all language in their laws that restricted tribal citizenship or other rights to Cherokees "by blood," calling that language "a relic of a painful and ugly, racial past."[47]

By contrast, the Pamunkey Indian Tribe still engages in Indian "blood" racism. During the Civil War, the Pamunkey enacted a "Black Law" that mirrored a Virginia law and forbade tribal members from marrying "any other person other than those of white or Indian blood." Violators were punished with banishment from the Pamunkey. While Virginia did away with their "Black Laws" in 1975, the Pamunkey Black Law remained until 2014, when it was finally eliminated by tribal politicians in order for the tribe to gain federal recognition from Congress. The Pamunkey received federal recognition in 2015, only to have tribal politicians turn around and deny enrollment to Black Pamunkey descendants.[48] The Pamunkey example illustrates the tribal internalization of abject Otherness and reproduction of internal oppression.

Indian "blood" ideology has also caused mass tribal disenrollments. For example, in 1954, a faction of so-called Northern Ute "full-bloods" caused the disenrollment of about five hundred "mixed-bloods," with the help of the Bureau of Indian Affairs (BIA) and Congress.[49] At the insistence of the "full-bloods," Congress determined that the criteria for Northern Ute membership were to include so-called "full" blood quantum: "one-half degree of Ute Indian blood and a total of Indian blood in excess of one-half, excepting those who become mixed-bloods by choice."[50] The BIA encouraged mass disenrollment as "the first step in terminating both full-bloods and mixed-bloods from federal obligations."[51]

In more recent times, tribal politicians have asserted pretextual claims of "inadequate blood quantum or blood from a different Native nation" to disenroll legions of tribal citizens, particularly as Indian gaming per capita monies have become common.[52] As of today, so-called Disenrollment Chiefs have terminated the enrollments of approximately ten thousand tribal citizens from nearly one hundred Native nations.[53] It is time for Native nations to end racist, exclusionary "blood" terminology and enrollment denial criteria.

Racial Blood Quantum Statutes Decimate Indigenous Kinship

By the late nineteenth century, Indian assimilation became federal law and policy, the cornerstone of which was supplanting Indigenous communal land tenure with private land ownership.[54] As Frederick Hoxie notes, the United States sought to "undermine the clan system and 'traditional modes of inheritance'" of Indigenous peoples.[55] To those ends, Congress passed the General Allotment Act—also known as the Dawes Severalty Act—in 1887.[56]

Under that law, large reservation-land tracts were divided into much smaller parcels of land and allotted and deeded in trust to individual Indians for a period of twenty-five years in the hope of transforming them into farmers and otherwise causing mass Indigenous assimilation into the newly dominant American society.[57] After twenty-five years, an allottee was to receive a fee patent for their allotment, rendering the parcel free of federal trust status and freely alienable.[58] The idea behind the twenty-five-year period was that the allottee's land would remain exempt from state property taxation and ineligible for sale for a generation—after one generation, all bets were off.[59]

In 1906, Congress passed the Burke Act, which amended the Dawes Act and allowed the Secretary of the Interior to issue a fee patent to an allottee before the expiration of the twenty-five-year period. Lands patented in fee under the Burke Act could be alienated, encumbered, and sold[60] upon an allottee's application for a fee patent and secretarial determination that the allottee was "competent and capable of managing his or her affairs."[61] Blood quantum became the determinative factor regarding whether, through "education and civilization,"[62] the allottee was competent and thus entitled to a fee patent for allotment.[63] Blood quantum was applied as a proxy for competency in order to release large swaths of allottees from land alienation restrictions.[64]

Under a 1908 statute, Congress released Eastern Oklahoma Tribal allottees from alienation restrictions according to the quantum of their Indian blood.[65] All lands of "mixed-blood Indians having less than half Indian blood" were "free from all restriction," while those of "three-quarters or more Indian blood" retained restrictions on all their land.[66] In other words, only tribal citizens of at least one-half "white blood" were deemed competent and capable.[67] The measure of Indian competence was overtly "racist," in keeping with then-prevailing eugenics ideology.[68]

In the early twentieth century, tribal citizens were arbitrarily deemed competent if they were either at least one-half white blood or recommended by a competency commission.[69] In 1917, the US Interior Department adopted a policy that directly correlated white blood percentage to competence. Interior Commissioner of Indian Affairs Cato Sells provided in the "Declaration of Policy":

> While ethnologically a preponderance of white blood has not heretofore been a criterion of competency, nor even now is it always a safe standard, it is almost an axiom that an Indian who has a larger proportion of

white blood than Indian partakes more of the characteristics of the former than the latter. In thought and action, so far as the business world is concerned, he approximates more closely to the white blood ancestry.[70]

Federal "competency commissions" journeyed throughout the country to determine which allottees were competent to receive fee patents, even without allottee applications or consent and even despite protest from those individuals.[71] After an allottee's competence was adjudicated based in great part on his or her blood quantum, a commission recommended to the Interior Secretary that an allottee's land restrictions be removed.[72] But before the Secretary could even free an allottee of inalienability restrictions, "tax collectors, auto dealers, and equipment salesmen descended on the newly patented Indians."[73] For most allottees, fee patent issuance was immediately followed by the sale of land.[74] Blood quantum was a great pulverizing engine.

Ironically, it was federal officials who were incompetent in regard to early tribal enrollment.[75] The federal government "formulated the official tribal membership rolls with frequent mistakes," for example, noting individuals' names and tribal affiliations incorrectly.[76] The same was true of federal blood quantum calculations for tribal members. "[T]he blood quantum information haphazardly collected in the early rolls is at best unsystematic, if not altogether unreliable."[77] Those rolls and blood quantum percentages are of "doubtful reliability."[78]

Meanwhile, the United States caused Native nations to form their own enrollment councils, which immediately grappled with blood quantum.[79] By the early twentieth century, many Native nations did not govern through any form of tribal council or business committee.[80] A great many Native nations lacked any discernable elected representative body.[81] But as a result of various federal laws calling for the allotment or surplus of Native nations' reservation lands, BIA superintendents caused the formation of tribal enrollment councils in order to identify individual members who were entitled to allotments or other federal benefits.

At the BIA superintendents' behest, blood quantum became the overriding criteria for enrollment.[82] As Alexandra Harmon explains: "By emphasizing that aboriginal 'blood' was a *sine qua non* of entitlement, they also expressed a conception of racial categories that underlay the department's enrollment policies."[83] BIA superintendents also urged tribal enrollment councils to exclude any individual with a low blood quantum because it would protect or enhance the economic interests of those already enrolled.[84] These practices were, and remain, wholly antithetical to traditional Indigenous kinship norms of inclusion and reciprocity.[85]

In 1919, Congress passed 25 U.S.C. 163, which usurped the inherent power of Native nations over tribal enrollment. The Interior Secretary was expressly authorized, whenever "in his discretion such action would be for the best interest of the Indians, to cause a final roll to be made of the membership of *any* Indian tribe" (except for the five Eastern Oklahoma Tribes and the Osage, Minnesota Chippewa, and Menominee Tribes).[86] Those rolls were required to "contain the ages and quantum of Indian blood," and once approved by the Secretary, they were "declared to constitute the legal membership of the respective tribes . . . be conclusive both as to ages and quantum of Indian blood."[87] Blood quantum, although not yet dictated in any specific percentage, was thereby proclaimed as federal criteria for tribal enrollment.

Worse yet, Congress assumed and delegated "exclusive authority to determine a tribe's final roll" to the Interior Secretary, "curtail[ing] an essential feature of tribal governing core powers."[88] The enrollment component of that 1919 statute has never been repealed.[89] As recently as 1965, the US Supreme Court affirmed that part of the statute and, more broadly, Congress and the Secretary's unbridled authority to regulate tribal enrollment.[90] In *Simmons v. Eagle Seelatsee,* a federal court made plain:

> [I]t was early held that included in this plenary power of Congress was the power to regulate and determine tribal membership. In short, Congress, or its delegated agents, had full power to define and describe those persons who should be treated and regarded as members of an Indian tribe and entitled to enrollment therein. The Act which authorizes the Secretary of the Interior generally to make up membership rolls of any Indian tribe directs that such rolls <u>shall</u> contain the ages and "quantum of Indian blood" of those placed on the rolls.[91]

As that 1919 statute reflects, it is also fiction that tribal enrollment has always fallen within the exclusive province of Native nations. Having invented tribal enrollment by no later than 1790, the United States has historically played a leading role in tribal enrollment.[92] The Interior Secretary still retains plenary control over the membership of almost every Native nation.[93] Blood quantum is mandatory according to that 1919 federal statute.[94] To this day, that statute subjugates Indigenous belonging and kinship, and it racializes and debases tribal citizenship.

Racial, Exclusionary Blood Quantum Laws Are Ubiquitous

In 1934, Congress passed the Indian Reorganization Act (IRA), also known as the Wheeler-Howard Act, prohibiting any further allotment of reservation lands and authorizing the Interior Secretary to acquire or reacquire lands in trust for Native nations and tribal members.[95] In order to reacquire land for Indigenous individuals and bestow other federal privileges upon them,[96] the IRA adopted the following "Indian" definition:

> The term "Indian" as used in this Act shall include all persons of Indian descent who are members of any recognized Indian tribe now under Federal jurisdiction, and all persons who are descendants of such members who were, on June 1, 1934, residing within the present boundaries of any Indian reservation, and shall further include all other persons of one-half or more Indian blood.[97]

As Spruhan explains, US Indian Commissioner John Collier originally proposed an "Indian" definition that included "all other persons" of at least one-quarter Indian blood.[98] By the late 1920s, the federal government had adopted a one-quarter minimum Indian blood hiring preference for federal employment.[99]

But in 1934, Senator Burton Wheeler of Montana said on the floor of the Senate that the United States should not "take a lot of Indians in that are quarter bloods . . . under this act."[100] Senator Wheeler believed only "Indians in the half blood" should be accepted under federal law, explaining: "What we are trying to do is get rid of the Indian problem rather than to add to it."[101] In turn, Congress rejected the one-quarter minimum Indian blood standard for federally identified Indians when passing the IRA.[102]

Under the IRA's "Indian" definition, a federally identified Indian must either possess at least one-half Indian blood, be enrolled with a Native nation, or descend from an enrollee who resided on a reservation on June 1, 1934.[103] In November 1935, Collier distributed a circular to federal employees "engaged in working with the Indians in the matter of organization," which addressed who qualified as "Indian" for purposes of membership under IRA constitutions.[104] The circular adopted the IRA's "Indian" definition, which, as Collier explained, "shows on the part of Congress a definite policy to limit the application of Indian benefits."[105] He proclaimed it Interior policy "to urge and insist" that any IRA constitutional membership for newborns be limited, in great part, to children of one-half Indian blood.[106]

Although Collier originally supported a one-quarter Indian blood metric, he made way for Congress's one-half Indian blood metric. In the final analysis, Collier supported the IRA as a "progressive transfer of municipal functions to the organized tribe."[107] He maintained that Indigenous peoples had lost their "ancient traditions of self-government."[108] As historian Elmer Rusco concludes, Collier was "operating under certain cultural and political presuppositions that elevated [his] own values and governing systems over those of indigenous nations."[109] Collier's vision for Native nations included tribal enrollment as an exclusionary governmental function.

With BIA urging and insistence, the IRA's "Indian" criteria for federal privileges—most notably blood quantum—became tribal criteria for enrollment in many Native nations. Blood quantum has since become the single most pervasive metric of tribal citizenship, with nearly four hundred Native nations having adopted that racial fiction as a metric for enrollment.[110] The federal Indian blood quantum fiction exists in countless Native nations' IRA constitutions and membership laws, operating to exclude Indigenous newborns and children from their peoples as the federal government intended. Those Indigenous youth are left without adequate tribal protection vis-à-vis the federal Indian Child Welfare Act.[111] The Indian blood quantum fiction has been internalized by Native nations to the point of sui-colonialism.

Exclusionary tribal blood quantum laws are ubiquitous. Over the last century, Native nations have wielded those laws to deny enrollment to Indigenous persons with purported low "Indian blood" percentages, in great part to protect the economic status of existing tribal members. Those Native nations are resolving the United States' "Indian problem" without the federal government having to dirty its hands. Tribal per-capitalism, in particular, has crystallized the racial exclusion of Indigenous persons according to fictional blood quantum.[112] Tribal blood quantum laws hurt Indigenous persons and jeopardize Native nationhood writ large. By racializing Native national citizenship, the political status—the very existence—of Native nations is threatened.[113]

Generations of Indigenous peoples have been excluded from tribal citizenship, and Native nations have been weakened as a result of Indian blood quantum, precisely as the United States intended. While tribal strength can be found in large citizenship numbers—take the Cherokee and Navajo Nations, for example—there can also be weakness in small tribal citizenries.[114] Indigenous peoples have always existed and survived as groups, duty-bound together in spirit and kinship, not small clusters of individuals tethered together by race and money.[115] If Indian blood quantum persists, Native nations will dwindle in political, cultural, and spiritual existence, and they will eventually self-extinguish—it is a statistical certainty.[116]

Native Nations Must Dispel the Blood Quantum Fiction

As exemplified by the first edition of *The Great Vanishing Act*, a growing number of Indigenous thought leaders are urging Native nations to reject the Indian blood quantum fiction—before it is too late.[117] In 2018, Congress amended the Stigler Act at the behest of the Eastern Oklahoma Five Tribes to eliminate a requirement that allotted land could only be inherited by heirs with "one-half or more of Indian blood" in order to retain its federal trust status.[118] That land can now be passed on to Five Tribes descendants regardless of blood quantum without losing its trust status. Native nations should take aim at other federal Indian blood quantum laws, most notably the IRA's "Indian" definition, which serves no practical purpose today.

More importantly, Native nations should reevaluate their own blood quantum laws. In 2020, Alan Parker urged the amendment of IRA constitutions to reestablish citizenship "rules" that "rely on traditional concepts of belonging" and "focus on the goal that there *will* be future generations."[119] Several Native nations have accepted such wisdom, as well as their own teachings, and dispelled the racial fiction through acts of their people. In the last few years, the Quinault Indian Nation, Minnesota Chippewa Tribe, and St. Croix Chippewa Tribe voters each passed constitutional amendments that eliminated blood quantum in favor of lineal descent.[120] Sealaska Corporation shareholders likewise voted in 2022 to remove blood quantum as a requirement to own shares in the Alaska Native corporations.[121]

A great many more Native nations must urgently confront and reject the Indian blood quantum fiction and restore culturally appropriate forms of kinship-based criteria for Indigenous national belonging.[122] There is great reason to worry that Indigenous existential reforms will not occur soon enough, if at all.[123] While generations of Indigenous peoples vanish right before our very eyes, the fiction persists. Bolstered by tribal racism, capitalism, and sui-colonialism, the status quo prevails on far too many reservations. A great many tribal citizens unwittingly believe the fiction or fearfully remain quiet while their children and grandchildren get left behind.

The writing on the wall could not be any clearer: End blood quantum before it ends us. Reawaken our respective kinship systems before it is too late. Only time will tell whether *our* original truth will prevail.

What does it mean to be Indigenous?
Who gets to decide?

Practicality: Native American Tribal Adoption in Historical Perspective

LAURENCE M. HAUPTMAN

Introduction

Native Americans have traditionally defined their identity through kinship, although there are other important factors, such as a sense of place, oral traditions, and language.[1] Yet today, many of the 574 federally recognized tribal nations in the United States have blood quantum as the defining requirement. Some also date tribal enrollment to a specific federal census or the preparation of a formal list. Yet others have a residency requirement. As a result of increasing intermarriage with non-Indians, blood quantum levels have rapidly declined, resulting in increased fears among Native Americans that their descendants will no longer be entitled to tribal enrollment and the rights and privileges that the status entails.[2] Legal scholar Matthew L.M. Fletcher has pointed out that by using bloodlines as a criteria for membership, tribes "with stringent membership rules limit their own population growth and in some instances, could shrink their membership down to nothingness, just as federal bureaucrats and policymakers may have envisioned decades or centuries ago."[3]

In the past, Indigenous nations have had their own unique ways of and rituals for incorporating members into their circle. The clan structure was essential in the process of integrating outsiders—men and women; Indigenous, European, and African; captives, orphans, and allies—into a particular tribal nation. In their book *Dismembered: Native Disenrollment and the Battle for Human Rights*, legal scholars David E. Wilkins and Shelly Hulse Wilkins have rightly pointed out that historically, Native American communities were inclusive, "incorporating—whether through force, invitation, or acceptance—individuals from other indigenous, racial, and ethnic groups. Native peoples had always managed to creatively and successfully augment their numbers and incorporate new blood and ideas." The Wilkinses added that these tribal nations "were bolstered, not threatened by inclusion."[4]

In her 1944 book *Speaking of Indians*, anthropologist Ella Deloria wrote that bloodlines were never the exclusive criteria for Lakota/Dakota kinship.[5] Anthropologist Raymond DeMallie noted that the Lakota/Dakota people speak of kinship in terms of attitudes and behaviors, not just in genealogical connections. Kinship was the "foundation for social unity and moral order"; it "provided the most basic cultural structures patterning the social system and related them as well to the sacred powers of the world at large."[6] DeMallie, citing Deloria, pointed out that strangers were seen as potentially dangerous, and to establish relationships with them, they had to literally become related as kin.[7] A similar reality existed among the nations of the Iroquois Confederacy, where the Condolence Council ritual was seen by them as bringing outsiders into the Haudenosaunee orbit. According to anthropologist William N. Fenton, one "can summarize Iroquois society in Iroquois terms, as a body of relatives, 'my people,' who are residents of a place—a village or settlement. The public includes *everyone*, therefore, any stranger must be adopted"[8] (emphasis mine).

The extensive and thorough incorporation of outsiders was so complete that today in Northern Cheyenne society, some refer to themselves as full-bloods even though "their great-grandmothers or grandfathers were Pawnee, Crow, or Lakota."[9] Equally significant, some Seneca, but not all, see themselves as more Onöndawa'ga:' [Seneca] if they could trace their genealogy back to Mary Jemison, the famous captive, the "white woman of the Genesee." George H. J. Abrams, former Seneca museologist, has pointed out that there are thousands of Jemison descendants in Iroquoia today and that some are generally proud of their ancestor, attending late-summer festivities held at Letchworth State Park, the site of the former Gardeau Reservation, a personal grant to Jemison by the Chiefs at the treaty grounds at Big Tree (Geneseo, New York) in 1797.[10]

Multicultural Indigenous Nations

Importantly, Indigenous communities did not just adopt individuals into their communities. Forty years ago, the noted historian Francis Jennings perceptively observed that Indigenous communities in the Colonial Era were multicultural in makeup. He maintained: "We know Europeans to be a conglomeration of peoples, but Whites are presumed to be homogeneous. Even racially categorized Indians are homogeneous and mythical; there never were such people."[11] One example is that of the Stockbridge-Munsee Mohicans. In 1740, Indigenous peoples began settling at the major mission community in Stockbridge, Massachusetts. In the next four decades, this "praying town" was a refuge for Algonquian speakers from diverse communities in the Hudson Valley, Long Island, and southern New England.[12]

A second example is the Iroquois Confederacy. In the late seventeenth and first half of the eighteenth century, the Five Nations "spread their blanket" and allowed refugee nations from the Mid-Atlantic and South—the Conoy, Munsee, Nanticoke, Saponi, Tutelo, and Tuscarora—to resettle in their territories, with some being incorporated into their population. But adoption for whole nations was at different levels of incorporation, and only the Tuscarora were fully adopted as the sixth nation of the Iroquois Confederacy. Even then, the Tuscarora were only allowed to present their views at Grand Council meetings through other nation's sachems.[13]

The Muscogee-speaking Creeks are a third example of a multicultural community. The Muscogee (Creek) coalesced along the Flint and Chattahoochee Rivers and along the Coosa and Tallapoosa Rivers. To reestablish their world after the collapse of the Mississippian Mound Cultures and the devastating impact of European-introduced epidemics, four of the Creek towns took the lead in expanding their world through adopting captives in war or allowing non-Muscogee speakers—Apalachee, Alabama, Catawba, Cherokee, Coushatta, Chickasaw, Choctaw, Hitchiti, Natchez, Shawnee, and Yuchi—as well as Europeans and Africans into their world. Through war and diplomacy as well as trade, they established a network of interconnecting towns from the seventeenth century onward. At the core of their cultural and political existence was their individual talwa (hometown), where they held Busk festivals and micos (political leaders) administered the flow of trade in deerskins.[14] Practicing inclusivity, the Creek facilitated this trade by adopting non-Indians, including Scottish traders who were incorporated through marriage into their society, adopted by prominent Wind Clan matrons. It was no wonder that some of the most famous Muscogee of the last decades of the eighteenth century and first decades of the nineteenth century had Scottish ancestry (e.g., McGillivray and McIntosh).[15] However, their growing intolerance toward African-Creek intermarriage and their offspring clearly reflected southern attitudes and led to extensive trade and enslavement of African peoples. Some of the most prominent Creek peoples even established plantations, housing numerous enslaved peoples. This racist carryover from the days of enslavement affects the contemporary debate about whether African Creek and descendants of Creek Freedmen should be eligible for tribal membership.[16]

Two Seneca Tribal Nations

Today there are two federally recognized Seneca tribal nations situated on four territories in western New York: the Tonawanda Seneca Nation, a government of chiefs with ties to the Iroquois Confederacy at Onondaga; and the Seneca Nation, an elected system of government outside of the Iroquois Confederacy's purview since 1848. In the past and in the present, both tribal nations follow a matrilineage descent rule as their requirement for membership. The Seneca, like other Iroquois communities, are also a multicultural reality, and outsiders' importance is recognized in Iroquoian religious traditions. They honor the Peacemaker, a Huron holy man, and Jikonhsasee, a Neutral woman, the legendary "Peace Queen" or the "Mother of Nations." Jikonhsasee is often credited with helping the Peacemaker establish the Iroquois League. Many of her contributions led the Peacemaker to assign women the traditional role of Clan Matron and allowed them the exclusive right to choose chiefs, assign the fields, and determine the fate of captives, among other important responsibilities.[17] Thus it is not surprising that some of the more famous people in Seneca history were adoptees. Besides the previously mentioned Mary Jemison, others include Kenjockety, Neutral ancestor of General Ely S. Parker; Half-King, a Catawba by birth who was a major figure in the onset of the French and Indian War; Harriet Maxwell Converse, a non-Indian journalist and reformer adopted by the Seneca as well as by the Iroquois Confederacy; and anthropologists Arthur C. Parker and William N. Fenton.[18] It should be pointed out that the Seneca in more modern times have used "adoption" as a tool to win favor with politicians for support for legislation. In these cases, they often played the stereotype "blood brother" for the cameras.[19]

Anthropologist Anthony F. C. Wallace has written that one of the major functions of Seneca warfare in the Colonial Era was not just to inflict casualties on the enemy, but to "maintain emotional equilibrium in individuals who were strongly motivated for revenge, or replace murdered kinfolk, and thereby to maintain the social equilibrium of kinship units."[20] He estimates that two-thirds of the Oneida could trace their ancestry back to captives who were adopted. These included Skenandoa(h), the famous Oneida chief of Susquehannock ancestry of the late Colonial Era right through the Early Republic.[21] Historian Daniel Richter has labeled this "mourning war," insisting that the Seneca and the other member nations of the Iroquois Confederacy were clearly motivated to take captives, men and women, as a way to replenish their ranks decimated by previous warfare and epidemics. Importantly, in the seventeenth century alone, they incorporated some of their enemy captives—Erie, Huron, Neutrals, Susquehannock, Wenro—into their universe.[22] Their Condolence Council ceremony was intended "to overcome the dysphoria of death and restore the euphoria of normal social relations." All outsiders to be adopted had to be "requickened," losing their past name, clan, and tribal affiliation, and become a replacement for a Haudenosaunee who had died. The outsider took the name of the deceased and became fully incorporated into the deceased's family and clan. They literally came back to life as a Seneca.[23]

The Cheyenne

Today, the Northern Cheyenne have a one-half blood quantum rule and the census roll of 1935 for membership, criteria that diverts significantly from the past. Encouraged by the Bureau of Indian Affairs to establish new governance structures and take advantage of government programs and federal monies available during the Great Depression, the Cheyenne came under the provisions of the Indian Reorganization Act (IRA).[24] Yet, as anthropologist John H. Moore has written, the Cheyenne traditionally encouraged exogamous marriage, and its society was hardly based upon "biological separateness" but rather on "extending and hybridizing the nation with other groups."[25] More recently, anthropologist Christina Gish

Hill has added that "Cheyenneness" traditionally was a "state of being, not based on birth and not based on a political contract—like citizenship."[26]

As was true of other Indigenous communities, Cheyenne tribal membership involved being incorporated into a family with all kinship obligations and requirements. Being fully adopted could take months or even years, since, in order to obtain full status, one had to reach certain cultural markers, such as becoming able to understand and speak Cheyenne, knowing religious traditions, and becoming able to participate fully in ceremonies. This was also true in Lakota/Dakota society. If a child in a Cheyenne family died, the family sometimes adopted a friend's child. An orphan, as in the Seneca case, could also be "requickened," thereby assuming the kinship role of the deceased youngster.[27] According to historian Leo K. Killsback, the "orphaned child grew up as part of the new family following the traditions of Sweet Medicine, Youngest, Red Buck, Red Hair, and Blood Bachelor—all of whom were also orphans."[28]

At a typical Cheyenne camp, in the second half of the eighteenth century and well into the nineteenth century, numerous people who were not Cheyenne were often involved in trade, ceremonies, and other purposes. In the 1790s, the French fur trapper Jean-Baptiste Truteau observed that in the camps of the Indigenous people in the Upper Missouri were "always some individuals of other nations, who in times of peace being allied either by marriage or by caprice meet their relatives there and are subsequently regarded as people of the nation, even in war."[29] As the Cheyenne moved from their Minnesota homeland into the Great Plains after the introduction and spread of the horse culture from the mid-sixteenth century onward, they made temporary or permanent alliances with the Arikara, Hidatsa, and Mandan and allied themselves with the Arapaho and Kiowa. As in the case of the Hidatsa, the alliance was consummated through participation in the Cheyenne Adoption Pipe Ceremony.[30] With losses as a result of epidemics and conflicts with the US frontier army, as Moore has suggested, in the 1860s, the Cheyenne Dog Soldiers even tried unsuccessfully to recruit and adopt Lakota warriors into their society.[31]

As in all Native American societies presented in this article, the guiding light to tribal membership was practical considerations more than bloodlines. To the Cheyenne, adoption was a strategic move. Establishing kinship across Plains Indian lines could produce obligations and lead to positive results: allies could be secured, trade could be expanded, and greater access to areas filled with buffalo herds and other needed resources could be obtained. In fact, the Cheyenne came to dominate a major trade route from the Plains into the Southwest.[32] Moreover, incorporating a non-Cheyenne and even a former enemy—male or female—could be useful not just in war, but also in diplomatic negotiations. Consequently, anthropologist Patricia Albers has perceptively observed that this practice of abducting captives was "not just a product of war, but one of reconciliation as well." Although fewer women than men were adopted by the Cheyenne, Albers has written that women captives served as go-betweens and opened channels between warring tribal nations.[33] The Cheyenne also valued intermarriage since women at times acted as major conduits in the fur trade. To further their strategic position and power on the Upper Missouri, the Cheyenne also adopted white traders such as William Bent after he married a tribal member.[34]

The Crow

The Crow Nation of Montana rejected the Indian Reorganization Act, which encouraged tribal nations to draft constitutions with blood quantum criteria. Yet today the Crow have a one-quarter or more Indian blood requirement for membership as set out in its constitution of 2001.[35] This definition of tribal membership is far different than what the Crow traditionally accepted in the past. The late Grant Bulltail—Crow elder, historian, and storyteller—has insisted that the Crow had no "orphans in the old days."[36]

Crow camps were composed of many non-Crow peoples. As late as 1902, a government survey listed that 985 of Crow Reservation residents were Native American and that 43 of 767 households contained individuals of non-Crow ancestry, including adopted and unadopted Arapaho, Assiniboine, Cheyenne, Cherokee, Chippewa, Piegan, and Yankton. Before that time, much like in the previous Northern Cheyenne example, other Indigenous peoples such as the famous Lakota warrior Young Man Afraid of His Horses would frequently visit their relatives and at least temporarily reside among the Crow.[37]

Much like other Plains Indians, the Crow saw the practical value in adopting. Three of the more widely written-about adoptees in the history of the frontier were Pine Leaf/Woman Chief, born to the Gros Ventre Tribe, and two African American mountain men, Jim Beckwourth (Bloody Arm) and Ed Rose (Cut Nose). All served the Crow in battle against other Plains Indians, although it is difficult in each case to separate their role from legend.[38] In May 2008, presidential candidate Barack Obama was "adopted" and given the name "One Who Helps People Throughout the Land." Although once again it showed the adoption was based upon practical concerns of a tribal nation, namely attempting to win support for an energy-dependent (coal) tribal nation, the one-day "ceremony" was hardly a version of traditional Crow adoption—a serious, complex, and sacred ritual that took months to complete.[39]

The adoption ceremony performed by the Crow Tobacco Society occurred right after the planting of tobacco—considered a sacred plant—began. This society contained at least thirty chapters, one of which was the Beaver Dance Ceremony. Each chapter had its own leaders, songs, and symbols derived from visions. Inclusion in the society was frequently based on a practical need or emergency; someone might vow to become a member if a sick relative didn't recover from illness or if a warrior was unsuccessful in battle. To members of the Tobacco Society, the primary aim of ceremonial adoption was to obtain a share of mystic powers that were associated with a medicine bundle.[40]

The Beaver Dance Ceremony commenced after a Crow Indian went into the mountains, fasted for several days, and received visions. Both men and women participated in the ceremony, which was composed of four separate ceremonies that usually took place one or two months apart. The one being adopted had to go through the same kind of ceremony three times, much like going through the stages of child development. The fourth time, the clan uncle would pick out four of his relatives, each of whom had to give the adopted person one of their favorite songs. Adoption aimed to establish a protective father-child or mother-child relationship—one that was to endure through a lifetime.[41] Grant Bulltail has also stressed the importance of the clan uncle in the adoption process. His responsibility was to instruct his adopted clan nephew "physically and spiritually" and be his promoter in the community, singing "a song of praise about him."[42]

Conclusion

By looking back at the past, one can conclude that tribal enrollment was incredibly fluid. Indigenous nations had their own unique ways of incorporating members into their circle. Incorporating the adoptee into a kinship network within the community was universal. All adoptions were based upon *practical reasons*: fears of strangers entering their world, depopulation in wars and epidemics, building alliances, setting boundaries, making peace, building trade for economic survival, gaining vital knowledge, or carrying out responsibilities they believed were mandated by the Creator.

How to Be a Real Indian

The first time someone asks you how Indian you are, lie.
On the blacktop, the soccer field, tell them
one hundred percent, your grandmother lived on the rez,
or you were born there, hooked up to machines running on bad
generators, in a bad hospital in a bad part of town. Say you dream in Oneida
at night, show-and-tell them rose rock and kachina,
give them exactly what they ask for,
the first time. Learn to read from that book
of the boy who falls in love with Minnehaha, invents
written language, discovers corn, and departs in a canoe.

In the third grade, when your class suggests "Ten Little Indians"
for the Thanksgiving theme, offer to teach them
the dances you don't know, but should. Swallow hard.
Imagine your ancestors, the ones you see each day
when you get home from school staring down at you from the walls
of your grandmother's house, draped in their turbans and regalia,
Tecumseh, Red Cloud; imagine their eyes—not sad, but fascinated
by the evenness of your buckskin fringe, the wild neon
in your store-bought feathers. Sing "Ten Little Indians."
Fan your hand across your mouth. Say "how."

The second time someone asks
how Indian you are, embellish. If you find out your mother's mother's father
was the son of a chief, tell them your mother was a princess. Tell them
your mother sang you songs at night while rocking the cradle,
in her native tongue, but she's forgotten all of it now. Tell them your tribe
waits for you, wants to embrace you as one of their own.
Tell them you are loved by your tribe. Memorize
the names of the Six Nations. You always forget Tuscarora.

After all, there is an agency for everything.
Call the BIA. Aren't you on the list? Dawes, Allotment,
can't you find your grandpa? And at first, this is a wonderful game:
Metoxens and Doxtaters, Hills and the occasional Cornelius.
No Antones in sight. When you find the man who might have cradled
your mother's mother's small head in his hands,
you must sniff out the whole line,
begat and begat and begat, married then divorced then
they split up the property and moved to Oklahoma.
All the people who passed down the blood,
the blood you wanted to be rid of, sometimes
the blood you wished could multiply.
Give them names. Tally up their fractions.

The third time you are asked how Indian you are, decide
it doesn't matter, exactly. Say, an eighth. Say, a thirty-second. Claim
to be Choctaw or Cherokee. Claim to be a princess, too. Talk about quantum
as though trying to find a way to name yourself.

Go back to the rez. Brenda's gotten clearance to open up a bar,
just in time for your coming of age. Take your white boyfriend
and play pool with him amid a cloud of smoke, where he will chat up
the locals, where he will talk about enterprise and fair trade. At the Pow Wow,
buy turquoise and the tail of a fox, and soft white cowskin
for your mother's moccasins. Eat fry bread every day of your life if you can.
On the way home a Chickasaw will sit down next to you on the plane
with his hair in two black braids and cowrie shells around his leathery neck.
Despite eagerness, opportunity, the sudden, improbable phenomenon
of two live Indians on the same plane together at the same time,
say nothing. If he says something first, stay quiet. Because you aren't just
two live Indians on the same plane together at the same time.
You're *one Indian and a fraud*, flying toward Delaware.

The fourth time, the fifth time, the eighth time they ask you how Indian
you are, your mouth is so, so heavy—let it hang open for a moment
so the spirits can enter. Let the woman who had your name and died

before you were born come into your body and speak the wisdom,
let her Grandmother Willow you. Let your head hang over the stump
of Chief Powhatan, ready to be bludgeoned by your own father
for love. Take Maria Tallchief into your limbs, eagle-graceful,
turtle-strong. Try to imagine your own face
on the face of a gold coin, the baby on your back
as recognizable as the way you point the way
and shut that open mouth. Make its flatness stretch
toward centuries of silence. Lead the men down the great river
to whatever they seek.

KENZIE ALLEN

In the Wake of Pretendians

KanyΛhtakelu (Snow scattered here and there)
REBECCA M. WEBSTER and

YakoyΛtehtauhi (She is continually going along learning)
AMELIA M. WEBSTER

We start with two simple questions, both having an array of complex answers. First, what does it mean to be Indigenous? Second, who gets to decide who is Indigenous? The answer to the first question is that Indigenous identity means different things to different people. It centers around community, traditions, family, and belonging. Indigeneity is biological, cultural, and political.[1] You can't base your Indigenous identity off a DNA test.[2] Further, self-identification alone does not make a person Indigenous. It requires the community, in turn, to claim the individual. This brings us to our second question of who gets to decide. Under our current system, tribal governments decide who officially belongs to federally (and state) recognized tribes. Tribes often rely on blood quantum—a colonizer-imposed system of determining who belongs. A system that Indigenous people never employed to determine belonging. This system can leave out individuals who would historically have been included in the community but are now left out. Even more confusion enters the scene when we consider our collective traumatic past of colonization, assimilation, and removal. Many people now find themselves removed from their Indigenous communities and struggle to find ways to rekindle kinship ties.

This chapter doesn't rely on colonized methods to determine who can justly present themselves as an Indigenous person. Rather, it focuses on the harm that comes when someone without any verifiable Indigenous ties fabricates an identity and presents as Indigenous for personal or financial gain. We will use the term that is gaining popularity: pretendian. A pretendian is defined as a "person who falsely claims to have Indigenous ancestry, who fakes an Indigenous identity, or who digs up an old ancestor from hundreds of years ago to proclaim themselves as Indigenous."[3] There is a growing base of literature dedicated to articulating the general harm that these individuals inflict.[4] This chapter provides a brief overview of that harm and then turns to two personal accounts of how pretendians impacted the chapter authors. We purposefully chose not to identify the individuals to avoid giving them more media attention. We are choosing to focus on our personal stories of their betrayal and where that leaves us.

Colonial Extraction of Resources

The phenomenon of pretendians is colonial in nature.[5] It extracts and shifts resources away from Indigenous people to white settlers. White settlers masquerading as Indigenous people take jobs, scholarships, employment, and other opportunities meant for Indigenous people. They take up space meant for Indigenous bodies and Indigenous voices. They speak on our behalf. They steal our stories, internalize them through their colonizer lenses, over-stereotype them, and regurgitate a warped version of the story as their own. They do all of this without our consent.

For generations, white settlers made Indigenous people feel shame for who they were. They tried to erase us. Now, they want to consume our identities. As Indigenous rights lawyer Jean Teillet explains: "If colonialism has not eradicated Indigenous people by starvation, residential schools, the reserve system, taking their lands and languages, scooping their children, and doing everything to assimilate Indigenous peoples, then the final act is to become them. It's a perverse kind of reverse assimilation."[6] This performance targets the holes in mainstream knowledge of Indigenous identity and feeds into existing stereotypes.

Indigenous Allies

Too many people are quick to defend pretendians because they sometimes do good work for our communities. However, doing good things doesn't erase the damage they inflict. All sorts of non-Indigenous people do good work for our communities and do so without masquerading as one of us. There is no need to pretend to be one of us to make a difference in our communities. Doing so is an insult to the allies who don't fabricate their identities.

I recently sat on the dissertation committee for a non-Indigenous ally, Kathleen Ratteree. Her dissertation focused on Indigenous plants and medicines, creating a learning experience for school-age children and providing guidance for teachers. However, the part of her dissertation that was most powerfully written was the way she articulated her responsibilities as a non-Indigenous ally:

> Allyship (a journey that never ends) requires a deep look into the very real effects of historical trauma that has been done and continues to be done to Indigenous peoples around the world. It requires recognition of the very real effects of the misuse of Western science. Most of all, it requires personal healing and reflection to step out of the spiral of despair and passivity to move forward with . . . "a heart for the work."[7]

Later, Kathleen further explained, "Throughout the project, I reckon with my own positionality, which is that of a white, non-Indigenous settler woman learning to be an ally. For this work, I assume the responsibility of honing my own ethic of non-interference as an outsider to the world of Indigenous knowledge."[8] Indeed, this process outlines the framework for non-Indigenous people to be allies while holding space for Indigenous people.

Personal Account—Rebecca

Right around the time I was going up for tenure at the University of Minnesota Duluth, I had to list several colleagues at other universities to be potential external letter writers to comment on my publication history. This was during a time when allegations were percolating about one pretendian in academia whom I had considered a friend and colleague. She had previously offered guidance on publication matters and navigating academia as an Indigenous woman. I chose not to confront the situation and simply removed her from the list of potential letter writers just as the deadline approached. When news sources and social media broke the story about her lack of Indigenous background and she released a public statement, I again did nothing. I didn't know what I was supposed to do or how I was supposed to respond. Instead, I stewed in a place of hurt, anger, and disbelief.

Fast-forward a few months, and another friend from out of town came to stay at our place. Our Oneida community was hosting a weeklong ceremony, and they wanted to attend. To be fair, I saw the warning signs that this friend might be a pretendian, and others even tried to warn me. For example, some of the birch bark baskets they gifted me, and I bartered for, turned out to have been made by a non-Indigenous artist. My former friend peeled off the original artist's signature to inscribe their own signature. This is one of the many red flags I chose to ignore, passing it off as a character flaw instead of the warning sign that it was. I refused to believe someone would weave such an elaborate web of lies based on imagined Indigenous connections.

When this friend was at our house, I brought up the recent news about our mutual friend who had been outed. This friend doubled down and talked about how it was such a disgrace to fake your identity and gain access to sacred spaces. We lamented how much we were hurt by her refusal to verify her own identity for so long. We were astonished anyone would base an entire persona around unfounded family lore. I thought we were on the same page with our stance on pretendians and the danger they pose to our communities. I thought this person was my friend. I was wrong.

Shortly after their visit, news broke about this person also being a pretendian. The more I stewed in the new hurt, anger, and disbelief, the more I saw others posting about them on social media. People posted photos of how they looked just a few years ago, with lighter hair and skin color resembling mine and my daughters'. It became apparent that they race-shifted with dyed hair and fake tanning, morphing into the stereotypical image white settlers assume we all have. I thought about the message this shift delivered to people: in order to be valid and to belong, you must look a certain way.

These two exposures left me mourning the people I thought I knew. But more than that, they broke my trust. I began questioning others around me, bracing for the next pretendian reveal to be among my network of friends. I became suspicious of old and new acquaintances. Whereas I previously thought the best in everyone and assumed they had the best intentions, now I question the identity and motives of people around me. I find myself limiting my exposure to those in my network whom I suspect might not be who they say they are. This isn't a good place to be, and I don't know how long I will be stuck like this.

Personal Account—Amelia, age seventeen

I had an experience with a pretendian, and it affected me and the people in my community. I first met them at a barter blanket event where people come to trade all sorts of things and share stories about the items they bring for trade. I thought this person had interesting stories about the traditional items they brought to trade. I didn't even consider that they might not be Indigenous.

After the barter blanket event, they helped me with a paper for one of my college writing classes. In the specific part they helped me with, we were talking about the cast of a movie that was centered around an Indian community. It just so happens that we got into the discussion of how much someone pretending to be Indian can hurt their community, especially when portrayed in the Hollywood film industry. This individual went above and beyond to show their knowledge on this topic and talked about many other famous movies and actors representing Indian people who weren't actually Indian. I didn't suspect anything at the time because it just seemed to me as though this individual had a lot of knowledge on the subject. Looking back on the experience, it makes me wonder if they researched some of the actors who pretended to be Indian to get a better understanding of how to fake it and learn what not to do to avoid getting caught.

When the news finally broke that this person was, in fact, not Indian, I almost didn't believe it. I heard about this happening in other places, but for the person whom I saw as a friend to our family, I just couldn't accept it. Even though this person broke my trust, it hurt to know that this individual felt the need to try to pretend to be someone they're not to feel accepted by my family. It was upsetting to know that this individual didn't own up to their own doing. I still don't understand why this person felt the need to pretend to be anything except what they were. They changed their appearance and life story to "fit in" our community. It made me realize that this person was going off a stereotypical image of what an

Indian is to feed into their pretendian image. I have so many unanswered questions. Did they think they weren't going to be accepted into this community if they weren't Indian? What caused them to pretend to be Indian instead of just being a strong ally of Indian communities?

Call to Action

Through it all, we're still not sure what our role is in keeping watch of other people's identities. Policing identities can discourage those who are disconnected from their communities from attempting to reconnect based on a fear of being labeled a pretendian. We don't want to get involved in investigating those around us, but we also don't want to stand by while others try to masquerade as one of us. As activist Rebecca Nagle explains: "Pretendians perpetuate the myth that Native identity is determined by the individual, not the tribe or community, directly undermining tribal sovereignty and Native self-determination. To protect the rights of Indigenous people, pretendians . . . must be challenged and the retelling of their false narratives must be stopped."[9] Further, the Native American and Indigenous Studies Association issued a statement in 2015 about the pretendian problem in academia. Their call to action emphasized that "we are all responsible to act in an ethical fashion by standing against Indigenous identity fraud."[10] Exactly how we systematically do this remains unclear.

What is clear is that we can and should ask each other to verify our identity when a question arises. An Indigenous professor shared her experience when someone on social media accused her of not being Indigenous. Instead of deleting the comment, she responded by identifying her family and clan. "Being accused of not being claimed by those you claim is not an indictment. It is an invitation. . . . Staying quiet will not address the pretendian problem; it will allow it to thrive."[11] We are often asked to prove our "pedigree."[12] While the need to prove our identity is certainly riddled with its own set of problems, it is the one thing that pretendians are unable to do.

When would-be allies decide to be pretendians and we find out, what happens then? The simplest answer is we hold them accountable. They need to stop holding themselves out as Indigenous and explain and apologize to the Indigenous community and the public. They need to acknowledge the harm they caused. They also need to understand that it will take time for people to forgive them and further understand that many never will.

Concluding Thoughts

Those with little experience with pretendians, and even those with plenty of experience, may wonder how they can be a part of the solution. The breeding ground of hate and negativity that is social media can serve as a platform for people to lie about their own identity as well as make false accusations about the identities of others. A little bit of research can go a long way. We need to stand by our fellow Indigenous people wrongfully called out while holding the people who are pretending to be Indigenous accountable.

The Explosion of the 2020 Census "Indian" Population and Its Implications for Tribal Policymaking

KARL ESCHBACH and JONATHAN TAYLOR

On June 30, 1920, J. C. Hart, superintendent of the Bureau of Indian Affairs Pawnee Agency, recorded a census of the Kaw Indians (Figure 1). In the rows, Hart used the column *Indian Name* to report the subjects' Kaw blood quantum. Hart typed for a certain Mr. Charles Curtis: 1/4. His wife, Annie E., is listed as "White."

Figure 1: Charles Curtis in the Kaw Census, 1920[1]

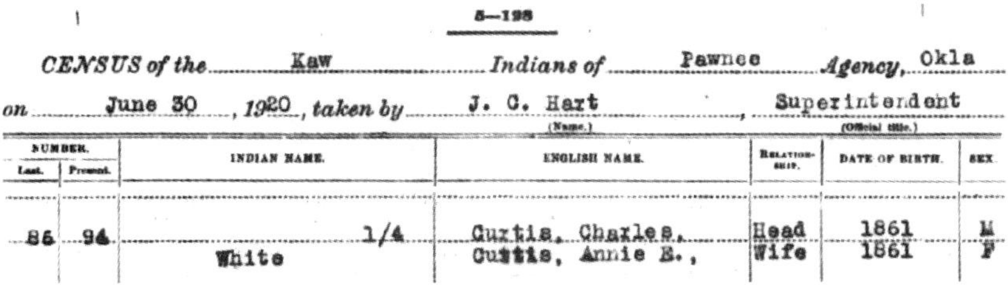

5—198

CENSUS of the Kaw *Indians of* Pawnee *Agency,* Okla
on June 30 , *19*20 , *taken by* J. C. Hart (Name.) , Superintendent (Official title.)

Number Last.	Number Present.	Indian Name.	English Name.	Relationship.	Date of Birth.	Sex.
86	94	1/4	Curtis, Charles,	Head	1861	M
		White	Curtis, Annie E.,	Wife	1861	F

Ten years later, a Census Bureau enumerator visited a home at 1101 Topeka Boulevard in Topeka Township, Shawnee County, Kansas (Figure 2). The enumerator recorded the presence there of a widower: the same Mr. Charles Curtis. In column 12, *Color or race,* the enumerator wrote "W." To the enumerator, Charles was white, as were all the other individuals listed on that enumeration sheet. The enumerator also charmingly (and accurately) recorded Curtis's occupation as "Vice President" and his industry as "United States."

Figure 2: Charles Curtis of Topeka, Kansas, United States Census, 1930[2]

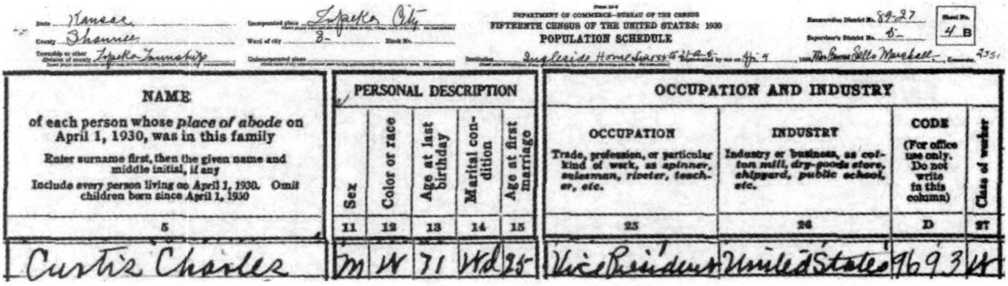
DEPARTMENT OF COMMERCE—BUREAU OF THE CENSUS
FIFTEENTH CENSUS OF THE UNITED STATES: 1930
POPULATION SCHEDULE

State Kansas
County Shawnee
Township or other division of county Topeka Township
Incorporated place Topeka City
Ward of city 3
Institution Ingleside Home
Enumeration District No. 89-27
Supervisor's District No. 5
Sheet No. 4 B

NAME of each person whose *place of abode* on April 1, 1930, was in this family. Enter surname first, then the given name and middle initial, if any. Include every person living on April 1, 1930. Omit children born since April 1, 1930	PERSONAL DESCRIPTION: Sex	Color or race	Age at last birthday	Marital condition	Age at first marriage	OCCUPATION AND INDUSTRY: OCCUPATION Trade, profession, or particular kind of work, as *spinner, salesman, riveter, teacher, etc.*	INDUSTRY Industry or business, as *cotton mill, dry-goods store, shipyard, public school, etc.*	CODE (For office use only. Do not write in this column)	Class of worker
5	11	12	13	14	15	25	26	D	27
Curtis Charles	M	W	71	Wd	25	Vice President	United States	9693	W

This 1930 census counted only 343,352 Indians in the United States, principally on the reservation lands of federally recognized Indian tribes. Notwithstanding his formal enrollment as a Kaw Indian, Herbert Hoover's vice president, the former US Senator Charles Curtis, was, to the Census Bureau, simply a white man.

Eighty-eight years later, the *New York Times* asked about another senator born in the mid-continent, "Elizabeth Warren has a Native American ancestor. Does that make her Native American?"[3]

These prominent opposites on the national stage obscure multitudes. Behind Vice President Curtis are those many Indians in the first half of the twentieth century whose identities were firmly under federal bureaucratic control (often to absurd results) and whose self-conceptions were under concerted social pressure to assimilate (often to tragic ends). Behind Senator Warren are millions of contemporaries deploying everything from family lore and Ancestry.com to DNA analysis and letters in the attic to integrate a self-construction that often encompasses "Indianness." Vice President Curtis and Senator Warren also bookend a story of evolving "Indianness" in the quantification of "Indians" in the US census. The story brackets millions under multiple, often countervailing social, demographic, and policy pressures as the US government counts and sorts them. This paper takes up that story, culminating in a radical and (as yet) poorly understood change in census categorization in 2020.

* * *

The Indigenous population of the Americas experienced a long decline from the first incursions of Europeans and the forced migration of Africans into the Americas. The causes of this decline include the effect of pathogens, military depredations, the destruction of life and livelihoods, and social disruption. The low point of the American Indian population, as reflected in the US census, was 240,000 reported in 1900.[4] From that point, the Indian population began to rebound slowly through the 1950 census. Counts were erratic at each census, as they varied with the emphasis on enumerating the Indian population. In 1950, still fewer than 360,000 Indians were counted.

After 1950, the American Indian population grew with increasing momentum. By 2020, the population of Hispanic and non-Hispanic American Indians or Alaska Natives alone and in combination with other races was counted at 9.7 million.

How does a country get from an Indian population of 360,000 to nearly ten million in seventy years? Certainly not through any routine demographic process of population growth via the excess of births over deaths. The answer lies in the changes in how people are classified as Indians.

A critical beginning point is that the population of the Americas as it emerged in the wake of the Columbian contact was an amalgam of Indigenous, European, African, and Asian people. Exogamy[5] (birth with partners outside the group) among groups in bounded populations can have explosive dynamics—doubling the descendancy population every generation under what would otherwise be replacement fertility (Figure 3). In other words, if two children per parent pair make for a steady population, the number of members of the descendancy population doubles each generation—a point well understood today in the context of Native debates about blood quantum on tribal citizenship and lineal descent policies. Descendancy dynamics are also applicable outside that context.

Figure 3: The Core of Descendancy Dynamics under Exogamy[6]

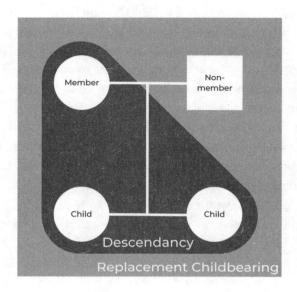

Seven Decades of Census Indians

After centuries of exogamy, when we consider the 360,000 Indians ostensibly counted by the census in 1950, the truth of the matter is that the Indian descendancy population in the United States numbered in the millions by that time, even setting aside the migrated descendants of Indigenous people from elsewhere in the Americas. Census Bureau classification policies and practices, expressing the presumptions of the Euro-American settler colonial population and its government, substantially restricted the use of the Indian identity category to members of recognized Indian communities living on or near designated reservations and a few similar locally recognized Indian communities. Even when Indians encountered sympathetic enumerators (or later the freedom to self-select race), evidence suggests they felt pressure to pass as white.[7] This reservoir of uncounted millions of Indigenous descendants lies latent through the chronology.

In Charles Curtis's day and up to 1960, racial identification on the census was assigned by a census enumerator. The enumerators were temporary workers over whom the Census Bureau had limited control. Indian identity was rarely assigned outside of states with federally recognized Indian lands, and the overwhelming majority of persons of mixed Indian and white or Black ancestry outside of these areas were not reported as Indians. The midcentury was also a period of growing urbanization of out-migrants from reservation communities. Some first-generation urbanizing Indian populations may have been counted as Indians, but it is unlikely that their mixed-race children and grandchildren would have been so counted.

Subsequent changes in Census Bureau practices combined with changes in the social forces bearing on the formation and expression of Indian identity fed the initially slow, later torrential growth of the census Indian population. Census changes occurred in several steps.

Beginning in 1960, the primary mode of administration of the census became a mail-out/mail-back form to be filled out by a respondent living in each household. The change of mode essentially remade census race into an expression of personal identity by the respondent. In other words, a change made initially for operational and fiscal savings yielded self-identification as a fundamental principle: You are who you say you are.

There is one partial qualification to this principle unique to Indians. Official guidance about racial classification incorporates two distinctive elements for American Indian identity. It defines an American Indian or Alaska Native as "a person having origins in any of the original peoples of North and South America (including Central America), *and who maintains tribal affiliation or community recognition*"[8] or *"attachment."*[9] The italicized part of this definition is included for no other group. For example, the definition of being Vietnamese does not stipulate engagement in Vietnamese community affairs. However, the qualification is only partial. It is up to the individual to decide what constitutes an affiliation, recognition, or attachment. For example, would that affiliation be to Pueblo (a category of Indian), Tewa (a linguistic/cultural group), or Ohkay Owingeh (a particular polity north of Española, New Mexico)? Three different citizens (or descendants) of Ohkay Owingeh could reasonably write three different answers. In 1980, changes in census collection and reporting joined "Alaska Native" categories with "American Indian" to yield the racial category American Indian or Alaska Native (AI/AN).

Beginning in the 2000 census, the race question was modified by introducing an instruction to report all races that applied rather than to choose a single race only (see the left panel of Figure 4, which shows the feature's continuation in 2010). With the introduction of this rule, the population reporting a single race started to grow more slowly. At the same time, the number of persons reporting the American Indian race in combination with one or more races appeared as a new group of 1.4 million multi-race, non-Hispanic Indians.

In 2020, changes to the race question were more subtle but nonetheless critically consequential.[10] The most visible change was the introduction of a write-in space into which Black and white respondents could report a more specific ancestry (right panel in Figure 4). Listed examples on the form include German, Egyptian, Jamaican, and Nigerian. This additional space and the inclusion of examples created more opportunities for persons with mixed Indian ancestry to report an Indian or tribal identity.

A second change entailed the addition of examples to the write-in space for American Indian respondents. One offered example was "Mayan," which modeled the selection of an "enrolled or principal tribe" neither federally recognized nor in a government-to-government relationship with the United States. This instruction implicitly encourages a broad view of Indigenous identity not tied to citizenship in or "affiliation, recognition, or attachment" with a federally recognized Native nation.

The third change was not visible to respondents but crucial to reported identity counts—the Census Bureau digitally captured and coded a substantially larger number of characters from the write-in responses in any of the spaces for disclosing specific identities than in previous censuses. For example, a 2020 resident of the Great Smoky Mountains might check the box next to White and write in "Scottish, Irish, and Cherokee." Even if she did not check the box next to American Indian or Alaska Native, the census coding procedures would record her as "American Indian or Alaska Native in combination with one or more other races." Respondents were advised, "You are not required to mark a checkbox category in order to enter a response in one of the write-in areas. You may respond by entering your specific identity or identities in any of the write-in response areas on the race question."[11] Together these changes encouraged and encoded greater attention to details of mixed ancestry in census race classification.[12]

Figure 4: Evolution of the Census Race Question, 2010 to 2020[13]

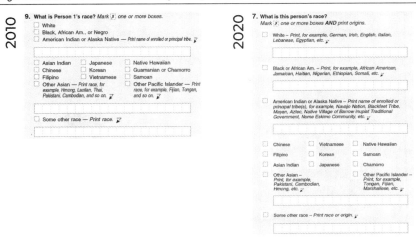

The large latent population of potential Indians, together with the changes in the wording and coding of the census race item, fueled subsequent growth in the census-reported American Indian population (Figure 5).[14] The background of these changes included broader social, cultural, and institutional challenges to systems of white dominance in the United States. For American Indians, these changes included the increasing autonomy of recognized Indian nations on the institutional side and the elevation of American Indian identities and culture on the personal side.[15] By 1990, the self-identified American Indian population had increased to 1.96 million, appearing not just in and near Indian communities.[16] The introduction of reporting multiple races with the 2000 census led to a scale change. The addition of a mixed-race AI/AN alone and in combination nearly doubled the identified Indian population.

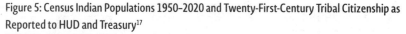

Figure 5: Census Indian Populations 1950–2020 and Twenty-First-Century Tribal Citizenship as Reported to HUD and Treasury[17]

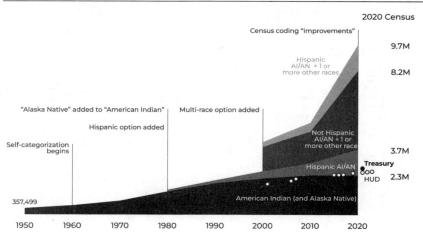

The emergence of a population that was both Hispanic and Indian was sudden and extremely rapid. In 1980 for the first time, a separate Hispanic identity item was added to the complete count form of the census. The population cross-classified as Indian and Hispanic in 1980 was 95,000, 7 percent of the total Indian population and just 0.6 percent of the Hispanic population. The count rose to 165,000 in 1990, 8 percent of the census Indian population. After 1990, the Hispanic Indian population grew much more rapidly than the non-Hispanic Indian population, growing to 675,000 (16 percent of all census Indians) in 2000 and nearly three million (30 percent of census Indians) in 2020.

The increase in the Hispanic American Indian population reflects in part the rapid growth of the Hispanic population through immigration and a high birth rate. However, another part of this growth reflects an apparent evolution in how Hispanics report race, given the available options. Through the 2020 census, the Hispanic population has been counted on a "Hispanic origin" question, separate from the race question. Hispanics have been asked to classify themselves on the race item, using available options. These options do *not* include Hispanic categories. The most common choice by Hispanic respondents has been "White," but a significant minority either leave the question blank or report that they are another race. That "other race" reported is typically a Hispanic identity category.

At each successive census, however, a small but growing minority of Hispanic respondents have chosen to identify as American Indians, reflecting the Indigenous component of their heritage. Given available options, this is a logical choice because the amalgamation of Indigenous and other racial populations was typical throughout the Americas. As in the United States, Indigenous identities elsewhere in the Americas have been persistent across time and have been expressed with increasing assertiveness in recent decades.

It remains a small share of all Hispanics who also self-report as Indian alone or in combination with another race. Less than 5 percent made this choice in 2020. Nevertheless, the large and growing Hispanic population makes Hispanic Indians the fastest-growing census Indian sub-population.

The rapid growth of the population reporting American Indian race in combination with some other race between the censuses of 2010 and 2020 caught many observers off guard. Changes in counts between 2000 and 2010 for non-Hispanic Indians were modest. We know from work by Liebler and co-investigators[18] that the relative stability of the count totals between 2000 and 2010 masks a high level of churn in who was counted in the different groups (Indian alone, Indian in combination, not Indian). However, the total counts may have stabilized by 2010.

This was not the case in the next decade. The non-Hispanic population reporting American Indian race combined with at least one other race grew by more than 2.6 million people, doubling this population. Nearly a million additional Hispanic Indians reported multiple races, nearly tripling the count in a decade. Why were these changes so significant? The Census Bureau has not released data that fully account for the shifts. It does appear that the changes to the race item that were designed to encourage greater reliability of results and discourage nonresponse to the race question and reporting of "some other race" played a role.

Census Indians and Tribal Citizens

Overlaid on the census racial categories in Figure 5 are plotted two separate data series on tribal citizenship published by other federal government departments. The white dots are the tribal enrollment totals from certain years of the Department of Housing and Urban Development (HUD) Indian

Housing Block Grant Program (IHBG) Final Allocation spreadsheets,[19] which are collected in service of implementing the IHBG formula under the Native American Housing Assistance and Self-Determination Act (NAHASDA).[20] The black dot is the sum of enrolled citizens of tribes that certified to the US Treasury their numbers of citizens and employees in applying for American Rescue Plan Act (ARPA) funds during the pandemic.[21] Whatever their omissions, limitations, and errors,[22] together these two data series show that the 2020 magnitude of the single-race Indian population (AI/AN) is on par with the tribal citizen population.[23] Moreover, the HUD data decisively do *not* show an increase from 2010 to 2020 on par with the multi-race Indian increase of 149 percent in the census data.

Variability in Growth in Different Areas

Insights into the explosion of the multi-race Indian population in 2020 can be gleaned from disaggregating the national picture. First, Indian Country does not drive the phenomenon. Figure 6 extracts from Figure 5 the data for all American Indian Areas, Alaska Native Areas, and Hawaiian Home Lands in the three censuses with multiple race identification: 2000, 2010, and 2020. No 2020 spike appears. Instead, the single-race Indian population gives ground to the multi-race category, and Hispanic Indians are a consistently small fraction. Over time, the census-recorded in-area Indian population is about half the tribal citizen population reported to HUD and the US Treasury. It is reasonable to surmise that adding the tracts near Indian areas to this analysis would close the gap between the in-area and citizen populations.

Figure 6: Census Indian Populations in Indian Areas* 2000–2020 and Twenty-First-Century Tribal Citizenship as Reported to HUD and US Treasury[24]

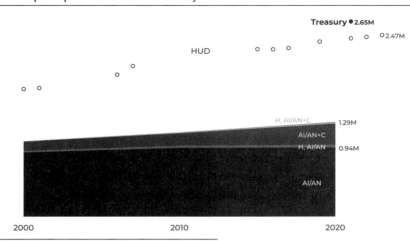

*Reservations, pueblos, rancherias, and Native/tribal statistical areas

Figure 7 decomposes the 2010 and 2020 data in Figure 5, plotting the states by the percentage of 2020 single-race Indians on the horizontal axis and by the relative growth of the multi-race Indian category on the vertical axis. Thus Tennessee (TN) experienced four times as much multi-race Indian growth as single-race Indian growth from 2010 to 2020. The states are further divided into three groups for convenience. Group 1 states include a higher Native proportion, spanning Wyoming (2.1 percent) to Alaska (14.4 percent). Group 2 states are those states that, together with Group 1, comprise 99 percent of the 2020 single-race Indians living in Indian areas. Group 3 is all other states. Above 2 percent (i.e., to the right of Wyoming), the relative change of the multi-race category declines with an increase in the Native percentage.

Figure 7: Relative Growth of AI/AN in Combination by State, 2010–2020[25]

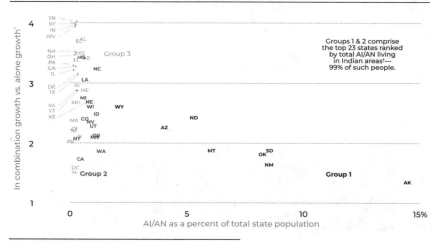

*Ratio = (AI/AN+C 2020 / AI/AN+C 2010) / (AI/AN 2020 / AI/AN 2010)
†Reservations, pueblos, rancherias, and Native/tribal statistical areas

Figure 8 breaks apart Figure 5 into the three groups identified in Figure 7. It shows the geographic concentration of multi-race Indian growth in the states with few single-race Indians and few on-reservation, single-race Indians, i.e., Group 3. Group 1 displays some descendancy dynamics (faster growth in the multi-race population) and Hispanic growth. Group 2, which contains California, shows substantial growth in the Hispanic Indian group and more multi-race Indian growth than Group 1. Group 3 overwhelms them both. Consider the growth from 1950 to 2020. In Group 1, it was 8X. In Group 2, 36X. And in Group 3, 192X, more than half of which occurred in the seventh decade. Texas contributes substantially to the growth of Hispanic Indians, and the southern states at the top of Figure 7 contribute massively to multi-race Indian growth. In Group 3 states, the Census Bureau identifies more than six times more people as mixed-race Indians than as single-race Indians.

Figure 8: Relative Growth of Census Indian Populations 1950–2020 by State Group[26]

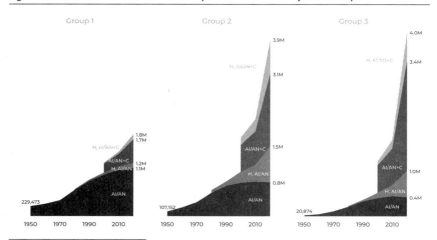

Group 1: AK, AZ, MT, ND, NM, OK, SD, WY
Group 2: CA, CO, ID, LA, MI, MN, MS, NC, NE, NV, NY, OR, UT, WA, WI
Group 3: AL, AR, CT, DC, DE, FL, GA, HI, IA, IL, IN, KS, KY, MA, MD, ME, MO, NH, NJ, OH, PA, PR, RI, SC, TN, TX, VA, VT, WV

Some Evidence of Contemporary Indian Exogamy

The start of this discussion highlighted the critical role of descendancy dynamics under exogamy in fueling the rapid Indigenous descendancy population growth. The Census Bureau's 2020 change in racial classification methodology brings the latent Native descendancy population into view, fueling the rapid "growth" of the census American Indian population in 2020. Nevertheless, the rapid growth of the Indian descendancy population through exogamy continues today.

This process is well known to many Indian nations that use tribal blood quantum to limit citizenship. For many, a growing number of children born to citizens do not qualify for citizenship. Tribes are thus caught between two conflicting but interrelated futures: exponential population growth with some tribal ancestry and rapid decline in the number of children who qualify for citizenship under blood quantum rules.[27]

As Indians and Native nations move forward from the present, the logic of descendancy dynamics will continue to progress at an exponentially increasing rate. Figure 9 shows a conservative view of Indian exogamy in 2021 using census data for the non-Hispanic AI/AN-alone population from the Census Bureau's American Community Survey. The box-and-whisker plots indicate the ranges of state average exogamy for Groups 1, 2, and 3. Nationwide, more than half of married persons reporting AI/AN alone were married to non-Indians. Even in the first group of states, which are home to large populations living in areas of tribal sovereignty, reported median exogamy rates above one marriage in three. Where the Indian population is dispersed, intermarriage rates range around eight marriages in ten to non-Indian spouses.

Figure 9: The Distribution of Exogamy of Single-Race Indians by State Grouping, 2021[28]

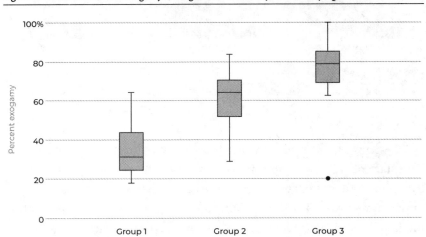

Group 1: AK, AZ, MT, ND, NM, OK, SD, WY
Group 2: CA, CO, ID, LA, MI, MN, MS, NC, NE, NV, NY, OR, UT, WA, WI
Group 3: AL, AR, CT, DC, DE, FL, GA, HI, IA, IL, IN, KS, KY, MA, MD, ME, MO, NH, NJ, OH, PA, PR, RI, SC, TN, TX, VA, VT, WV

Implications for Native Nations

The extreme number of multi-race Indians recorded in 2020 begs the question of whether they should be compared to earlier data at all. Confounding as they may be for analysis, the 2020 "improvements" in collecting racial data[29] and the resulting explosion in multi-race Indian numbers point to four important contemporary features of defining an "Indian."

First, the federal census-surveying principle that "you are who you say you are" stands in contrast to a core principle of federal Indian policy:

In the relationship between Native nations and the United States, Native nations determine the boundaries of their citizenship. These opposing principles will always complicate the application of federally gathered information to citizenship questions and demographic analyses of and by Native nations.

Second, internal Census Bureau dynamics that amplify counts of the population of American Indians or Alaska Natives in combination with other races will persist independent of the needs of Native and other governments for demographically well-behaved numbers. The designers of census survey questions and response coding protocols face professional incentives to improve engagement and consistency, both of which will tend to "pull" more ethnic information from Americans. The professionals in the Census Bureau probably do not care if there are two million Indians or four. On the other hand, they might be professionally offended (if not called to testify to Congress) if the churn of American Indians or Alaska Natives entering and departing the census count[30] were to continue to appear in the Indian data.

Third, *whenever* distinctions between Indian and non-Indian were drawn, and there was exogamy across that boundary, the Census Bureau's encouragement to be detailed, thorough, and consistent about the race question will tend to recover—to bring forward in time—the effects of historic descendancy dynamics created by exogamy. Genealogy does get lost to history, but the recollection of Great-Grandma's Indian heritage behaves like a lineal descent population to everyone who does remember it. We should not be surprised to see ballooning multi-race Indian numbers in the age of Ancestry.com and concerted census excavation of remembered lineage.

Fourth, while the descendancy dynamic may have been remote from Indian Country in time and space, it is moving closer, if not already arriving. Yes, the multi-race Indian populations of reservations (Figure 6) and Group 1 states (left panel of Figure 8) appear to display demographically plausible population dynamics. Nevertheless, because exogamy rates are high (Figure 9) and generally rising, the population of Indian descendants will continue to accelerate even in those areas.

* * *

Were he still alive for the 2020 census, Charles Curtis might have been enumerated as a person of mixed white and Indian race. Kaw planners would undoubtedly want his census record in their statistical portrait of the Kaw Nation. Elizabeth Warren's census record might be of less practical interest, as she is not a citizen of a tribe.

Regardless, everyone's freedom to self-identify would drive the data. Unfortunately, tribal prerogatives of self-government weigh little in most census respondents' race choices. Furthermore, in 2020, the number of non-Hispanic people reporting American Indian or Alaska Native alone or in combination with one or more races (6.69 million) outnumbered the enrolled citizens of recognized tribes reported to the US Treasury (2.65 million) five to two. Most census respondents may not be aware of the sensitivity of Indian citizen populations to others' claims of Indian identity. Of the few who do, many may not care.

The Census Bureau probably cannot be counted on to stem the tide. If anything, the bureau will improve its capacity to reveal latent historic descendancy populations. Tribal governments will have to take matters into hand. Here are four implications for doing so:

1. **Non-Hispanic AI/AN *alone* may be a temporary, imperfect safe harbor of plausible census information about tribal citizens.** The AI/AN alone data in Indian areas has imperfections; most importantly, it is not a closed population (i.e., it does not stay the same from survey to survey because it is affected by identity and geographic migration). It is also subject to undercount and now differential privacy fuzzing. That said, it is the available census population with the most substantial overlap with tribal citizens, especially on and near Indian lands. For the time being, it gives a plausible picture of the socioeconomic status of tribal populations.

2. **The premium on tribes' knowing off-territory citizens and descendants is rising.** It has always been essential to tribal politics and policymaking to know who the *self* in self-government is and where the relevant people reside. Moreover, it has always been a challenge to know the socioeconomic status of, for example, *Oglala* Lakota in Rapid City, South Dakota, *Fond*

du Lac Chippewa in Milwaukee, Wisconsin, or *White Mountain* Apache in Phoenix, Arizona, relying only on census Indian data. Tribal governments can expect to receive even less precise census information about the socioeconomic status of Indians living off-territory, especially in further-flung cities and as multiracial self-identification increases.

3. **Tribal governments can amplify their information gathering.** The US census is arguably the country's most expensive, studied, and calibrated data-gathering effort. The learning, policy, and infrastructure needed to replicate even a small segment of it could be prohibitively expensive for most tribes. Nonetheless, for specific high-value statistics, Native governments may find that they can leverage their existing enrollment, public outreach, and administrative data and staff to systematically develop more statistics about their citizenry. In 2013, the Cheyenne River Sioux Tribe completed an oversampled, one-in-four-household survey comprising 157 questions, some as detailed as "How often do you forage or hunt for food?" Deepening intertribal communities of practice in survey design, anonymity protection, response rate development, demography, and related expertise is likely a worthwhile investment.

4. **Tribal governments should advocate for more detailed Census Bureau reporting of the effects of its imputation "improvements."** National and tribal policymaking directed toward "Indians" would often be distinct between, for example, (a) census respondents who *do not* self-identify as American Indian or Alaska Native but *are* identified by the bureau's Indian imputation from their self-identification as, say, Scottish-Irish-Cherokee, on the one hand, and (b) census respondents who *do* self-identify as American Indian or Alaska Native, on the other. As of this writing (February 2024), the Census Bureau has not released data or analysis of the many permutations of race identification across the self-reported vs. imputed distinction. Doing so should be an urgent priority. At the moment, apples-to-apples comparisons to prior censuses of unimputed, self-identified, multi-race American Indian or Alaska Native populations are impossible.

The Census Bureau's 2020 methodology takes the unprece-
dented step of classifying people as American Indian or Alaska Native
who themselves did not self-identify as AI/AN using the available check-
box. Until the Census Bureau decomposes the census-classified and
self-identified multi-race Indians in 2020, policymakers and social
scientists will be flying blind about the intercensal demographic
dynamics in that population.

Now What?

SUZAN SHOWN HARJO

It's been nearly a half century since the US Supreme Court affirmed in 1978 that the Santa Clara Pueblo had the sole right to determine its own citizenship and eligibility criterion, rejecting any authority of a federal housing agency or any outside entity to make such decisions. And it's been almost a century since the federal government imposed boilerplate tribal constitutions that changed "citizen" to "member" and set the "membership" threshold at one-quarter blood quantum.

It has taken all that time for more and more Native Peoples to change their constitutions, while others have yet to do so.

Citizenship decisions are inherently sovereign, meaning they do not arise from anything outside the sovereign. Native Peoples have been under colonial rule for so long that many subjected to it have come to accept it as the first and last word. Once colonial rule was ensconced in constitutions, many thought there was nothing they could do to change it. Some are just appreciating that they can do something to make change and that they are the only ones who can do anything.

Over the same period of time, federal and even state institutions grew comfortable with making their own decisions about who is or is not an Indian, and most universities still do not rely on tribal determinations. Educational institutions' reliance solely on the word of a person seeking job or student placement has resulted in numerous instances of fraud, rampant and unchecked, with little movement away from the self-declaratory prac-tices. The entertainment, publishing, and sports worlds—operating with no checks at all—have raised up myriad pseudo-Natives over actual Natives.

So, while Native Peoples were doing as colonizers intended with the quarter-blood rule—breeding themselves out of existence—outside influences were deciding who were the Native writers, teachers, actors, and athletes, often to the exclusion of Native individuals.

Now What?

For the next quarter-century, four areas are in need of new and continued attention by Native Peoples:

1. deracializing tribal constitutions and law to provide for future generations;
2. advocating congressional action to craft specific provisions or laws;
3. advocating that nonfederal institutions do their part; and
4. exposing pseudo-Natives and making it more difficult for them to rise.

Taking the last item first, a host of pseudo-Indians have been unmasked during the past half century. Most of them have claimed to be Cherokee, but they have not been claimed by Cherokee Nation, Eastern Band Cherokee, or United Keetoowah Band of Cherokee Indians. Here are a few examples of pseudo-Cherokees:

- Nadema Agard, artist (claimed to be Eastern Band Cherokee and Standing Rock Sioux, but neither Band nor Tribe agreed; settled on current claim: "Cherokee/Lakota/Powhatan;" New York born)
- Forrest Carter, author (Asa Earl Carter, the Ku Klux Klan organizer and segregationist; Alabama born; Caucasian, both parents)
- Ward Churchill, author, educator (claimed to be Cherokee and Creek and "enrolled Keetoowah," but the Band and Nations disagreed; fired from University of Colorado for plagiarism, academic misconduct, etc.; Illinois born; Caucasian, both parents)
- Iron Eyes Cody, actor, "Crying Indian" (Oscar Espera DeCorti; Louisiana born; Italian American, both parents)
- Roxanne Dunbar-Ortiz, author, educator (Roxy Amanda Dunbar; switched from Sioux claim, to Cheyenne, to Nez Perce, to Cherokee, to Unknown, to Cherokee again, but no tribal agreement; Texas born; Caucasian, both parents)
- Jimmie Durham, painter (also claimed Wolf Clan; not claimed by Cherokees; expelled from International Indian Treaty Council,

denied entry into Santa Fe Indian Market; Texas born; Caucasian, both parents)

- Rayna Green, folklorist, curator (claimed Cherokee Nation, which did not claim her, and that her first language was Cherokee, which she does not speak at all; Texas born; Caucasian, both parents)
- Jamake Mamake Highwater, author (Jackie Marks, Jay Marks; also claimed to be Blackfeet; California born; Caucasian, both parents)
- Princess Pale Moon Rose, singer, ran "Indian princess" contest (Rita Ann Sentz, also claimed to be Chippewa; opened Washington R*dsk*ns NFL home games in fringed buckskin and feathers, performing "Indian sign language" to national anthem; Caucasian, both parents)
- Andrea Smith, author, educator (her claimed Cherokee Nation found only non-Native ancestors, relatives; one university denied her tenure, another entered into disengagement agreement disallowing further claims of Native-ness while employed)

Pseudo-Indians who claimed Native Peoples other than Cherokee are included in this list:

- William Dietz, coach ("Lone Star," pseudo-Sioux, Wisconsin born, raised; German American, both parents; ringer football player at federal boarding schools; unmasked in early 1900s court case; continued to be touted as "full-blooded Sioux born in South Dakota" by the Washington NFL franchise; exposed again in the early 2000s)
- Yeffe Kimball, artist (Effie Goodman, pseudo-Osage, Missouri born; Caucasian, both parents)
- Melody Lightfeather, artist (pseudo-Pima; required to withdraw from Santa Fe Indian Market and New Mexico State Fair)
- Sacheen Littlefeather, actor (Maria Louise Cruz, pseudo-White Mountain Apache/Yaqui; California born; Caucasian mother, Mexican father)
- Nasdijj, writer of "memoirs" (Tim Barrus, pseudo-Navajo; Michigan born; Caucasian, both parents)
- Hyemeyohsts Storm, writer (Arthur Charles Storm, pseudo-Cheyenne; also claimed Sioux and "spiritual adoption" by a Crow man; German father, Irish mother)

- Joanelle Romero, actor, runs "Native" film-awards group (after Mescalero Apache Tribe did not support her "Muscalero" claim, declared herself elaborately as "citizen of Mescalero-Chiricahua Apache-Dinétah-Paiute Spanish Sephardic. A relative of Pawnee-Pojoaque-Southern Ute-Lakota-Haudenosaunee"); Caucasian, both parents
- Chris Spotted Eagle, photographer, filmmaker (Chris Corpus, from Sioux, to Cheyenne, to Creek, to Mohawk, to Chippewa, to Houma; New York born; Filipino American, both parents)
- Randy Whitehorse, artist (Randy Lee White, pseudo-Brule Sioux, also claimed to be South Dakota born, raised on several Sioux reservations; actually, Texas born and raised; Caucasian, both parents)

The lists above represent only a small percentage of proven pseudo-Natives in their fields and a *de minimis* sampling of those imposters as yet unmasked. They do not include any person who is adopted or whose background is open to further question.

Most of the work to uncover the true identities of the pseudo-Natives has been done by small groups of people with varying levels of skill and more determination than resources, making it difficult for thorough exposés of all those who don a Native persona. The numbers of pseudo-Natives have escalated with the intense publicity surrounding tribal casino profits and the increased visibility and status of Native individuals in numerous professions.

One group working on these issues at this time is seriously discussing a social media structure for placing red arrows next to people's names to certify that they are Native. When reminded that Native Peoples do that with sole legal authority respecting citizens and artisans, a leader of the group responded that the tribal governments cannot be trusted, which plays into the thinking of non-Native agencies, universities, and Hollywood that they can best decide who is Native and who is not. Putting aside the potential for extortion and corruption in such a scheme as the red arrow seal of Native-ness, no outside group should be able to substitute its judgment for that of a Native Nation (nor should any want to do so).

This is not to say that tribal governments and systems are the best they could be or are without problems. But they are the entities most familiar with all the many facets of Native "identity." Their job is to keep focus on families, kinship, relations, language, culture, well-being, and other unique, essential aspects of tribal life and identity, as well as to address potential threats to their people, such as pseudo-Natives and other predators.

Part of that tribal focus must be on those Native persons caught in a blood-quantum trap of their own nation's complicity with antiquated racist federal standards, leaving them unenrolled when one or sometimes both parents are enrolled citizens. One way to curb the steep rise and aggression of pseudo-Indians is for Native governments to correct the unjust exclusions from tribal rolls and to reinstate those who should be recognized citizens. Pseudo-Indians, who deceive others and make material gains from the deception, often gain sympathy for themselves by holding up examples of real Native persons who are wrongly outside tribal protection, suggesting that they (the con artists) also are victims of unfair exclusionary laws or practices.

Indian Arts and Crafts Act and Related Laws

In 1990, Congress attempted to deal with the "fell through the cracks" issue when it amended the half-century-old Indian Arts and Crafts Act (IACA). The amended IACA bows to tribal sovereignty and defines "Indian" as one who is a tribal member. Congress added a provision that tribes also are the sole determiners of who is a tribal "artisan," meaning one who is not enrolled, but whom the tribe wishes to be known as one of its artists. Native Nations have handled this in a range of ways, from documenting tribal artisanship on a case-by-case basis to making the criteria for artisan the same as for citizen. Native governments do not need any outside authority to codify their own classifications—such as scholars, writers, contractors, filmmakers—as many now do under their inherent authority in establishing criteria for those certified as heritage language speakers or culturally competent teachers.

The IACA now covers only visual artists and craftspersons and their promoters (galleries, museums, and individual or business partners). It needs further amending to cover all artists, including but not limited to

writers, curators, dancers, singers, actors and all performing and direct-
ing artists and filmmakers, educators, and their promoters. When IACA's
penalties were increased thirty-five years ago, many pseudo-Indians traded
their visual art careers for writing, curating, or teaching careers, and they
continue to prey on the same Native Peoples.

The Federal Trade Commission (FTC), which operates under its
own statute, has an Indian arts and crafts section that should be amended
to include all arts marketed to the public. The FTC pursues these cases
as consumer fraud and encourages arts and crafts outlets to clearly mark
products as Native made and non-Native made. The signs or notices must
be placed at the point of purchase, that is, at or next to the cash register.
The FTC has required this kind of placement as part of past settlements
with trading companies in the Pacific Northwest and elsewhere.

FTC representatives have explained this approach in this way:
Bookstores do not differentiate between books written by Native authors
and those whose authors are not Native. Anyone can write about anything
they want, but the public should be informed about which books are in a
Native person's voice and experience and which are not.

New Statutory Authority

Often, pseudo-Indians hold on to their fictionalized personae until hope
runs out and then adopt a belligerent "so what?" attitude. "So what if I'm
not actually Indian? I'm now an Indian expert." Their thinking would seem
to be that, after playing Indian for so long, they've gained the "expertise"
to be considered Native. They then shape-shift their way into higher,
entitled expert status, with even less accountability. And what happens
to the damage they caused, the money they made, and the accolades they
garnered under false pretenses? They abscond with the money and goods
and leave the mess for the people they impersonated.

The pseudo-Indians' actions are not victimless crimes, and they
should not be held harmless but should be made to pay. In the vast
majority of these cases, the non-Natives are deriving benefits from their
false Indian identities—tenure, a job, a book contract, a record deal, a
movie role. The pseudo-Indians are descendants of those white men our
ancestors warned us about—look away, run away from those with gold
in their eyes.

During hearings in the late 1980s on IACA amendments, I testified on behalf of the National Congress of American Indians that Congress should establish a new law that would authorize a tribe to bring a federal action against those who profit from false claims that they are people of that tribe. But the cognizant committees of Congress had charted another, softer approach, contained in the law as it stands today. A cause of action for Native Nations should be more than a cease-and-desist order. Budding pseudo-Indians should know that there are serious consequences for identity theft.

The new statute should be enacted as a right of action for Native Nations to pursue impostors across state lines, try them in tribal courts, and impose triple damages against those found to be guilty. These are offenses against a particular People, who have the responsibility to do something about them and should have the authority that is accepted in other jurisdictions. This authority does not exist under current law.

The second part of such a new law could read, in effect:

In the alternative, the US Attorney(s) shall—

- commence action on behalf of the Native Nation(s) making the complaint;
- advise on its valuation of the pseudo-Native's injuries, including damage to its reputation and good name, damage to specific tribal citizens who suffered from the pseudo-Native's corrupt actions, and damage for the crime of stealing tribal identity;
- seek recovery of triple damages and court costs for the Native Nation; and
- provide for the perpetrator's appearance in court.
  (Note that triple damages is standard in numerous existing laws.)

Enact an Updated Version of the Pseudo-Indian Act

Enact an updated version of the Pseudo-Indian Act, first introduced in 1933 as part of the Indian Reorganization Act package and morphed into the IACA. The Pseudo-Indian Act, proposed but not enacted, would have made it a "crime to represent one's self to be an Indian, and providing punishment therefore." Its language was simple and direct:

> It shall be unlawful for any person other than an Indian to represent himself to be an Indian for the purpose of obtaining employment or any contract for the rendition of services, or of obtaining pecuniary or other assistances, or of securing to himself or to any other person any of the privileges or benefits conferred by law upon Indians. Any person violating the provisions of this Act shall, upon conviction thereof, be fined not more than $2,000 or imprisoned for not longer than one year, or both.

The above language would need considerable updating, starting with elimination of gender-specific terms for perpetrators, conversion of monetary amounts into modern fines, and strengthened penalties commensurate with the modern understanding of the severity of the crimes. In service of enforcing the latter point, the name of the new law should retain the title. While there are other useful terms for this class of offender, none conveys the serious nature of the crime as does "pseudo-Indian" or "pseudo-Native." The currently popular "pretendian" is clever but gives the impression that a person is doing something usually harmless, such as a writer using a nom de plume.

What Federal Entities and Outside Institutions Could and Should Do

Congress needs to enact new authorities and to remove present restrictions against Native Peoples acting on their own behalf in these areas. Congress also needs to exercise its oversight responsibilities, let the federal agencies know that this is a priority, and provide monies to enforce existing laws.

Educational institutions need to rely on Native Nations for their Native identity questions and to end their race-based self-declaration policy respecting tribal citizenry. They also should work with tribal authorities to edify their faculty, staff, and students about the distinction between race-based and political or policy-based laws and determinations.

Tribal and federal actions should be taken with an eye toward cleaning up racialized "Indian identity" language—imposed, parroted, or merely confused. This involves eliminating any "blood" language or requirements—because blood is directly racial—and replacing it with familial, cultural, locational, or other terms and tests. This also involves edifying others that longstanding federal and tribal treaties and laws are premised on allied sovereigns with political, policy relationships and dealings. Native Nations determine their own citizenship standards, and their citizens have a political, not racial, status from the nation-to-nation relationships.

Some non-Native interests, including some nontribal gaming businesses, want to abolish treaties, laws recognizing tribal inherent sovereign prerogatives, and the federal-tribal relationship. Those interests take the position that Native Peoples have a race-based status that violates the constitutional rights of non-Natives. The US Supreme Court has ruled that tribal citizens do not have special rights; they simply are different and do not interfere with the constitutional rights of non-Indians. These non-Native interests are pushing toward their goals of getting rid of Native business competition through the Indian Child Welfare Act (ICWA). ICWA was enacted in 1978 to stop the wholesale adoptions of Native infants and children away from their extended families and tribal cultural context by recognizing grandparental rights and tribal child custody proceedings.

Given the current fevered litigation activity to end ICWA and its "racial preferences," it's more important than ever to insist on federal and tribal language reflecting tribal citizenry as political and not racial. Of immediate importance is to prevent a return to the pre-ICWA chaos of lost generations. The gains we have made in the last half century and the very identities and futures of Native Peoples depend on it.

Saving Seeds

To new waters, am I mouth or tributary?
Let me be not ending but start.

Descendant, finding the fireside.
Ancestor, clearing the path to the door.

Our bodies are not a fraction.
Let my blood speak of more than loss.

Let it sing kinship. Let me offer
this gift, responsibility, inheritance,

to my children, and their children,
and their children, and theirs,

and theirs, and theirs, and theirs.
Let it be a flourishing,

how a strawberry plant blooms
from one corner to all across a field.

Let the corn grow high and higher,
year after year, as we save and replant the seeds.

Let us give back—and forward;
let us nation build and return.

Like rivers carried by rain clouds.
Like snowmelt strengthens the stream.

Let us gather and honor
our family in its wholeness.

Like our Mother, like Turtle's back,
the seasons and the moons.

KENZIE ALLEN

"There's More at Stake Than Just My Love Life!" Understanding Tribal Enrollment as a Reproductive Justice Issue

DANIELLE LUCERO

Introduction

Before reading further, it is imperative for the reader to know who I am. My name is Danielle Lucero. Like my mother and grandmother before me, I am an Isleta Pueblo woman of the Red Eye Corn Clan. I am also Hispano/ New Mexican; my father is from the town of Santa Rosa, New Mexico. I grew up just south of the Pueblo of Isleta in the Village of Los Lunas, on the border between the reservation and the barrio, a beautiful and vibrant blend of Nuevo Mexicano cultura and traditional Tiwa Pueblo culture. As a child, I was surrounded by strong Isleta Pueblo women who taught me how to be a Pueblo person and the important roles I have as a Pueblo woman. I am also a daughter, a beba (Tiwa for godmother), an auntie, a partner, a granddaughter, a sister, a niece, and a cousin.

Talking with other Native American women, I have often heard the statement, "You don't have to marry them; just have a baby with them." I have also heard, "I want an enrolled child, so I can't leave him." These types of statements offer a glimpse into the deeply personal impacts that tribal enrollment policies have on Indigenous people in the United States. While these decisions are inherently individual, they also hold a great deal of significance for thinking about the larger landscapes of Native nationhood in the United States due to the implications women's lived realities have on shaping the future of tribal membership in both political and demographic terms. Studies of tribal enrollment practices have traditionally been the domain of legal scholars and anthropologists who approach these issues through political frameworks that focus on federal Indian policy and constitutionalism, or cultural preservation. In these cases, understandings of Indigenous identity tend to be based on self-identification or specific sets of ascribed cultural practices and characteristics. Such frameworks, however, obscure the tangled webs of sexual politics, reproductive choices, and tribal enrollment logics that in turn inform the complex landscape of Native American identity and belonging in the twenty-first century.

Using the Pueblo nations of New Mexico as a case study,[1] this essay explores the complex history of these Native enrollment-reproduction relationships in the United States and draws upon ethnographic research with and by Pueblo women to introduce and conceptualize the importance of *reproductive nation building* for Native nations and people. Notably, Pueblo women's personal stories reveal the correlation between tribal enrollment requirements and reproductive expectations placed on Native women. These stories illustrate how Indigenous people engage in belonging that transcends enrollment via concepts such as responsibility, accountability, permission, and protocol. I argue that the most common current tribal enrollment practices (blood quantum and lineal descent) have significant impacts on Native women's reproductive choices, whose generational legacies hold long-lasting implications for the future of Native nations. Seen in such a light, blood quantum and other forms of tribal enrollment practices are reproductive justice issues. We must engage reproductive health and body sovereignty as foundational to tribal sovereignty. Centering women's experiences and stories is an imperative first step to the political reclamation of kinship, clanship, and other traditional forms of belonging that have been used within Native communities since time immemorial.

Blood Quantum, Tribal Enrollment, and Reproductive Choices

The concept of blood quantum is deeply implicated in the creation of the current contradictory landscape surrounding Native American identity and tribal enrollment in the United States. According to Kim TallBear,[2] "Scholars generally explain that 'blood quantum,'... emerged as an incisive social technique for managing Native American lands and peoples." Blood quantum relies upon antiquated and problematic notions of blood and race to measure an individual's amount of "Indian blood" in order to determine if they are "authentically" Native, that is, "full-blood," "half," "quarter," and so on.[3] Formal blood quantum policies were introduced within the framework of the US reservation system during the late nineteenth century as a means to dispossess Native peoples of their lands and to contribute to their eventual elimination from American society.[4]

As Alan Parker posits, "for those Indian nations who are committed to maintaining requirements that require future members to meet a specific degree of descendancy as a condition of membership, they should seriously consider the impacts of intermarriage with nontribal members on the degree of blood that children and grandchildren will possess in the near future."[5] The impacts of intermarriage with nontribal members and the intersection of race and gender within the conceptualization and deployment of Native nation citizenry is important to unpack for Native communities. With these decisions and dilemmas becoming exceedingly more common due to the relatively small populations and increase in the number of interracial/intertribal marriages and children in Native communities, the relevance and timely nature of this discussion is evident given the realization that soon there will not be any children eligible for tribal membership.[6]

Across the United States, it is very likely that parents and their children could soon hold different political statuses within the same Indigenous community—enrolled and unenrolled, citizen and noncitizen. As seen through this lens, tribal membership laws may often appear arbitrary to the larger settler society that "does not comprehend that membership is not a 'right' per se but a privilege determined under a given tribe's sovereignty over its own internal affairs."[7] However, tribal sovereignty and self-determination are foundational to the existing structures of tribal membership, and, as I argue throughout this chapter, tribal sovereignty and body sovereignty are interdependent.

It is important to understand that "shadow systems" originating in Western colonial structures of governmental control have been internalized by contemporary Native nations.[8] There are shadow systems currently in use within Native nations, and it is necessary to identify these systems to better understand their complex histories and their relationship with the traditional non-Western systems of belonging that are rooted in Indigenous knowledge systems. For example, many Native nations continue to adhere to the blood quantum system of tribal membership that was imposed more than a century ago as a way of honoring the importance of biological kinship in Native communities, a goal that in itself is not inherently negative. However, the preference for and strict application of the Western logics of blood quantum and biological lineage over other more traditional criteria for community identity and belonging have created a seemingly unsolvable dilemma for Native nations—decisions about partnership, marriage, and having children are being made within a shadow system of colonial control.

Similarly, the *marry out, get out* policies that currently exist in a few Native communities in the United States and Canada can be understood as another type of shadow system. These policies stipulate that if a woman enrolled in her Native nation marries a non-Native/nontribal member, she must forfeit her enrollment and any land or homes held in her name, and she can no longer reside within the reservation boundary. The root of this policy, which on the surface appears to be deeply problematic, came about because of the historical manipulation and exploitation of Native women by Anglo settlers. Up until the late 1900s, settler men would enter marriages with Native women for the sole purpose of gaining access to matrilineally controlled lands and then usurping these resources through the patriarchal Western legal system."[9] The "marry out, get out" policy was created to *protect* Native women, resources, and land.[10] The use of exogamy laws to protect Native women, land, and resources was not an uncommon tactic in the 1900s. For example, the Mohawk Council of Kahnawake passed a law that prevented non-Native people from living on the Mohawk territory south of Montreal in Canada. It became known as the "marry out, stay out" law. The council created and enforced this law to protect the community's culture, traditions, and land. However, the law has been the topic of much debate over the past two decades as the community's demographics have changed, which ultimately led to a Quebec Superior Court decision ruling the law unconstitutional in 2018.[11] Currently, settler shadow systems and Indigenous systems work simultaneously in many Native communities, and much can be done to think critically about how membership policies such as "marry out, get out" will continue to impact the lives of Native people for years to come.

This type of critical thinking is all the more important because, as documented elsewhere across Indian Country, European Americans launched fierce campaigns to devalue and subordinate Native women. In these campaigns, they often would enlist Native men. For example, Brianna Theobald's 2019 book *Reproduction on the Reservation* reveals the very intentional quest of an early-twentieth-century Bureau of Indian Affairs agent to eliminate Crow women's autonomy over both their reproductive choices *and* their political status within their communities. More specifically, land ownership and land politics were deemed men's concerns, and government agents sought to limit Crow women's involvement in what had been their traditional domains—land and politics. A letter written by the Indian agent calls on Crow men to "use their influence to eliminate this practice [of reproductive autonomy],"[12] showing just how much federal Indian policy hinged on the destabilization of gender norms in Native communities. The incorporation of Native men into the patriarchal colonial agenda became a necessity to strip women of their control over the land *and* their bodies. These efforts were echoed in many other Native communities at the turn of the twentieth century, including the Pueblos, shifting the traditional gender balance and allowing men to adopt new positions controlling women's roles, ceremonial participation, and—most poignantly—their reproductive choices.

Exploring the Impacts of Colonial Shadow Systems on Reproductive Choices, Enrollment, and Inheritance in the Pueblos

Within issues of tribal enrollment, questions about land, property, and "benefits" become central to the conversation.[13] Land is a fundamental component of what it means to be a Pueblo person. Without our land, we are lost as Native people and disconnected from our ancestors and culture. As such, it is no surprise that land is also a key consideration when Native people make decisions about dating, marriage, and having children. Naya, a young Acoma Pueblo woman, articulated the pressures she feels as the only granddaughter in her family and as someone who is not "full-blooded Acoma." Naya has been told that there is more at stake than just her love life, including the house that her great-grandfather built and the land her family holds in her Pueblo. Because land can only be passed through the maternal line, it falls on Naya, as the only granddaughter, to ensure she has children who are enrollable at Acoma.

While part of this is due to tradition, it is important to highlight that tribal *membership* is a specific requirement in order to hold land and homes in your name at Acoma. This creates situations like the one Naya finds herself in, where land, gender, and inheritance are intimately connected in Pueblo communities, and enrollment status has been elevated above all else as *the* most important requirement.

One of the reasons why tribal enrollment currently plays such a central role for the Pueblos can be traced back to the early nineteenth century, when New Mexico was part of the Spanish Empire. Under Catholic-influenced Spanish civil law, men were the heads of households, and land, goods, and other material things were the sole property of the man/husband. This conflicted greatly with the traditional gender structures of Pueblo communities, in which material things, specifically houses, land, and children, were stewarded by women. Pueblo women in the colonial period were free to form relationships with whomever they liked, and if a woman chose to enter into a relationship with a Spanish man, she had every reason to believe her Pueblo society's rules would be followed.[14] However, the Spanish, and later the Americans, held different ideas about women's sexuality and inheritance. As such, during the eighteenth and nineteenth centuries, many Euro-American men deliberately sought relationships with and married Pueblo women in order to eventually acquire their possessions through lawsuits in the patriarchally organized Spanish civil courts.[15]

Conflicts over property rights inevitably arose in northern New Mexico as Spanish civil law took precedent in the colony, causing Pueblo women to lose their stewardship rights to land and suffer diminished economic autonomy and political status. The dominance of Spanish civil law inevitably led to responses within Pueblo communities that changed traditional laws, social mores, and cultural customs. This can be clearly seen in the enrollment practices of some Pueblos, which require women who marry out of the Pueblo to forfeit their enrollment, theoretically protecting Pueblo lands from being lost to non-Pueblo husbands or descendants.

In other instances, a few Pueblos have switched from being matrilocal or bilocal to primarily patrilocal, where the Pueblo woman must follow her husband to his homelands. Other Pueblos maintain the practice of "women are raised to stay in place," and men are raised to be in-laws.

"There's More at Stake Than Just My Love Life!" Understanding Tribal
Enrollment as a Reproductive Justice Issue
101

One woman I interviewed, Tess, is in her mid-twenties and lives on her Pueblo's reservation in the northwest region of New Mexico. In Tess's Keres-speaking Pueblo, for example, it is considered traditional that when a woman gets married, she has to follow her husband. Whichever community the man is from, the woman must move to it. Tess described it in our interview: "Women from my Pueblo don't have materialistic stuff like land . . . [i]t's all held by their husband or by their male relatives. Women can't own anything without a man's say-so, such as land." Tess said that in her Keres-speaking Pueblo, there is a very real threat of losing land if "there is no man to hold the land." This is why marrying within the community is so important to people from her Pueblo.

While this is a challenging situation, I should highlight an important change Tess noticed in her Pueblo: "Not a lot of people follow the traditional teaching of 'following the man,' but my mom did because she was raised very traditional, and that's why we live in [my dad's Pueblo] and are enrolled in [my dad's Pueblo]." This move away from practicing strict patrilocality is important because it is a recent change, probably within the past two decades. However, the pressure to be viewed as traditional remains quite strong and translates to the woman following her husband. In Tess's mother's case, when she married a man from a different Pueblo, she relinquished her rights and lands in her Keres-speaking Pueblo, and everything then went to her brothers.

On the other hand, we have Pueblos like Zuni, which Lyla, a young Zuni tribal member, describes as a place where "women are raised to stay, meaning the men come to the women; we stay in place while the men are raised to be in-laws." In Zuni, land is primarily passed down through the women. Additionally, only the women's clans get passed down in Zuni; this is something that remains true for all of New Mexico's nineteen Pueblos.

Reproductive Justice and Tribal Enrollment

Reproductive justice is defined as the human right to maintain personal bodily autonomy, have children (or not), and parent the children we have in safe and sustainable communities.[16] I found that Native women actively struggle for reproductive empowerment and self-determination in the context of imposed Western patriarchal norms. In my study, Pueblo women demonstrated a desire to control their own bodies and maintain their own identities and sense of belonging to their communities. For example, despite contending with shadow structures and systems that placed social (and in some cases physical) limitations on their family-planning abilities, they subverted these structures by asserting their status as Pueblo women within the traditional cultural context of the Pueblos. In other words, as Pueblo women, they hold tremendous responsibility in their Pueblos, and as such they take an active role in their community. By doing so, they ensure their children's sense of belonging within the Pueblo regardless of their enrollment status. Rather than viewing Pueblo women as complicit in patriarchal systems that overburden them with responsibilities as *only* mothers, their ability to negotiate multiple and often contradictory and competing roles and expectations actually demonstrates both their durability in the face of difficult circumstances and their refusal of the colonial systems that aim to destroy Native families.

In the Pueblos, women are expected to be mothers and raise the children. With the imposition of colonial patriarchal gender roles, this requirement of motherhood translated to a devaluing of women's historical roles in which women were able to be both the center of the household *and* hold political and social power in the community. Although the dark shadow of patriarchy constrained many Native women's mobility and choices, many women negotiated more fluidity and autonomy in their roles, essentially subverting patriarchal colonial norms in favor of more egalitarian gender norms and political participation.

My research highlights how expectations for Pueblo women include a specific form of motherhood that pressures women to have "enrollable children" for the dual purpose of land/property tenure (political continuity) and for continuing traditional language and practices into the future (cultural continuity). However, with the dislocation of women from political positions, effectively half the Pueblo population must contend with governmental structures like tribal enrollment that place serious limitations on their reproductive decisions. For this reason, I argue that issues surrounding tribal enrollment (i.e., politics, practices, and structures) are inherently reproductive justice issues and must be viewed as such. Doing so places the power over bodily autonomy back into the hands of Native women, further ensuring that women are involved and prioritized in the decision-making processes for Native nations' futures, including tribal membership requirements.

It is evident that structures like a tribal government or tribal enrollment requirements hold significant sway over how Native people are making decisions about family planning, dating, and children. For something like blood quantum to determine how and with whom Native people have sexual relations is deeply troubling and deserves attention. For the Pueblo people that I spoke with, many were taught in school or at home that having sex was *only* for procreation. This concept weighed heavily throughout many of their stories on how they learned about safe sex and what they were teaching their children. This understanding of sex and sexual partners connects directly to reproductive decisions and how social, cultural, and political factors influence the intimate choice of whom to have sex with. Lyla shared her thought process when she considered a sexual partner:

> Lyla: *You have to think about, "What if I get pregnant?"*

> Danielle: Do you feel you've had to ask yourself even with the people you're meeting on Tinder? Do you think about, "Okay, if we have kids, what is that going to mean?"

> Lyla: *Yeah, I really think about that myself. My mom was in that area of just dating. She didn't know she was going to get pregnant. I'm on birth control. And even if that 0.1 percent comes through, I'm like, "Okay, yeah, you have to think about it, you have to think about some things because you just have to make sure, cover yourself, and protect yourself, too."*

Lyla is the product of an unplanned pregnancy between two young people who were just starting college. Lyla has thus been keenly aware of the consequences of having sex and like many others understands sex as a serious responsibility that brings children into the world. However, external structures such as tribal enrollment and cultural structures like Pueblo belonging and kinship are major influences on people's reproductive decisions.

This rather "logical" approach to sex often removes the pleasure and exploration from sexual intercourse. It is these structures, which evolved from patriarchal colonialism and heteronormativity, that have deeply impacted the sexual behavior and expression of Pueblo people, specifically women.[17] In an ideal world, sexual relations are not just about conceiving a child but are also about pleasure and intimate companionship. In the Native world, however, whom you have sex with matters because, as Lyla and others articulate, the decisions that go into having children have deep and personal consequences for oneself, the families, and the community.

Reproductive Nation Building

Reproductive matters are at the heart of the experiences of Native women. Reproductive decisions cannot be separated from broader political struggles or from the political, social, and cultural contexts that shape women's lives.[18] As such, to capture the way reproductive decisions are intimately connected to tribal sovereignty, I use the term *reproductive nation building.* Nation building refers to "the process by which a Native nation strengthens its own capacity for effective and culturally relevant self-government and for self-determined and sustainable community development."[19] According to the University of Arizona Native Nations Institute, "Nation building involves building institutions of self-government that are culturally appropriate to the nation and that are effective in addressing the nation's challenges. It involves developing the nation's capacity to make timely, strategically informed decisions about its affairs and to implement those decisions. It involves a comprehensive effort to rebuild societies that work."

While useful, this definition of *Native nation building* does not address the expectations placed specifically on women to—literally—carry tribal nations into the future, or the relationship these pressures have with tribal enrollment and membership policies. Native women are relied upon for their reproductive and social labor in regard to cultural continuity and the ability to carry tribes into the future. As philanthropist and advocate Se-ah-dom Edmo writes, "While the pressure to maintain culture and [blood] quantum may be felt by all tribal people; the ultimate responsibility to produce potential tribal members remains with and in the hands and wombs of Indian women."[20] Adding reproduction to the nation-building

"There's More at Stake Than Just My Love Life!" Understanding Tribal
Enrollment as a Reproductive Justice Issue

105

equation repositions reproductive matters as central to questions of tribal sovereignty and self-determination. In doing so, reproductive nation building calls attention to the extent to which colonial and tribal politics have been—and remain—reproductive politics.

Conclusion

I do not claim that the information presented in this chapter represents the experience of all Native people in regards to dating, marriage, and family planning. Instead, it is based upon my personal engagement with Pueblo people from my own network and my knowledge of Native/Pueblo history and anthropology. There is always the chance that the portrait of Pueblo life that I have drawn here might be altered entirely with the inclusion of differing Native/Pueblo perspectives and social identities. I have done my best to make it clear on what basis I have constructed my interpretations and my positionality within that stance.

It is important to understand the social, cultural, political, *and* reproductive politics that Native people navigate when they make choices of romantic partnerships and family rearing/planning, and the consequences of those choices for the future of Native nations. This chapter follows in the footsteps of the many Indigenous people (specifically women) who have articulated their support for upholding tribal sovereignty *and* advocating for change and reimagining relationships and enrollment from within, not imposed by outside norms or legal systems but through internal dialogue and reflection. As such, this chapter is intended to start dialogues within communities. It offers no answers or solutions, but it posits essential questions and prioritizes the experiences of Native women.

Generally speaking, the impacts of tribal enrollment on reproductive matters in Native/Pueblo communities give rise to a multiplicity of answers, all complicated and contradictory to varying degrees. This chapter aims to contribute knowledge on how Pueblo people (Native people) think about dating and relationships in the context of tribal enrollment, cultural belonging, and identity. I hope this exploratory work will further our knowledge in developing effective programs to promote healthy relationships and strengthen Pueblo sovereignty with the voice of women and queer folks included.

*How can we encourage connection and belonging
for our Native youth so they grow up
with strong identities?*

Gidoodeminaanig

KADIN MILLS

Every angsty teen and twentysomething is trying to figure out who they are, where they come from, where they are going, and how they are going to get there. As much as I like to believe I have always known these things, I have only recently come to the daunting realization that not everyone is so sure of who they are. And yet, such a rude awakening is a weight lifted off the shoulders and a heavy responsibility, especially since beginning my lifelong road to reconnection.

I went to a small high school in a rural Midwestern town. Buchanan, as it is called, was settled on Potawatomi land in the southwest corner of Michigan in 1833, after much of the area was ceded in the 1828 Carey Mission Treaty. Today, Buchanan is mostly working class and white, and I fit in.

I am white, and I am also Ojibwe. I have blond hair and green eyes, though I somehow manage to look exactly like my dark-haired, dark-eyed Ojibwe mom. But based on my phenotypes, Native American is likely far from the first thought that enters one's mind upon meeting me.

I am a first-generation descendant of the Keweenaw Bay Indian Community, one of twelve bands of Lake Superior Ojibwe, meaning I am unenrolled due to blood quantum. I come from a line of Ojibwe women— my mom and aunties, my grandma, and my great-grandma—all of whom are recognized as American Indian. My pedigree, however, doesn't qualify for enrollment in our tribe, nearly four hundred miles away.

Growing up, I spent most of my time with my dad, who is white. My parents separated when I was just a few years old, and shortly thereafter, my dad took custody of me. He kept me from my mom and her family for years. Consequently, she fell back into a pattern of substance use. I saw her about eight days every month, every other weekend, and three hours on Wednesdays, plus every other holiday.

During the summers, when I wasn't with my mom, my dad would take me to his mom's house while he went to work. My grandma Elaine and I were best friends. The time I spent with her afforded me some of my life's most valuable lessons, at a time in which they were most needed. We would watch the sunrise over morning coffee and cookies, though in retrospect she probably shouldn't have been giving me coffee as a kid. Then, she would teach me how to cook my favorite breakfast foods. Most important, however, were the raspberries.

Every year, for about three weeks, my grandfather's pile of disfigured cars and gas pumps—iron rusted beyond recognition—was transformed by vibrant reds and purples. Amid the slow decay was an annual birth of wild black raspberries, makade-miskominag. I couldn't wait to forage for them and see how many new ripe berries there were. Every day, it seemed like there were twice as many as the day before.

For three weeks, we would eat berries with sugar, in pies, and off the vine. She told me how the birds brought the raspberries there, and she taught me to always leave enough for them. I remember walking with her, cereal bowl in hand, trying to get as many berries as I could. And I always wanted to eat them right away, which often made baking the pie difficult. In good time, I learned to take only what I needed, but it wasn't quite an issue, considering the brambles extended far past my reach. My grandma is not Native, but she taught me important lessons about respect, patience, and reciprocity. She first instilled in me the notion of being in community with the more-than-human.

As I've matured, my mom and I have grown very close. But from a young age, I was acutely aware of the fact that my dad hated her—he made sure to tell me I was just like her every time we butted heads, which was often when I lived under his roof. He also took every opportunity to invalidate who I was, only acknowledging my mixed heritage when he wanted to take advantage of tribal health care and telling me I wasn't Native when he would mock our ceremonies, singing, and communities. Meanwhile, he claims his side of the family are descendants of Tecumseh—a claim for which I have found no basis. To me, this was a gross display of white privilege, to erase my own identity while asserting himself as Native instead.

At the same time, I have struggled to wrap my head around the influence Grandma Elaine had on my identity, even though she is not Indigenous. For years, I wished I had the same relationship with my Ojibwe grandma, Donna, as well as my Great-Grandma Jo, who died in 2011.

Indibendaagoz

When I was thirteen, my mom took me to my first powwow. I remember being anxious after a Native person I knew teased me and said I was "gonna look like John Smith" out there. Up until this point, I was used to being told I wasn't Native or that I was pretending, so I was by no means unaware of my whiteness or the way I was perceived. I always hated this. I felt invisible, not only to Native people, but to everyone.

It was the Labor Day weekend Kee-Boon-Mein-Kaa Pow Wow at the Pokagon Band of Potawatomi, about thirty miles from my hometown. An old friend of my mom's had invited us to camp with her and her sons, who were twins about my age. They showed me around the powwow grounds; taught me how to use tobacco, sage, sweetgrass, and cedar; and introduced me to fry bread. Later that day, my mom's friend taught me to barter. "Make sure to ask 'em if it's Indian price," she told me, and that night I strung together a medicine bag around the fire.

I remember when we entered the drum circle for the first time. As for me, this was my mom's first powwow—her mom, my grandma, had never taken her before. For both of us, this was the beginning. My mom couldn't stop crying, and her friend said, "That is your spirit bubbling up." Those words stuck with us and put us both on a path to reconnection. Prior to the powwow, all we knew was that we were Chippewa, but this didn't mean too much. Now we are proud to be Anishinaabe.

When I returned to school for the start of the new school year, I was excited to show everyone my medicine bag. Some of my friends made snide comments about keeping tobacco, and one classmate called me a "redneck redskin," a line he seemed to think was pretty clever. At the time, I wasn't even sure if I should be offended. On one hand, I was extremely uncomfortable but laughed along anyway (I didn't know better at the time). On the other hand, it felt like the first time a non-Native acknowledged me as white *and* Ojibwe. I don't know if he meant to hurt me, but I realize now his nickname communicated that I was different to him: that I wasn't like other Natives because I was white.

But how can I be unlike other Natives when I'm not sure they were too similar either? I knew of Native people in Buchanan who flew confederate flags and drove the same diesel trucks as the sweet-corn-fed farm boys. I also knew Native people who were on their traditional homelands and Native people who were far from their relatives. Even me—I was on Anishinaabe land, but not our own tribal lands. My first important connections were with Potawatomi people, not with "my" community. And while I wasn't on the rez, I wasn't an urban Native either. I was left to consider whether I was Native at all.

These feelings followed me throughout high school and shaped the way I think about myself, even now. I still catch myself saying things like "my mom is Ojibwe," or "my family's community." While both are true, I become complicit in my own erasure by removing myself from my family, as well as from the processes that have dictated who I can be, like blood quantum, which places countless limitations on Native people of mixed heritage.

When I started my studies at Northwestern University, I was greeted with open arms. It was September 2020, so there was very little social interaction, but what little we had went a long way. I was invited to come to campus for a weekly fire, hosted by one of our faculty and my chosen "auntie," Pam Silas. At the time, I felt so out of place, and I was hesitant to attend the community events. I had convinced myself that upon arrival, I'd be asked to present my tribal ID and Certificate of Degree of Indian Blood (CDIB) card. Then everyone would find out I was a fraud.

But I am not a fraud, and I can very easily document who I am and from whom I come. But *still* I had internalized this fear of not fitting in for lack of a citizenship card, or for not being "Indian enough," or not *looking* Native, or not knowing enough about who my ancestors are, who my family is, and who I am.

I was embraced with open arms, and Pam took on the responsibility of telling it to me like it is: that these feelings are by design. Centuries of federal Indian policy—of dispossession, of disconnection—have attempted to sever ties between Native peoples and their lands, waters, and more-than-human relatives. And here I was, now forever a part of the Native community at Northwestern and in Chicago.

College gave me the opportunity to finally learn from Native people. I studied the history of Native resistance movements and started learning Anishinaabemowin. I started writing, and the pieces to this impossible jigsaw puzzle started to come closer together. I began to understand why I had to reconnect in the first place after I stumbled upon a photo of my Grandma Jo. On the back, it was inscribed "Flandreau school," and I soon learned she had graduated from the Flandreau Indian School in South Dakota in 1949. She was a part of a generation discouraged from being a part of their communities and cultures. For many reasons, she did not pass down the practices and traditions of her parents and the generations before her.

Instead, my chosen family has filled in those lapses, all in the effort to ensure my family continues to be Anishinaabe, not only for my sake, but for the next generation and those to follow. But I wish it weren't that way. I wish I had a strong support network of my Ojibwe family to nurture and encourage me in our culture. I have had to reckon with a certain feeling of resentment that I have held against my Grandma Donna and her mom for not being the Noomokisag (grandmothers) I feel like I deserved. I have resented how this loss has hurt my mom and her sisters. And me. But I am learning to give them grace and trust that healing will take time.

I realize now my grandmothers were hurting the most.

In 2021, my grandma's cousin, Deb, invited me to a family cookout while I was visiting Baraga for the annual summer powwow. I traveled up north with my friends Dawson and Nora. Dawson is Pokagon Potawatomi. This was our second trip to Keweenaw Bay together, and my third visit. We went to my Great-Great-Aunt Dianne's elder care facility, where I met more than twenty members of my extended family for the first time. Numerous cousins and great-aunts and uncles. They only knew of me as Donna's grandson, but my family welcomed me home. While I was there, I heard stories about my great-grandma. They said Grandma Jo was the life of the powwow, and they recounted all the times she made them laugh. Like my community at Northwestern, they welcomed me with open arms. This time, they really were family.

They teased us and poked fun, and it felt so good. I knew they really saw me as Ojibwe when Cousin Pat, who is my grandma's age, warned us, "Don't be tipi creepin' either, 'cuz they're probably your cousin!" and everyone erupted in laughter. We left that day with our bellies full and a roasting pan full of fry bread to take back to camp. Later that day, I won a spot dance held in honor of our relatives who were taken from their families and placed in boarding schools. I could feel Grandma Jo smiling.

Since then, I have made the annual trip, and in 2023, I returned with my mom. I was honored to introduce her to our family, and it made me so happy to see the joy and belonging she felt there. Plus, she got teased by Pat too.

Nimizhishawab

Native people often hear things like "Oh it's so great you chose to be a part of your culture." The usual pushback is that we do not choose to be who we are but that we live it every day. And while I believe this is true, I think there is also a sliver of reality in this ignorant praise.

I am white, and I am Ojibwe. I didn't choose to be Ojibwe or white, but I have chosen to learn what those two identities mean. I have the privilege to choose reconnection without fear of being attacked for my identity. I don't experience personal racist attacks because I am not a person of color. But my writing and my community have, and I do experience the pain inflicted on us as a result of it.

As an increasing number of Native youth are cut off from their communities by minimum blood quantum requirements, we are faced with a crisis. If we don't have citizens, we don't have a nation. My mentor, Dr. Patty Loew, has told me over and over again, "Our nations are writing ourselves out of existence."

Blood quantum divides us into parts, both as individuals and as communities. It pits us against each other to compete for who is more Native. It keeps families from attending ceremonies together or exercising their treaty rights. This system of classifying Native people like horses or dogs is dehumanizing, and it is an active process of erasure, with the end goal of eradicating Native American people and stripping us of our sovereignty.

I believe that as a white man, I have a responsibility to stand up to settler colonialism. As an Ojibwe man, I have a responsibility to my ancestors, lands, waters, and relatives. I have a responsibility to my descendants—to teach them to speak Anishinaabemowin and to walk in a good way.

I will be reconnecting for my entire life, from building new relationships to learning the Ojibwe language. Reconnection takes time. By holding on to my Indigeneity, I can share the teachings that should have been passed on through generations with my mom, my aunties, and the generations of Ojibweg who will come after us. I have a responsibility to them.

I do not have a strong connection to the Keweenaw Bay Indian Community. I have stronger connections to other communities, like Bad River and Minneapolis, through my work with Dr. Patty Loew and the relationships I am fostering in college. Imagining my road forward, I realize it will be long and built upon centuries of Indigenous resistance. Colonization has been all about telling Indigenous peoples who they are and who they should be. "Uncivilized savages." "One-eighth degree." "Not Native enough."

Reconnecting with my family on the rez will be hard after two generations of lost contact. But I have to try. And I have to be patient. And I choose to be a part of my community so that one day little "Shnaabz" can pick makade-miskominag—Indigenously.

I am white and I am Ojibwe, and I am proud to call myself Anishinaabe. To say that I am not is a victory for the colonial processes of blood quantum that define Indigeneity for me, and for so many other Native people.

Mii iw.

Who's Your People?
Living with a Multi-tribal Native Identity

JENNIFER HILL-KELLEY and SADIE KELLEY

One topic that is not discussed much in tribal identity conversations is the experience of being a descendent of multiple tribal nations. This experience, which we are calling multi-tribal identity, is becoming more common as Natives are traveling beyond their homelands for education, jobs, powwows, and vacations. In the United States, most tribal enrollment law legislates a tribal citizen to be enrolled with only one tribal nation, even though they may be eligible to enroll in more than one. This means that if you have ancestry from multiple tribes, you must choose which tribe to be a citizen of and which tribe you will legally only be a nonenrolled descendant of. The need to choose only one of your tribes is a complex and dynamic decision that evolves throughout your life, especially when you are actively engaged in multiple tribes through family and ceremony. This decision directly impacts your identity as a Native person and sometimes comes with family and financial implications.

It is common practice for parents to apply to enroll their minor children in the tribe of choice so that they may enjoy the connection and benefits of tribal citizenship as soon as possible. This important responsibility of a parent contributes to the development of one's identity as an Indigenous person, yet enrollment in a tribal nation is not the only contributing factor to tribal identity and belonging. The richness and benefit of growing up being engaged in multiple tribal cultures is important to recognize as Indian Country continues to dialogue about tribal enrollment and identity.

In the process of writing this article, we spoke with family members and friends to see what their perspectives were on this issue. Some Natives who grew up away from their multiple reservations talked about how they didn't pursue significant connections until they were adults. As children, they didn't have the opportunity to visit their tribes but once a year or less and didn't have access to experience their tribal lands or culture. They knew they were from multiple tribes but did not know what they were missing in the connection to their land, history, and cultural practices. As adults, they chose to visit their tribal lands and to participate when they could. This "being there" reinforced their identity through connection to place as they experienced interacting with the land, people, and practices that made them feel like they "belonged" to the tribe. We also learned that some tribes, like those in the Haudenosaunee Confederacy, require tribal citizens to choose one nation to be identified with, even if the person has parentage from multiple tribes. Another situation we learned about was making the decision as an adult to switch enrollment to another tribe after one's parents died, or to move to a tribe that provided better benefits and services. This situation results in members of the same family belonging to different tribes and comes with angst over some family members now identifying as another tribe.

Jennifer's Story

My experience of living and growing up with multiple tribal identities as a descendant from three tribes is not unique, as more of the Native population is increasingly multi-tribal. I identify as Kiowa and Comanche and Oneida, while I am enrolled in the Oneida Nation in Wisconsin. I fortunately grew up in both of the places where my parents grew up. I know the places that were significant to their upbringings. We lived in both Oklahoma and Wisconsin during my lifetime and were engaged in the cultural activities of each tribe. The lands and places that my families come from are a significant force in the person I am and how I identify myself today. I know the important places, like Jimmy Creek in southwest Oklahoma and Trout Creek on the north end of the Oneida reservation. I did not realize how fortunate I was to have learned the histories and participated in the cultural practices of all my tribes until I was an adult.

Chief Oren Lyons, Onondaga, has said, "We think in circles," and I think of my different families in circles—circles of dance and songs. My earliest realization about being multi-tribal was when I first went to a social dance in Oneida. It was the late 1970s, and the dance was held in the one tribal building at Chicago Corners. We had recently moved to Wisconsin and, up to that point, I had gone to the Kiowa Gourd Clan Ceremonial and other powwows. I wondered why this dance was held inside a building and everyone wore their regular clothes, not their "Indian clothes." The dance felt so different to me since I loved outdoor powwows, which were mainly in the summer, and we usually camped with family and friends. Yet the social dance was much more engaging, with a smaller crowd, and the songs were so inviting to sing. Both dances were great fun with lots of laughter and visiting and events I still participate in today.

The Kiowa Gourd Clan, an annual summer gathering that happens to be around the Fourth of July, is an event that connects me to history and place. I have attended this gathering since I was about eight years old. There is a strong sense of belonging, as it is called these days, while you are in the arena, surrounded by hundreds of your direct and indirect relations, surrounded by songs that are hundreds of years old, and moving to the drumbeat together. Moving together but apart, you feel that there is so much more there with you. The connection threaded through this feeling is to your family, your ancestors, and your tribe, and it bears the weight of knowing the need to connect the next generation for this to continue. It is a trust exercise to get your kids to believe in the importance of this place before they really know the importance of this gathering. It is what Paul Chaat Smith, Comanche, calls "remembering what you can never know." The dance has evolved much from what it was in the past. Being privileged to attend the Paiute Sun Dance, I can see similarities at the Kiowa Gourd Clan that remain today.

Language is also important to identity, and as someone who is multi-tribal, I can say it is challenging to learn one Native language, much less three. The yearning to know the language is an individual feeling that gets me closer to being more of one of my tribes, and it takes an individual endeavor to make it happen. Yet no amount of immersion programming can make someone learn the language if you have no one to talk to. My Kiowa relative Bernadine Rhoades made the bittersweet point so eloquently: "I am happy and sad at the same time to hear the language and know that those I used to hear it from are gone."

As an adult, deciding where to raise a family was a choice that impacted my multi-tribal identity. My daughter is a descendant of eight tribes and eligible for enrollment in one tribe with one-quarter blood degree requirements and two tribes that enroll based upon lineal descent, which means that members must have descended from an enrolled family member; there is no blood quantum requirement. The choice to live in the Oneida community where my daughter could be enrolled was a decision I was fortunate to make. Although I spent some of my childhood in Oneida, I did not receive an Oneida name until my daughter received hers. I had a Kiowa name given to me by my Kiowa grandfather when I was very young, which was the custom. It was a source of pride and identity for me to know that I had a Kiowa name, even though I didn't use it. I wanted my daughter to feel that same pride and identity. In Oneida, it is now common to hear and see Oneida names everywhere. Today, it is so fulfilling to hear and see many people using their names in their tribal languages in all settings. And although we, as parents, selected the cultural setting that our daughter grew up in, we wanted her to know all the peoples from which she came, so she could make the choice for herself when she was ready to pursue her own connections to family and traditions.

Sadie's Story

I am Haudenosaunee, Mvskoke, Ka'igwu, Numunuu, Numu Newe, Aniyvwiya?i, tsa-la-gi, and sawanwa. I use the names we call ourselves to honor my ancestors and the people that came before me, not the government English name that we are known by.

Applying to college was the first time I realized my upbringing was a little different. Not only was I surrounded by my Onʌyote?a·ka· community, but I was consistently surrounded by my other tribal communities during winter and summer months when school was out. I grew up knowing where I come from because my parents were gracious enough to instill all our generational practices in us. Taking thirteen-hour drives to Oklahoma to visit family was routine to me because that is where five out of seven of my tribes are located today. It was a drive that I took for granted, and I thought frequently, *Why don't we move back to Oklahoma to be surrounded by most of our family? Why did my parents make the decision to be one of the few to move to Oneida?* Thinking of those questions now that I am in college and living away from any of my homelands or tribes, I realize it was an innocent time in my life when I didn't understand the uniqueness I had within myself and throughout my family. I only thought of it as a time when I could see my cousins, aunties, and grandparents. Now, whenever I have a chance to see my relatives, I am reminded of the sacrifices my parents and the generations before me made, to encourage me to be proud of who I am and to tell my story.

Because I wasn't enrolled in my other tribes, there was sometimes a false feeling that I was not a member of that tribe. When people would ask me what tribe I belonged to, it was almost like I had to prove myself and my connections. I know now that this narrative of being enrolled in one tribe stems from colonialism and doesn't have anything to do with my identity as a multi-tribal person. The first time I went to Duck Creek stomp dance grounds near Mounds, Oklahoma, I was reminded of Oneida and the social dance songs that are sung. At that young age, I discovered a sense of belonging to both places. I still feel it to this present day, after being away at college, whether attending a powwow in Oklahoma, hearing the drums and hearing my family sing, or hearing social dance songs. Now I understand my parents moved to Oneida so I could grow up surrounded by my people, teachings, and traditions. I understand why my parents made the long drive to Oklahoma two to three times a year and the longer trip to Owyhee, Nevada. It was all a part of the bigger picture, so I would know who my people are and to keep me connected to generations of people who live with me every day. I have insight into all my tribes, and now it is up to me to engage and travel to see my family. I cherish the times I get to be in person at ceremonies. I appreciate social media, which helps to keep me connected while still away.

Now that I am entering my mid-twenties, I am thinking more about the complicated situation of blood quantum requirements for enrollment. Thinking about my future children, as they won't be enrolled into a tribe unless I find a partner from one of my two lineal descent tribes, or unless my future partner brings enough blood quantum with them to enroll our kids in one of their tribes. I feel restricted in these choices. It seems like we have not moved beyond the historic federal government policies previously designed to eradicate our future. But we are still here, and we have the collective ability as participants in sovereign governments to create alternatives. So how do we as Onʌyoteʔa·ka· people address the blood quantum issue while ensuring our cultural practices and languages are taught and shared to reinforce our tribal identities?

By sharing our stories, my mother and I wanted to focus attention on one area of tribal identity that comes from deciding which tribe, out of your multiple tribes, you want to actively be a part of, beyond having to decide which one to enroll in. The tribal enrollment process is a significant act of tribal sovereignty, and the tribe, as a community of people, should decide citizenship criteria. For Oneida, enrolling citizens through the one-quarter blood quantum policy will lead to fewer Oneida citizens, as our enrolled population is currently declining. If we change our citizenship policies toward more inclusion, we will increase the opportunity for the transfer of knowledge of practices and language. By excluding descendants who are family, who are we excluding that could contribute to the passing on of tsiniyukwalihuta (our ways)? The decision about eligibility is up to us as a community and our government, which, according to our governing tribal laws and constitution, includes all Oneidas over eighteen years old. Addressing enrollment eligibility is the most important sovereign act of self-governance that will shape our future.

My mother and I are both strong Native women, yet the internal dialogue about knowing enough and questioning our connectedness to our tribes remains. We both continue to learn our tribal histories and languages and make it a priority to participate in current events. We wonder how many others feel the need to know more about or be more involved in a tribe in order to claim that tribe as part of your identity. We know many don't have the access or ability to connect for many different reasons. How can we encourage connection and belonging for our native youth so they grow up with strong identities? The message we would share with them is, as a descendant of many tribes, you already have a connection to a rich cultural identity, and blood quantum requirements don't prevent you from learning from your people how to be a good ancestor to your future descendants.

How do we honor our unique histories
while also blending them
with our current-day circumstances?

Life at the Intersections:
A Black Oneida Perspective on
Blood Quantum and Belonging

MARENA BRIDGES

Introduction

When I was eight years old, I moved from Milwaukee, a city with a vibrant Black culture, to Green Bay, a predominantly white community near the Oneida Nation reservation. I became a student at Oneida Nation Elementary School, and as a newcomer among deeply interconnected Indigenous peers, my outsider status was affirmed. I found my identity wasn't based on personal attributes but on the pedigree of my ancestors, where the concept of blood quantum, quantifying Indigenous ancestry, dictated tribal membership. I found myself where the rich tapestry of my Black and Oneida identity was reduced to conflicting fractions.

In this chapter, I invite readers to navigate the intricate dynamics of multiracial Indigenous identity and scrutinize the tribal membership paradigm. I challenge using blood quantum, matrilineal descent, and cultural knowledge as membership criteria, as these often overlook the diasporic realities of Indigenous people who may be disconnected from their ancestral lands and marginalized within their communities.

I urge us to rethink outdated norms that suppress multiracial voices within Indigenous communities and critically examine racial negotiation within Native communities to expose anti-Black racism within such spaces and reveal the discord between the blood quantum construct and genetic reality. Personal experiences and critical insights aim to stimulate discussion toward a more inclusive Indigenous community identity.

A Tale of Two Cities

Born in 1986 to a mixed-race family in Milwaukee, Wisconsin, I was a vibrant thread in a diverse tapestry, navigating a complex world shaped by my dual Oneida and Black identities. Amid the urban hum, I confronted misconceptions about Indigenous people, fueled by cliché television portrayals, from an early age. In the second grade, I had the opportunity to dismantle these stereotypes for a classroom presentation. Drawing on my mother's wisdom, I painted a vivid portrait of the Oneida people for my classmates, challenging the tipi-dwelling, feather-headdress-wearing Native American trope. Simultaneously, I was exposed to my father's Black heritage, absorbing stories of his upbringing in a de facto segregated Milwaukee. This dual cultural immersion planted seeds of understanding my multiracial identity.

The year 1994 brought a family shift. Our move to Green Bay was not merely geographic but a pivot in my cultural narrative. Green Bay was quieter, a stark contrast to Milwaukee's urban pulse. Enrolling in school at the Oneida Nation "turtle school" initiated deeper exploration. But my immersion was challenging, particularly confronting linguistic gaps during language classes. Each learned word, every formed sentence, bridged my understanding of my Oneida roots. Despite these challenges, my dual identities—Black and Oneida—presented a complex dance I was learning to master within the Green Bay milieu.

In my first "language and culture" class, grouping by clans was a novel concept that signified my lack of understanding about my Oneida heritage. This was one of many experiences emphasizing my alienation and feelings of being an outsider within my tribe. The disparity between my lived experiences and those of my classmates became apparent when I aligned myself with the Wolf Clan, oblivious to my actual Turtle Clan heritage, a fact later conveyed to me by my grandmother. Tears from my first day at the Oneida school signaled more than just new-school jitters; they were a testament to my sense of displacement and longing to belong.

These experiences played a pivotal role in shaping my multiracial identity. They underline the complexities of navigating cultural terrains, representative of the struggles faced by many multiracial Indigenous individuals. These narratives emphasize the need for more flexible notions of identity and belonging. My life's journey between Milwaukee and Green Bay became a crucible for my identity formation, evidence of the profound resilience and understanding forged through struggles.

The Erasure Within: Confronting Anti-Black Racism and Identity Negation

Children are like blossoming flowers, full of life and innocence. I was no different until I had to navigate my multiracial identity in a society that adheres to a racial hierarchy. The school hallways, usually a sanctuary for learning, became a battleground, filled with taunts about my Black heritage.

My hair, a symbol of my Black roots, was often the target of jokes. Influenced by our community's biases, classmates would laugh about my "afro puffs," using rap lyrics to caricature me. Though seemingly harmless, their laughter masked the uncomfortable truth of my marginalization. One memory stands out: a classmate—we'll call him Jay—pointed out that my palms were lighter than my skin because that's where I rubbed them when I washed. His words were a harsh reminder of the prejudice in our community, where my identity was seen as a stain needing to be cleaned. This was my reality, caught between my Oneida and Black identities.

These experiences highlighted a more significant issue of how Indigenous identity is defined. Traditional views held that Indigenous identities were determined by blood quantum. My life showed that experiences, relationships, and cultural ties shape identities. Yet my dual identity was often questioned and belittled, underscoring the need for a more inclusive definition of Indigenous identity that recognizes the realities of multiracial individuals and actively works to dismantle these harmful attitudes.

Moving from high school to university, the overt racial mockery I faced became a more subtle form of identity erasure. Interactions with Indigenous peers at university displayed a troubling pattern: non-Black Natives often negated my Black identity, exposing a deeply ingrained racial hierarchy.

One unforgettable incident was during officer training for my university's Indigenous student organization. I was asked to choose my race from a list of distinct categories, none recognizing my multiracial heritage. I objected, but a Native classmate suggested I identify solely as Indigenous, casually dismissing my Blackness. This dismissal highlighted the frequent marginalization of my Black identity within the Native community. The identity erasure I experienced went beyond negating my Blackness; it diminished the complex experiences that shape the identities of multiracial individuals. Recognizing the intersectionality of our identities broadens our understanding of what it means to be Indigenous.

As a Black Oneida, my life reflects the complexity of mixed-race existence—interwoven cultures, traditions, histories, and struggles. To deepen our understanding of Indigenous identity, it's crucial to acknowledge the wholeness and complexity of mixed-race individuals, challenging the standard view of us as fragmented racial components. This approach, which respects the entirety of a person's identity, offers a more inclusive perspective. Our identities are not diluted but rather amplify our unique perspectives and experiences. We are not fractions. We are not half-this or part-that. We are whole.

Genetics versus Blood Quantum: Decoding Ancestry

In my younger days, my grandmother, a proud Oneida woman, often claimed she was "100 percent Indian" with unwavering certainty. I took this at face value, weaving it into my understanding of self as I grew up. I was, as the tribal enrollment records stated, seven-sixteenths Oneida, and this fraction became an integral part of my identity. However, a simple DNA test, a promotional offer from the genetic testing company 23andMe, challenged my understanding of my ancestry and spurred a deep examination of the complex landscape of multiracial identity.

As my DNA analysis results came in, I stared at a puzzling array of percentages. Half of my genetics traced back to Africa, consistent with my father's Black heritage, while about 28 percent suggested Native American ancestry, contradicting the 44 percent or seven-sixteenths Oneida identity I had long accepted. Moreover, 22 percent of my genetic makeup was attributed to European descent. The discord between my genetically inferred heritage and the blood-quantum-based definition of my Indigenous identity revealed blood quantum's socially constructed and often inaccurate nature.[1]

While it might seem a personal anomaly, this genetic data underscores the limitations of the blood quantum system for defining Indigenous identity. Developed by colonial administrators, the blood quantum approach fails to account for historical complexities and dynamics, such as intertribal adoptions and intermarriages.[2] It overlooks historical events like the Oneida people's welcoming of European immigrants during their migration from New York to Wisconsin in the 1800s.[3]

This divergence between genetic reality and calculated blood quantum questions the binary framing of Indigenous identity. It challenges the oversimplified notion of racial quantification, which often fails to capture the richness of multiracial lived experiences and identities.[4] As multiracial individuals, our identities are not mere arithmetic combinations of racial fractions or genetic percentages; rather, identity is represented by the multiplicative essence of our diverse experiences and heritages. These experiences, not blood quantum or genetic makeup, truly define us.[5]

The genetic versus blood quantum paradox begs for a nuanced understanding of Indigenous identity, calling for an appreciation of our diverse stories and experiences. The laughter shared with my mother over our surprising genetic results, and my grandmother's confusion about reconciling her perceived "100 percent Indian" identity with my genetic makeup, provides an opportunity to examine the notion of racial purity. From a genetic standpoint, a "100 percent Indian" identity claim is practically unachievable, similar to the crumbling credibility of blood quantum under scientific scrutiny.[6] Race and Indigeneity transcend biological borders.[7]

During a Sustain Oneida community meeting regarding our dwindling membership, I voiced these concerns, arguing against blood quantum's scientific validity and insisting on it being a flawed social construct. Yet the resistance to revising blood quantum requirements was palpable, reflecting a fear of cultural dilution and loss. However, to survive, we must challenge the notion of racial purity and embrace a more inclusive understanding of identity. This understanding should celebrate our rich diversity and intricate histories. The path forward requires us to acknowledge our shared past, embrace our genetic variability, and respect the complexity of our multiracial identities.

Unjustifiable Gatekeeping:
A Critical Analysis of Oft-Proposed Alternatives

I often think of Grace, my cousin, a child entangled in a tumultuous cultural tug-of-war. After the suicide of her Oneida mother, my Aunt Amy, Grace moved in with her non-Oneida father. The tangle of emotions clouded her world, yet she held on to our community threads. But cultural immersion wasn't as fluid for her as for me. The turning point arrived at the Oneida museum, where a mere word in our Native tongue escaped Grace's grasp. She couldn't pronounce "ten" in Oneida. It was a small thing, but its implications rang loudly—would this disconnection deem her "less" Oneida?

This highlights the deficiency of cultural knowledge as the sole membership criterion for tribal identity. Nearly 78 percent of Indigenous people in the United States live outside reservations, often lacking ready access to cultural rituals, languages, and traditions.[8] This mirrors Grace's situation; her Oneida heritage is diluted due to geographical and familial circumstances. Yet does her lack of full cultural knowledge invalidate her Oneida roots? I argue it does not. It merely underscores the need for a more inclusive, nuanced understanding of tribal membership.

My cousin Arthur's story further complicates the narrative. Born to an Oneida father and a mother of Irish descent, Arthur's connection to the tribe remained unswerving despite his parents' separation. He grew up navigating between the Oneida Nation School System and public schools. His commitment to our Oneida roots led him to engage with tribal council meetings and dream of an environmental science career to contribute to our Nation.

Yet traditional lineage-based membership models, which favor maternal lines, pose a question. Where does Arthur stand in this system, given his non-Indigenous mother, despite his heartfelt dedication to our tribe? I contend that excluding tribal members based on matrilineal descent overlooks their sincere commitment to the community, thereby underscoring the insufficiency of such restrictive models.

My mother, an urban Oneida woman, further broadens this conversation. Born and raised amid Milwaukee's diverse cultures, she frequently visited our Oneida relatives on the reservation, maintaining a dynamic interplay between her urban life and cultural heritage. Far from our ancestral lands while growing up, she remained an integral part of our tribe. Her experience challenges the perception of Indigenous identity as bound by geographical ties to reservations or blood quantum alone.[9] Shaped by a confluence of experiences, my mother's Indigenous identity transcends these parameters and opens a broader dialogue on the rich diversity within Indigenous experience, ranging from reservation life to urban Indigeneity.[10]

Personal narratives spotlight the inadequacy of alternative membership criteria like cultural knowledge, matrilineal descent, and geographical ties. They underscore the imperative for a more nuanced understanding of Indigenous identity—one that beautifully weaves the threads of individual experiences into the rich tapestry of our collective Indigenous heritage.

Conclusion: Rewriting the Rules
of Indigenous Community Membership

When I was a child, my mother's stories of the entwined struggles of my ancestors as Indigenous peoples and as Black descendants of enslaved people resonated deeply. Conversations with my mother awakened an appreciation for our interconnected histories. Indigenous peoples and Black descendants of enslaved people have been woven together by shared experiences of adversity: colonialism, imperialism, and the attempted eradication of our cultures. My mother's narratives did not fragment my identity but instead fused my Blackness and Oneida-ness. This melding did not dilute our unique identities but strengthened them, reflecting resilience and defiance against oppressive forces.

Our understanding of Indigenous identity must evolve beyond genetic, geographic, or cultural markers. It's time to acknowledge the inter-woven experiences that shape who we are, from our shared histories to our lived realities. My identity, for instance, is not a fraction of Oneida or Black; it's an integrated, resilient response to cultural erasure attempts. It's time to recognize and cherish the diversity within our community, the many hues of Indigenous identities, each one complex, resilient, and whole.

A broader understanding of Indigenous identity demands more than mere acknowledgment. It calls for action, dialogue, and further explora-tion. It requires us to question traditional boundaries and constructs, and to expand our understanding of community. My mother's experiences, my journey, and the narratives of countless others call us to redefine Indig-enous identity and membership, not based on blood quantum, but on shared histories, experiences, and cultural connections.

Redefinition won't come without challenges. The journey requires tenacity and resilience, traits our communities have shown time and again. It calls us to reexamine our shared past and use it as a foundation to construct a more inclusive, realistic future. Our stories, our experiences, and our identities have the power to ignite a transformation. Woven from the narratives of our past and the realities of our present, we are beckoned to a future of inclusivity and recognition. This is not just my mother's legacy, mine, or yours—it's our collective journey toward a more inclusive understanding of Indigenous identity.

Food, Sovereignty, and Belonging

TONI HOUSE

A Dream

Many years ago, before ever growing corn, I had a dream I was standing on Old Seymour Road in Oneida, Wisconsin, where I have been told my great-great-grandmother's homestead was. She was tending to corn, not yet a foot tall, in front of her house. As I got closer, I saw a baby who I came to realize was my father. Upon waking, I wondered why I had been given a dream of my father as a baby, never considering my great-great-grandmother, nor the corn, until many years later.

* * *

Unfortunately, I was not born in this community with our Indigenous corn. I was born in Los Angeles, California. On my eighth birthday, my grandmother and I left to go to my parents' home, the Oneida Reservation in Wisconsin. My mother and siblings followed shortly thereafter, and my father with his second family some years later. We moved back and forth from the reservation to urban areas a few times before settling in Oneida. Even though I have lived here in Oneida, Wisconsin, for about fifty years, a feeling of disconnect still prevails.

A Theory

My disconnect became most evident with the fear I experience entering gardens and fields where corn is growing. The experience pushed me to reflect upon the origins of this fear. Instead, what I found was a theory. Throughout my life experiences with our Indigenous teachings, I have come to believe a natural critical bonding period with creation begins around conception and forms a foundation of belonging within three years. During this time, acknowledgment of and relationship to all of creation is established. Should this period be interrupted, disconnection to the whole prevails.

Before I even attended school, I already had the belief that little girls did not play in the dirt, much less crave it. I remember playing in the dirt while often tasting it. Later, through my teachings as a midwife, I learned that cravings usually indicate a necessity of specific nutritional contents in the foods one craves. Dirt cravings often indicate mineral deficiencies. I suffered from anemia throughout my childhood. Upon moving to Wisconsin, so our aunts and uncles could help care for us, it became evident my mother lacked the resources and knowledge to provide the sustenance we needed.

Reconnecting with Corn

My first recollection of corn was a time when I was staying with my aunt and uncle in Milwaukee. My aunt used to make corn bread and corn soup; it was very foreign to me. Today, when I watch people eat corn soup, I often know whether they were raised around these foods by their dislike of corn soup, as I had never been fond of corn soup either. Soon after, I encountered corn soup again at my first of many longhouse Midwinter Festivals in Oneida, located near London, Ontario. Corn soup is served at just about every longhouse ceremony.

I have fond memories of sitting on the bench at longhouse waiting for the women to serve us corn soup, beans on white bread or biscuits, and potatoes with onions. I did not understand much, as I did not speak our Oneida language and the ceremonies are all in our language, but I could dance and eat. This would become my second home, as my Wolf Clan family took me right in. This experience of finding our ways and family encouraged me to bring my children up with our teachings and language, further highlighting the importance of Indigenous foods.

Learning to Grow Corn

My children grew up eating corn soup and corn mush. However, we did not have our first successful crop of corn until they were the ages of four, nine, and eleven. When we attended our harvest ceremony that fall, we took our longest cob of corn to the longhouse to show one of our elders. She had worked and advocated for sharing, producing, and understanding the nutritional value of our Indigenous foods for years. I still remember her fond expression as we shared our cob with her. When it came time to dance and acknowledge our harvest—the corn—I came to an understanding about our ceremonies in a way I had never experienced before.

Learning to grow corn inspired me to learn how to make corn soup the old way, by cleaning the corn with ash. I failed multiple times. I then started to make corn soup the easier way, by using baking soda to clean the corn. This came to a stop when one of my older brothers stood up during a longhouse ceremony and spoke in English. This was something I had never seen him do in all my years of going to our longhouse ceremonies. He explained the importance of making our corn soup with ashes. Ironically, this ceremony was about our ancestors.

Seven Generations

When my grandmother died, my first grandchild was almost a year old. It was at this time, I realized, that I have had the privilege of knowing six generations of my family line: one of my great-grandmothers; my grandmothers; my aunts, uncles, and parents; my siblings; our children; and now our grandchildren. Many times, when I look at the different years of the corn seed, I see how the corn is just like our family and the generations.

Our family is now a part of Ohe·láku, a corn-growing cooperative of families. We have traveled together for various events since 2017. In 2019 we attended a gathering at the original territory of the Cayuga Nation in what is known today as New York. The gathering included activities such as eating our Indigenous foods, preparing them over an open fire using ancient methods of preparation, and a seed exchange. I did not have any seeds to exchange, so I sat to the side and watched. Some women entered, and one caught my eye, as she was wearing a rebozo, a Mayan wrap employed in many capacities, including carrying infants and in childbirth practices. The women sat alongside me, and we began to converse about birth, ceremony, and sexuality. Such an appropriate conversation to have during a seed exchange; is that not what it is all about?

It was amazing to sit with women who thought even deeper about the subjects of birth, ceremony, and sexuality. The woman wearing the rebozo shared some of her teachings as a Mayan woman. Although much was said that day, what I took from this encounter was how this woman looked at the corn and concluded: most think we are here to learn how to grow, prepare, and share this food together, but it is more than that. The corn has come back to teach us. I have seen her, the corn, do this in many ways.

Through a dream, I was able to see my great-great-grandmother and the corn. My grandmother often told me how her grandmother only spoke Oneida because she refused to speak English, and she was a midwife. However, she never told me about her growing corn. My father's family tree indicates Louisa (Denny) Christjohn was born in 1861, and she married Moses Christjohn, born in 1879. They had eight children and many grandchildren. With this dream I was able to see the seventh generation of my family line. Decades later, I have come to realize the gifts of this dream. First, I was able to see my great-great grandmother. Furthermore, I was also able to embrace two important cultural components: the concept of looking out seven generations and the realization of how long the corn has been with us.

Sovereignty

Both the seven generations and the corn are strong components of our ancient governing system, the Great Law of Peace. I have been taught how all the Oneida Good Men and Good Women leadership (interpreted as chiefs and clan mothers today) are to keep seven generations in mind when decision making. An interesting note in regard to the first three titles of the nine Oneida Good Men is that they are all named according to what they were doing when they were first encountered by the Peace Maker who brought the Great Law of Peace. These three titles all related to guarding the corn. It makes sense in that our leaders needed to have the wherewithal to feed their people. This in turn gives clues as to how we exercised sovereignty as nations within our ancient governance.

To grow food as nations, a territory must be established in order to exercise food sovereignty. Not only that, knowledge of how to care for the territory and work with the natural resources in a harmonious way is needed. If one were to only look at one resource, the human resource, one would find the need for a diversity of skills and gifts. Growing a vast acreage of corn to feed a nation requires a great magnitude of human resources. In turn, recognizing the necessary diversity of human resources validates each person who belongs to the nation. This cannot be done if people do not have a mindset that acknowledges a diversity of skills and gifts.

From my perspective, creating such a mindset goes back to my belief that a natural critical bonding period with creation begins around conception and forms a foundation of belonging within three years. Having this type of mindset requires one to see how everything in creation is related. Being that so many are disconnected, we need an antidote that fosters reconnection. The method I have used to examine this theory is learning to plant and harvest corn to reconnect. As reflected in our words of acknowledgment to all of creation, we know that all of creation has diverse responsibilities; therefore, it would only make sense to speculate there is no one method to establish reconnection to creation. This method is just one of many.

Illustrating Planting and Harvesting Corn

I have created two figures (10 and 11) to illustrate some of the diversity of resources necessary to plant and harvest corn. Neither is all-encompassing; they are only snapshots of a few considerations necessary to grow corn. The figures are intended only to share one aspect of how planting and harvesting corn requires multiple skills and gifts of the diverse resources necessary to exercise our sovereignty through the growing of our own foods to sustain our nation.

Figure 10 highlights planting corn and harvesting. A few of the considerations regarding planting corn are the process of acquiring seeds, knowledge of the growing season, and knowledge of how much to plant. And a few considerations for harvesting corn are baskets for gathering, processing, and drying corn. Each consideration illustrated has a few subjects to expand upon the capacity of the resources required in planting and harvesting corn. Figure 11 is intended to illustrate the impact one grower has on the community/nation. The illustrations are not complete and are only intended to show how one grower interacts within the community/nation. In reality, the capacity of the whole is very broad; no one person does it all.

Figure 10

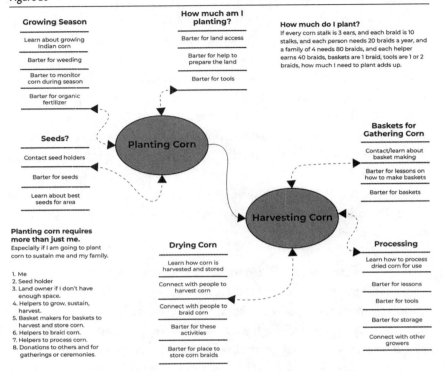

Growing Season

Learn about growing Indian corn

Barter for weeding

Barter to monitor corn during season

Barter for organic fertilizer

How much am I planting?

Barter for land access

Barter for help to prepare the land

Barter for tools

How much do I plant?
If every corn stalk is 3 ears, and each braid is 10 stalks, and each person needs 20 braids a year, and a family of 4 needs 80 braids, and each helper earns 40 braids, baskets are 1 braid, tools are 1 or 2 braids, how much I need to plant adds up.

Planting Corn

Seeds?

Contact seed holders

Barter for seeds

Learn about best seeds for area

Baskets for Gathering Corn

Contact/learn about basket making

Barter for lessons on how to make baskets

Barter for baskets

Harvesting Corn

Planting corn requires more than just me.
Especially if I am going to plant corn to sustain me and my family.

1. Me
2. Seed holder
3. Land owner if I don't have enough space.
4. Helpers to grow, sustain, harvest.
5. Basket makers for baskets to harvest and store corn.
6. Helpers to braid corn.
7. Helpers to process corn.
8. Donations to others and for gatherings or ceremonies.

Drying Corn

Learn how corn is harvested and stored

Connect with people to harvest corn

Connect with people to braid corn

Barter for these activities

Barter for place to store corn braids

Processing

Learn how to process dried corn for use

Barter for lessons

Barter for tools

Barter for storage

Connect with other growers

Figure 11

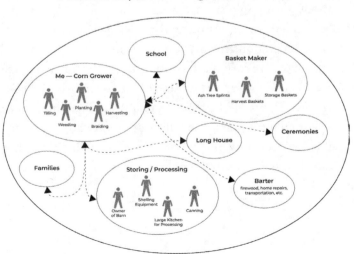

Nation / Community
Potential Impact of a Single Corn Grower

School

Basket Maker

Ash Tree Splints   Storage Baskets
Harvest Baskets

Me — Corn Grower

Tilling   Planting   Harvesting
Weeding   Braiding

Long House

Ceremonies

Families

Storing / Processing

Owner of Barn   Shelling Equipment   Canning
Large Kitchen for Processing

Barter
firewood, home repairs, transportation, etc.

People who grow corn realize that this work cannot be done independently. We must also acknowledge the small pockets of people throughout the generations who have persevered in preserving our seeds. The corn has stayed alongside our ancestors through hundreds of years of genocide, oppression, war, poverty, sickness, relocation, and assimilation.

The Golden Goose

Many years ago, I was taught how corn is precious, equating "her" to the value of gold. It took me many years to relate to this concept. Recently, someone reminded us in a General Tribal Council (GTC) meeting that there used to be a man who referred to our casino as the "Golden Goose." Instead, my thought went to our corn. What if corn is the "Golden Goose" for our Nation today? I shared this with an elder, and his response was, "George Washington knew this!" He was referring to how, during the Revolutionary War, Washington sent out the Sullivan Campaign to destroy and burn many Longhouse homes and acres of orchards, various crops, and stored foods, our corn being one of them. From what I understand, a part of successful warfare is to take out the primary resources people cannot live without. The targeted attack points to our corn as a critical resource, to be held high in relation to the survival of our Nations as the Haudenosaunee (They Build a House).

* * *

Through a dream I was able to see how we have survived, both our Nation and our corn. It has taken many years of experiences and reflection to interpret the value of this dream. The strongest pull was seeing my great-great-grandmother. When I became a grandmother, this dream enhanced my understanding of seven generations. It also taught me the importance of looking back. Finally, seeing my father as an infant with his great-grandmother and the corn validated my sense of the natural critical bonding period with creation.

My reconnection with creation began by facing my fears of the gardens and fields. Over time came an understanding of the vision and knowledge our ancestors held not only to preserve our corn, but also our communities and the environment. As I walk this path of learning about our Indigenous foods, I am constantly amazed at how the diversity within creation works together to grow the corn. In turn, this understanding has helped me to transfer this core knowledge of creation and how these concepts have been woven into how we are intended to govern ourselves, our communities, and our nations. This dream has helped me to embrace the power of bonding with creation to foster belonging.

How Memory Works

A thousand years ago
The wind blew against you
And you turned to walk backward
And as you turned
You dropped something shiny
It fell out of your pocket and
Landed on the ground
You walked away from it
And never realized it was gone

LOTNI

The Long Arc of Time: Who Are You?

KCHEYONKOTE BURTON W. WARRINGTON

One of the most important questions you can ask any human being is "Who are you?" Today, as it pertains to the original people of this land, commonly referred to as Native Americans, we are confronted with important questions related to how we identify ourselves, how others identify us, and for what purposes we are being identified. Although generations before us have confronted similar questions, in our current moment in time, we find ourselves faced with unique modern challenges and opportunities as we navigate our inherited histories, our current circumstances, and our responsibilities to our future generations.

I have often heard the saying "It's hard to know where you're going if you don't know where you've been." Understanding our histories are critical to gaining perspective to appreciate, understand, and develop solutions to current and future challenges. One concept I have found helpful in putting the topic of identity into perspective is the concept of the long arc of time—a framing that a close friend first shared with me in 2016, shortly after the Resistance at Standing Rock.

To illustrate the concept of the long arc of time, I will use a general reference point of ten thousand years, understanding that the histories of tribal peoples are much older than ten thousand years. If we start there, consider that if a generation can be summed up as twenty-five years, within one hundred years there are four generations, in a thousand years there are forty generations, and in ten thousand years there are four hundred generations.

To put the arc of time into perspective, consider that the United States was founded about ten generations ago, the boarding school era started about six generations ago, and the Indian Reorganization Act, passed on June 18, 1934, was less than four generations ago. The last six generations, in particular, have brought about a great deal of change to our collective and individual experiences as Native Americans. From broad common experiences with nonsensical federal Indian policy, to individual tribal experiences, to the increased mobility and connectedness of the overall population at large, the circumstances we are faced with today are unique to our place in the world and our moment in the arc of time.

Specific to questions related to identity and for what purposes we are being identified, it must not be lost on us that we are fortunate to have long, rich, and beautiful histories to draw power and wisdom from. Using a ten-thousand-year arc of time, consider that for well over 396 generations our people were the architects of our own value-based identification systems. Modern disruptions to those systems have largely been present only over the last four generations. Specifically, foreign concepts such as blood quantum have been part of the Native American experience only over the last four generations.

As my friend explained his understanding of the arc of time, I realized the concept was not at all unfamiliar to me. Rather, it was very familiar, but I had not used that frame to gain a more holistic perspective on modern challenges. In reality, the arc of time concept should not be foreign to Native Americans. Most, if not all, tribal peoples I know of have some variation of a creation story that has been passed down for countless generations among their people. Similarly, the concept of making decisions for unborn or future generations is present in the ethos of most, if not all, tribal peoples across the land. That past and future connection to something greater than ourselves is what solidifies our place in the arc of time.

I have come to appreciate that no human being alive today knows with 100 percent certainty what life was like for my Menominee ancestors twenty generations ago, let alone one hundred generations or four hundred generations ago. However, I believe wholeheartedly that through all those generations, my Menominee ancestors shared certain common characteristics that were acquired through shared lived experience. Those characteristics are, in part, what identified them as Menominee, including experiencing life on Omāēqnomenēw Ahkēw, (Menominee ancestral lands), experiencing life as Kayēs Mamāceqtawak (ancient movers), communicating through Omāēqnomenēweqnesen (Menominee language), and learning Enātesen (way of being) through Kaehkēnawapahtam (learning through observation), which included an expectation of a reciprocal relationship with the larger group of people.

I have also come to appreciate that as foreign belief and value systems were imposed over multiple recent generations as part of state- and religious-sponsored cultural genocide, many Native Americans, through no fault of their own, became less and less exposed to the lived experiences that our ancestors experienced for more than 396 generations. As Native Americans continue healing from the genocidal trauma inflicted over many generations, more meaningful discussions related to identity are sure to occur. When they do, what, if anything, can we learn from our long, rich histories? How do we collectively go about gaining more insight into ways of being that carried our ancestors for thousands of years? And most importantly, how do we honor our unique histories while also blending them with our current-day circumstances?

I am wholeheartedly convinced that a major key to addressing identity challenges, including blood quantum, can be found through the revitalization of our tribal languages.

Native Americans—for tens of thousands of years—have predominantly relied on oral history and lived experience as opposed to written or documented history. Framing this thought through the long arc of time, consider that for more than 390 generations our tribal languages and lifeways were the receptacles of our history, worldview, philosophy, and understanding of our relationships. It wasn't until the boarding school era began that the English language began its meaningful intrusion into our communities. Thus, if we want to gain perspective to appreciate, understand, and develop solutions to current and future problems, our tribal languages and lifeways as our receptacles of history, worldview, philosophy, and understanding of our relationships should show up prominently in those discussions.

The general question of "Who are you?" is a complicated and deeply personal question that is highly influenced by individual circumstances and the context in which the question is being asked. In its most basic form, a person's identity is a combination of multiple elements including an individual identity, a family identity, and a social identity. With respect to the modern challenges Native Americans face with identity, it is worth first acknowledging that just being alive today as a distinct Native American is something special in and of itself. The attempted literal and cultural erasure of our people and how that erasure impacts the individual, family, and social identity of every Native American is important to acknowledge as conversations continue to evolve. We have inherited the challenges of that history, and we now must answer the question of whether we are equipped to address those challenges or whether we will pass them on for our future generations to address.

The most important identity any of us have is our own individual identity. This identity is specific to us and is influenced by things we have little to no control over—for example, inherited or genetic characteristics such as our height, hair color, skin color, eye color, and other physical characteristics or other appearances. These characteristics could be described as *what* we are. Our individual identities are also in part largely influenced by acquired or learned characteristics such as our belief and value systems, which may more accurately describe who we are or what type of person we are.

Our family identity is also closely tied to our individual identities. Within our family identity, who we were raised by and who influenced our belief and value systems is important. Our family units are naturally the most common places where we acquire and learn our initial belief and value systems—the language(s) we use, the religion(s) we follow, appropriate behavior(s) and ways of being, and our earliest understanding of where we belong in this world in relation to others. It is worth noting that within one's family identity, an inherited or genetic connection is more often than not present; however, there are countless examples of familial belonging in tribal communities where there is no genetic connection.

Social identity is perhaps the most complex, as it involves multiple external factors to be considered, such as who in society is identifying us and for what purposes. Human beings are social beings, and, as such, we all have an innate need and desire to be a part of a larger group of people. Over the long arc of time, there were very practical considerations for groups of tribal peoples to associate in larger groups. Food and physical security, diversity of gene pools, and various skills and knowledge were needed to support the larger group. Similarly, collective recollection of cultural ways of being, protocols, medicines, songs, and dances required a larger group of people to carry out certain customs, traditions, and religious functions in a society. The life experience of tribal people has been substantially altered from what was. As communities practice reclamation and repair the fractures to cultural connection, community, and identity, we also grapple with belonging.

The elephant in the room in most tribal communities today is the concept of blood quantum as a means to define who is or isn't considered a part of the organized governmental institution. In regard to blood quantum, I would like to reiterate three key points. First, a US law, the 1934 Indian Reorganization Act, is credited with being the primary source of the widespread adoption of blood quantum requirements for enrollment. Second, our existence as distinct peoples was never part of the larger plan in this country. This country saw tribal ways of being and connections to the land as obstacles to westward expansion and long sought to rid itself of the "Indian Problem," one way or another. Third, Native Americans always have—and still to this day have—the inherent power to define ourselves. That power isn't afforded to us by any piece of paper, government, or court of law, and, as such, that power cannot be taken away or controlled unless we allow it to be. This is true self-determination.

Our identities are complex concepts that include our individual identity, our family identity, and our social identity. Our individual and family identities are not based purely on nature or nurture, but rather a combination of nature *and* nurture. One challenge with blood quantum as a means of defining one's social identity is that the concept is purely based on the inherited genetics of nature and leaves no room for the *acquired* characteristics of nurture. Setting aside the fact that records documenting blood quantum were measured at an arbitrary point in the long arc of time, the concept is worth questioning. Does the concept of blood quantum honor who our ancestors were for more than 396 generations prior to the 1934 Indian Reorganization Act? Does it honor what they persevered through dark chapters to retain? Most importantly, how much does that even matter to Native Americans today? It also begs the question of whether our individual, family, and social identities can or should align.

Four years ago, I was personally inspired by Nēmat (my close friend/brother) to shift my primary focus to community language revitalization work. Over the previous twenty years, I maintained a close connection to home through family, ceremonies, and community but spent time away attending advanced schooling and gaining meaningful modern-day professional skills in business, management, law, and politics. Throughout this time Nēmat remained deeply engaged in the Menominee language revitalization efforts. During my frequent visits home, we always made it a priority to catch up on life and dream about what the future could hold. After many years of dreaming we took a leap of faith in organizing the grassroots-led, community-based nonprofit Menomini yoU, Inc. to serve as a vehicle for the community language revitalization work.

As we embarked on this new organization, the concept of the arc of time was not lost on us. After all, the language revitalization work was not starting with our efforts, and it surely won't end with us. Rather like our ancestors, we are merely stepping into our moment in the long arc of time to do what we can to honor the generations before us, contribute to our community, and do our part to ensure the generations to come are in a better position than what we inherited.

In the fast-paced globalized world we navigate today, it can be difficult to find the time, energy, and space for reflection on blood quantum, identity, and our place in the world. What I know is that the experience of being involved in something bigger than oneself is what solidifies our place in the long arc of time. Some people might say we are trying to save our language, but what I truly believe is that it is our languages that are trying to save us.

How do we collectively go about gaining more insight
into ways of being that carried our ancestors
for thousands of years?

Learning Our Path into the Future

ARTLEY M. SKENANDORE

The Oneida Nation, like many tribal nations across Turtle Island, is dedicated to sustaining the specific cultural understanding of one's identity into the seventh generation. The challenge, however, is renewing the practice of sharing cultural learning stories from the past to guide future learning. Original knowledge is the foundation of our origin—past, present, and future. The Oneida Nation embarked on a sovereign learning journey for education fifty years ago with the opening of the Oneida Nation Elementary School (K–8) as the first step in renewing the cultural learning system. The learning journey began by encouraging clan discussions, reflection by individuals and families, and community experience of "learning to be Oneida." The motivational purpose for creating a cohesive learning environment for expanding cultural knowledge: strengthening the cultural identity of families of the Oneida Nation.

The original teachings of Creation, Ceremonies, Great Law, and Kaliwiyo serve as the cultural principles and foundation of the Haudenosaunee. The original teachings are messages of respect, responsibility, and relationship that span thousands of years of interaction. The purpose of this essay is to encourage everyone the opportunity to delve into and renew the stories of original knowledge and reflect upon the relevant application to illuminate our path into the future as individuals, families, clans, and Indigenous nations. The collective future of our Indigenous civilizations rests upon our educational practices of embracing the ancestral knowledge that has carried us to this moment of reflection, thereby sustaining our learning foundation today and into the future.

Encouraging opportunities for community interactions, sharing individual and family stories, broadens the foundation that contributes to the future of fortifying our *learning to be* context of knowing our origins to embrace the future. This sovereign framework illustration represents the methodology for continuous renewal of our Indigenous identity as individuals, families, and clans to guide and sustain our path as Indigenous nations.

Figure 12

Sovereign Educational Framework

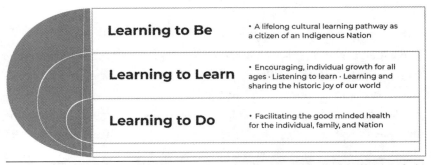

Learning to Be	• A lifelong cultural learning pathway as a citizen of an Indigenous Nation
Learning to Learn	• Encouraging, individual growth for all ages · Listening to learn · Learning and sharing the historic joy of our world
Learning to Do	• Facilitating the good minded health for the individual, family, and Nation

The Sovereign Educational Framework for learning represents a physical, spiritual, emotional, and intellectual foundation for the individual, family, community, and Indigenous Nation as a whole.

Jo-Ann Archibald, author of *Indigenous Storywork*, provides an emphasis on the interweaving principle and practice to guide the application of cultural teachings. Archibald's idea of holism illustrates the interrelatedness of how our teachings contribute to the development of the whole person. This emphasis of learning by the individual, family, and community are the concentric circles that emerge as holism.[1] The concept of holism describes the journey of *learning to be a whole person*. Each story in *Indigenous Storywork* attests how someone has traveled along and gathered knowledge to understand who they are as an individual. Embracing the understanding of becoming a family is a similar learning journey to discover and share the cultural stories that influence our thinking and the feeling of learning to share within family. Looking into the future commences with facilitating the gathering of stories and fortifying the framework of cultural practices. Renewing the fabric of original knowledge embraces the challenges of learning to be Oneida through the past and present to create a pathway into the future.

Learning to Be

Navigating the learning pathway is the architecture of sharing the relevance of cultural stories of the past and present as the bridge into the future. According to Lomawaima and McCarty,[2] American Indian education, throughout history, has experienced relentless attempts of standardizing, assimilating, and recasting Native people by secular and religious agencies.[3] Following the original teachings of the Oneida people as a blueprint, creating a responsibility enriches the pathway of learning. The application of responsibility is the sovereign footprint that exercises choice in the process of learning consistency, which underpins the process of *learning to be* from the content of original knowledge.

The learning journey of original knowledge is one of consistency, starting with the teachings of creation. Scanning across Turtle Island, Indigenous nations all possess stories that speak specifically to their intimate origin with the land. Archibald[4] describes learning consistency as starting every morning by asking for guidance from the Creator through prayer because it creates a cultural learning process that promotes respect, reciprocity, and reverence.[5] The Oneida as part of the Haudenosaunee share a specific cultural practice of Kanehelatuksla. The opening statement of relationship with the natural world, Kanehelatuksla expresses our gratitude for where our feet fall upon this earth daily. The acknowledgment of creation and the Kanehelatuksla is an exercise of consistency and responsibility. We witness with our eyes, hear with our ears, and gather knowledge through interactive experiences from others sharing and retelling the lessons and stories of our past. This is what begins the process of *learning to be*. In the future, this practice will continue to renew our place, where our feet are upon our Earth Mother.

The ability to demonstrate cultural competence through the learning pathway is best described as self-determination, which helps an individual continue their learning pathway. Individuals learn through watching others. According to Simpson,[6] learning is described as modeling and sharing desirable behaviors for children to mimic.[7] Exercising this dialogue is the essence of educational sovereignty, representing renewal of a learning paradigm that bundles three important learning methodologies: learning to be, learning to learn, and learning to do. The challenge, however, is where to begin telling the story of individual and collective experience, the essential educational resources, and cultural practices of a tribal nation. Since settler contact, Indigenous communities have struggled and continue to struggle to determine a definitive strategy and approach to protect their Indigenous learning systems. The constructionism of settler expansion across the territories of tribal nations has posed challenges for cultural practices of Indigenous nations. What will be our challenge in the future? Our commitment to be responsible for renewing our Indigenous learning systems, speaking our original languages to share the first-person experience, and interacting with creation as a daily practice.

An essential cultural practice that acknowledges our interactions with all of creation is Kanehelatuksla (expressing heartfelt gratitude). Each person is encouraged to acknowledge the families of creation in a daily statement of gratitude. Kanehelatuksla continues to serve as the foundational platform to represent the uniting of our minds as one as we come together, ˆtwahwe?nu.ni yukwa?nikuhla? A vital practice during the learning journey into the future, Kanehelatuksla will help support the individual, family, and clans carry out the methodology of learning to be, learning to learn, and learning to do as the pathway into the future.

Reciprocity, respect, and relationships are at the center of continuously renewing our interactions with creation today and in the future. Learning to learn is a shared practice that strengthens our identity and interactions within our families and contributes to enriching our cultural knowledge.

Figure 13[8]

___

Our Knowledge Sources

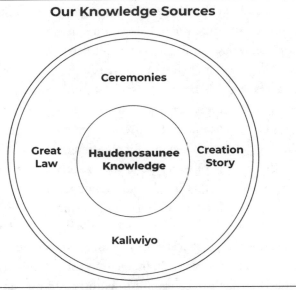

The Dr. Antone Cultural Knowledge Model demonstrates the Haudenosaunee knowledge of Ceremonies, the Creation Story, Great Law, and Kaliwiyo.

Learning to Learn

The cultural framework of the Haudenosaunee is the foundational content for the *learning to learn* journey. Drawing upon the cultural learning stories of Kanehatunksla (Creation), Kayeniyoliwake (Ceremonies), Kayenlakowa (Great Law), and Kaliwiyo (good words), the cultural stories share a relevant context of the sense of purpose, place, and relationship between people and the natural world. The relevance today is the fusion process of the learning stories that convey the sense of responsibility of individuals to embrace learning and carry forward the sense of purpose to strengthen families. The cultural content is a source of learning to motivate each person to embrace the understanding that influences a good mind—an epistemological platform common and shared by all nations of the Haudenosaunee. The way of knowing is embedded in the language, which is key essential content. Understanding the language and the teaching within the language is a twofold challenge for individuals. Learning the language becomes a foremost goal. Language learning has emerged as a spectrum of individual experiences to achieve linguistic fluency. Embracing the personal mission of becoming proficient in the language supports the cultural fluency and comprehension of our ancient teachings, which are embedded in the language.

Envisioning the future was introduced to the chiefs of the Haudenosaunee by the messages of the Peacemaker, who traveled among the Nations of the Haudenosaunee to encourage the application of the good mind and word to strengthen relationship within and among communities. The Peacemaker encouraged the leadership to symbolically extend their hands to each other in a circle. Within the inner circle, no one would fall too far without the assistance and support of the other chiefs. The strength of the chiefs collectively would hold the leadership together. The symbolic strength of the teachings from the Peacemaker continues to resonate within the Nations of the Haudenosaunee as an essential cultural practice.

Cultural knowledge is the foundational resource, the compass that one follows to learn to be a contributing citizen as an individual to their family, clan, and nation. The vision for the future is rooted in the renewal process of embracing the cultural practices as learning the lessons found in our Indigenous thinking and expressions of language. Our challenge is to create a learning climate that allows for interaction and sharing, which will contribute to brightening Yukwatsistay^ (Our Fire, Our Spirit within Each of Us).

The learning journey into the future begins with the individual and how that individual relates to the family and the collection of families that we have come to know as clans. The relationship that guides the interactions is learning the cultural characteristics and ensuing responsibilities that rest within each clan family. There is no beginning point to this journey other than to celebrate learning and the connection to the natural world. Envisioning the future is bundled with the task of reflecting on the effort and energy to create a path of cultural learning. How does the citizen of an Indigenous nation identify the essential cultural practices that create the relevance of *learning to be* for the individual, family, clan, and the nation?

Essential to the journey is the celebration of cultural content that continues to expand across Indigenous communities across Turtle Island. The emphasis of the learning journey is not an accumulation of cultural knowledge but learning the context and application of the cultural teaching as the spirit of brightening the fire of the individual and the families and creating a brighter path for the Nation.

Learning to Do

The learning process as the methodology of revitalization, regeneration, and envisioning, when combined, become a powerful learning pathway to strengthen Indigenous self-determination. Linda Tuhiwai Smith demonstrated, in *Decolonizing Methodologies*, the urgency of Indigenous research as a tool where the content outcome is not to learn about but to learn from the efforts of discovering and retelling the story to articulate the journey of Indigenous peoples. Smith highlighted twenty-five Indigenous projects that serve as a framework to describe the efforts of Indigenous struggles. These included the survival of the peoples, cultures, and language; the struggle to become self-determining; and the need to take back control of our destiny.[9]

The learning journey methodology for embracing learning to be, learning to learn, and learning to do renews the community narrative structure, ensuring the families of our Indigenous nations have a responsibility to contribute to the future. The community contributes to the expansion of cultural knowledge through their collaboration in developing and strengthening the learning system.

The commitment of *learning to be* guides our Indigenous thinking and feelings in a constant mode of dynamic growth of sharing our ways of learning and contributing to the collective understanding and application as we journey into the future. The power of offering a good word of encouragement to each other is encouragement to keep learning and a celebration of the joy of cultural learning. The cultural learning journey will ensure our original knowledge is timeless and a sustaining contribution to future generations. Peoples of Indigenous nations today celebrate cultural renewal and share confidence in each other as citizens, Yukwatsistay^ navigating the future!

Blood Quantum and the Auto-Colonization of the Michigan Anishinaabek

MATTHEW L.M. FLETCHER

Anishinaabe storyteller Basil Johnston described the chronological path of life in four stages, what he called the four hills of life.[1] The first stage, linked to the East, is infancy and early childhood, a time of preparation and listening. The second stage, linked to the South, is youth, a time of doing things. The third stage, linked to the West, is adulthood, a time of vision. The fourth stage, linked to the North, is Old Age, a time of the fulfillment of the vision and a time of sacred learning and teaching.

The twelve Michigan Anishinaabek tribal nations are in many respects ancient, pre-dating the United States by centuries or more. But the modern incarnations of those ancient tribal nations are only a few decades old. After all, Congress did not adopt and enable tribal self-determination policies until the 1970s. Michigan tribal nations are still in childhood, perhaps still infants. Most Michigan tribal constitutions are documents all but dictated to the tribes by the United States because of a federal law that grants approval power of new tribal constitutions to the Secretary of the Interior. As a consequence of self-determination practices that require tribal governments to meet federal standards, Michigan tribal governments are essentially federal government contractors, spending federal money under federal rules. As a result of being asked to follow federal rules, Michigan tribal governments have heavily borrowed state and federal laws to build their codes. They also borrowed state and federal models to build their justice systems. And the work is ongoing.

Critically, the federal government also coerced most Michigan tribal governments to adopt blood quantum requirements for enrollment, expressly to keep the numbers of tribal citizens to whom the United

States owes a duty of protection to a minimum. It worked, to the twisted benefit of the federal government. Contemporary tribal governments do not have to maintain those requirements, but sadly most of the Michigan Anishinaabek and their ogemaag (leaders) have embraced blood quantum, internalizing and even fetishizing blood quantum. The embrace and internalization of a colonizer's political principle like blood quantum is evidence of governmental immaturity, but there is great hope.

This essay surveys the origins and the substance of the blood quantum rules of representative Michigan Anishinaabe tribal nations. The essay then compares the modern rules to traditional Anishinaabe notions of belonging and citizenship, which are rooted in the core principles of Mino-Bimaadiziwin and the Nizhwaaswi Mishomis/Nokomis Kinoomaagewinawaan. The final part of this essay includes suggestions for moving forward, focusing on the possibility of tribal nations resetting their internal blood quantum determinations and on a recent Anishinaabe tribal court decision on enrollment matters.

Origins and Substance of
Michigan Anishinaabek Blood Quantum Rules

By my count, seven of the twelve federally recognized Anishinaabe tribal nations in Michigan currently utilize a minimum blood quantum requirement for enrollment as a tribal citizen. Most of these tribes use a one-quarter minimum. This section surveys the historical background of representative tribes' blood quantum rules, focusing on the Saginaw Chippewa Indian Tribe and the Grand Traverse Band of Ottawa and Chippewa Indians.

The collective histories of Michigan's federally recognized tribal nations directly informs this discussion.[2] Fifteen to twenty tribal nations negotiated treaties with the United States from the late eighteenth century until the 1860s. Despite their status as treaty tribes, there were only four federally recognized tribes in Michigan until the late 1970s, tribes the federal government allowed to organize under the IRA in the 1930s: Bay Mills Indian Community (BMIC), Hannahville Indian Community (Hannahville), Keweenaw Bay Indian Community (KBIC), and Saginaw Chippewa Indian Tribe (Saginaw Chippewa). During the 1970s and 1980s, two tribes split off from two of the original four tribes: Lac Vieux Desert Band of Lake Superior

Chippewa Indians (LVD, splitting from KBIC) and Sault Ste. Marie Tribe of Chippewa Indians (Sault Tribe, splitting from BMIC). The remaining six had been administratively terminated, meaning that the Department of the Interior unilaterally (and illegally) ended the federal-tribal relationship, in the 1860s and 1870s[3]: Grand Traverse Band of Ottawa and Chippewa Indians (GTB), Little River Band of Ottawa Indians (LRB), Little Traverse Bay Bands of Odawa Indians (LTBB), Match-E-Be-Nash-She-Wish Band of Pottawatomi Indians (Gun Lake Tribe), Nottawaseppi Huron Band of the Potawatomi (NHBP), and Pokagon Band of Potawatomi Indians (Pokagon). Several other Anishinaabe tribal nations remain nonrecognized but continue to press their claims against the United States.

As noted, seven of the twelve federally recognized tribes in Michigan require a minimum blood quantum for eligibility to be a tribal member:

- The Bay Mills Indian Community requires membership petitioners who descend from persons listed as members of the Sault Ste. Marie Ojibwe residing on the Bay Mills Reservation on the Durant Roll to show they possess one-quarter Indian blood in order to be eligible for tribal membership.[4] Recently, the BMIC general membership voted to maximize the blood quantum of enrolled tribal citizens as a matter of tribal law.

- The Grand Traverse Band of Ottawa and Chippewa Indians requires membership petitioners who are descendants of current members to show that they possess one-quarter Indian blood, of which at least one-eighth must derive from "Michigan Ottawa and/or Chippewa" ancestors.[5] Others can be adopted into the Tribe if they possess one-quarter "Indian blood" and can show "substantial ties" to the tribe.[6] GTB also relies on the Grand Traverse portion of the Durant Roll.[7]

- The Hannahville Indian Community requires nonresident children of tribal members who are petitioning for membership to possess one-half Indian blood.[8] Children of one member and who reside on the reservation when they are born[9] and children of two tribal members regardless of residence[10] are also eligible, regardless of blood quantum. Hannahville also provides for adoption of persons who are descendants or married into the Community and can show they will "assist the Community in the fulfillment of its purposes."[11]

- The Keweenaw Bay Indian Community requires membership petitioners with a tribal citizen parent to possess one-quarter Indian blood.[12] Alternatively, a petitioner can show one-quarter "Chippewa" blood, residence on the reservation, and ancestral ties to KBIC.[13] The KBIC Constitution allows for persons to be adopted by the Tribe, but those persons possess limited membership rights.[14] Enrolled members may be disenrolled for fraud, mistake, or dual enrollment.[15] News coverage of the struggles faced by first descendants is prevalent.[16]
- The Little River Band of Ottawa Indians requires membership petitioners to show descendancy from a person listed on the "Grand River Ottawa" portion of the Durant Roll and possesses one-quarter "Grand River Ottawa or Michigan Ottawa blood.[17] LRB has closed future enrollment to all persons not under the age of 18.[18]
- The Little Traverse Bay Bands of Odawa Indians requires membership petitioners to show descendancy from a person listed on the Little Traverse portion of the Durant Roll and one-quarter Indian blood.[19]
- The Saginaw Chippewa Indian Tribe requires descendancy from four specific rolls (listed in the Tribe's constitution by date only) and one-quarter Indian blood.[20] Children of tribal members may also be adopted.[21] Saginaw Chippewa also expressly authorizes the disenrollment of citizens and adopted citizens who are enrolled in another tribe[22] or who "abandon Tribal relations" with Saginaw Chippewa.[23] Saginaw Chippewa closed its rolls to new members many years ago. The Tribe also has embarked on a decades-long series of campaigns to disenroll members it claims were enrolled by mistake.[24]

In the Indian Reorganization Act of 1934 (IRA), Congress required the Secretary of the Interior to decide whether to approve initial tribal constitutions.[25] That means all Michigan Anishinaabe tribal constitutions have been analyzed and approved by the federal government. Though the IRA authorized the secretary to approve the proposed constitutions unless they were "contrary to applicable laws,"[26] history shows that federal bureaucrats exercised domineering control over the substance of the proposed constitutions. We will focus on Saginaw Chippewa and GTB, both of whom have engaged in litigation over enrollment and membership issues affected by historical federal intervention in the origins of their blood quantum rules.

Saginaw Chippewa is one of the four tribes in Michigan that the United States allowed to participate in the IRA upon its passage in 1934. The IRA allowed tribal citizens to vote in a secretarial election to decide whether to reorganize their governments.[27] Tribal leaders drafted a constitutional text soon after learning about the IRA and proposed it to the Bureau of Indian Affairs, which promptly rejected it, insisting on holding an election to decide whether to opt in to the IRA.[28] The secretarial election was delayed by the difficulty of establishing a list of tribal citizens eligible to vote, which at that time included persons residing off-reservation.[29] Once the tribal citizenry voted to opt in, the Commissioner of Indian Affairs used its IRA powers to dictate to the Tribe who could be a member and who could not, deciding that the tribal membership could come from only those persons then residing on the reservation.[30] The Tribe agreed to these new rules in a secretarial election held in 1937 to ratify the constitution approved by the federal government.[31] It appears that the federal government's choice privileged those Saginaw Chippewa citizens who were able to successfully select and perfect an allotment within the reservation boundaries, a process dominated by federal incompetence and corruption.[32] The Tribe successfully prosecuted a land claim arising from the failed allotment process in the 1970s, leading to several years of lobbying Congress to appropriate funds to satisfy the judgment.[33] In 1985, after both the Interior and Congress insisted that the judgment funds be distributed to nonresident nonmembers who were harmed by the allotment process,[34] the Tribe sent proposed amendments to the tribal constitution that removed the residency requirement for membership.[35] Congress adopted a judgment fund act that assumed the Tribe would enroll the nonresident nonmembers.[36] In 1996, the Saginaw Chippewa began its efforts to disenroll nonresident tribal members.[37]

The conflict within the Saginaw Chippewa tribal community arising from the federally imposed and influenced membership criteria is apparent from a review of the text of those rules. The 1937 text excluded persons who were direct relations of tribal members if they did not formally reside on the Tribe's reservation. As a functional matter, the 1937 rule excluded persons who could not acquire or select an allotment from within the reservation boundaries due to federal incompetence and corruption, creating two classes of tribal citizens, those with allotments and those without.[38] The 1986 text retained the exclusion of persons who did not meet the one-quarter blood quantum requirement, but included persons who had benefitted from the land claim arising out of the allotment process. The Tribe did not change the membership criteria imposed in 1986, but the political disdain for non-resident nonmembers is apparent from its aggressive and patient efforts to disenroll those persons since 1996.

The political reasons for the 1934–1935 actions of the federal government and the 1937 and 1986 membership rules are distressing, to say the least. The 1934–1935 actions of the federal government including non-resident Saginaw Chippewa Indians in the election to adopt the IRA were governed by the federal government's hope for more votes favoring the IRA. The 1937 rule came from a federal bureaucrat interested in confining Indian people to reservation lands and limiting the federal government's duty of protection to a smaller number of citizens, even to the extent that it excluded nonresidents who a few years earlier were eligible to vote in tribal elections. The 1986 rule came after the tribal community seemingly internalized its exclusion of nonresident nonmembers and hoped to deny them from benefitting from distribution of the judgment funds. That tribal political choice was undermined by federal officials who wished to resolve its liability to as large a tribal class of plaintiffs as possible, ironically expanding the Tribe's membership criteria. The Tribe quickly moved to undo the inclusion of nonresident members. In this respect, the Saginaw Chippewa is a bit of a pariah in Indian country.

The story of the Grand Traverse Band is not as dramatic as the Saginaw Chippewa story but is similarly dominated by federal interference. GTB initially hoped to open its enrollment to all Michigan Ottawa Indians beyond the Grand Traverse region, but the United States forced the tribe to adopt restrictive criteria. Decades later, the Tribe's internal politics have internalized this restrictive enrollment criteria, evidenced by aggressive denials or objections of enrollment of plausible petitioners and even some disenrollment of tribal citizens.

GTB was administratively terminated in the 1870s, denying the tribe a chance to reorganize under the IRA until the Bureau of Indian

Affairs promulgated an administrative process for federal recognition in 1978.[39] GTB's federal recognition petition included a draft constitution and a roll of 297 purported tribal citizens. The draft constitution's membership criteria would have allowed the tribe to enroll any person with Michigan Ottawa ancestry. Upon federal recognition in 1980,[40] GTB and the federal government proceeded to negotiate about the Tribe's initial constitution. The federal government objected to the expansive membership criteria and instructed GTB leaders that it would block federal-tribal relations until GTB limited its membership to the 297 persons listed in the petition.[41] The Department of the Interior, without a scintilla of authority to do so, even threatened to revoke the tribe's federal acknowledgment if GTB did not relent.[42] GTB partially relented (after filing a federal lawsuit to force the government to approve a tribal constitution[43]) and agreed to a one-quarter blood quantum requirement and the exclusion of Michigan Ottawa not descended from GTB ancestors, paving the way for the approval of the tribe's constitution in 1988.[44]

The restrictive enrollment criteria demanded by the federal government has generated several hotly contested GTB tribal court cases in several areas. First, in *In re Menefee*,[45] the tribal court held that the tribal enrollment office was correct in not counting Indian blood from Canadian First Nations and was further correct in concluding that a membership petitioner's enrollment in a Canadian First Nation did count as dual enrollment. Second, in *Cholewka v. Grand Traverse Band of Ottawa and Chippewa Indians Tribal Council*,[46] the court affirmed the disenrollment of tribal members who had been enrolled without the requisite blood quantum. Finally, in *Ance-Berry v. Grand Traverse Band of Ottawa and Chippewa Indians*,[47] the Tribe's efforts to exclude an adopted child of a tribal member were rebuffed by the tribal appellate court. In each of these situations, GTB attempted to deny membership or disenrollment of Anishinaabe people who had close ties to the tribal community but who did not meet blood quantum requirements of the tribe, prevailing in all but one case.

The *Chowleka* matter is particularly exemplary. The dispute there arose from likely federal incompetence in determining the blood quantum of two sisters in 1910; one census listed them as four-quarters degree of Indian blood (DIB), but another listed them as three-quarters (DIB).[48] As a consequence of GTB's compromise with the Department of the Interior in the 1980s, nearly two thousand persons were enrolled in 1988, including the descendants of the two sisters.[49] This federal roll listed them as three-quarters DIB,[50] a roll that the GTB enrollment office relies upon to this day. Several years later, many of the sisters' descendants who were the issue of unions between tribal members and non-Indians were ineligible for enrollment because their blood quantum had dropped below one-quarter.[51] In 1996, a closed-door meeting of the GTB council led to a resolution altering the blood quantum of the descendants of one sister but not the other, allowing some descendants to become eligible for enrollment.[52] Later, the council reversed itself, concluding that the federal government's determination that the sisters possessed three-quarters DIB could not be reversed by the tribal council.[53] That reversal undermined the potential claims of the descendants of the other sister. Rather than welcoming whole families into the GTB fold, the tribe chose to reject their citizenship claims entirely.

The Saginaw Chippewa and Grand Traverse Band disputes are simply examples of the conflict that arises directly from the tribal enrollment criteria imposed by the federal government long ago over tribal objections that has since been internalized and weaponized by tribal leadership to exclude people who are Anishinaabe relatives and have substantial ties to tribal communities. This is auto-colonization.

There is another way.

Traditional Anishinaabe Inaakonigewin on Citizenship

It is my sense that the Anishinaabe Inaakonigewin (law) on belonging is analogous in a useful way (for this essay) for understanding contemporary Anishinaabe laws on citizenship or membership and enrollment. The manner in which I understand Anishinaabe Inaakonigewin in general starts with Mino-Bimaadiziwin and the Nizhwaaswi Mishomis/Nokomis Kinoomaagewinawaan. This portion of the essay attempts to extrapolate legal principles from these notions of Anishinaabe Inaakonigewin that are helpful in developing laws and practices on tribal citizenship and membership in the modern era in which tribal governance is respected but still dominated by federal superintendency.

Anishinaabe elders have described Mino-Bimaadiziwin as a kind of unwritten constitution of Anishinaabe people. In Anishinaabemowin, the phrase means something like "the act of living life the right way," but the meaning and import of the phrase is much more extensive. Kekek Stark explains that the phrase invokes "the concept of achieving harmony in life, to live in balance with all of creation. . . [,] the central goal of Anishinaabe existence[,] and . . . an embodiment of the essence of creation, flow[ing] through every aspect of Anishinaabe life."[54] Mino-Bimaadiziwin is a quest for harmony and balance in governance, personal relationships, and Anishinaabewaki. Unlike Western political thought, which dominates American law and politics and elevates humans to a place of superiority over the world and its inhabitants, Anishinaabe political thought presumes that humans are humbly a mere part of the world, not the most important part. Anishinaabe people are supposed to play roles that interact with and complement the roles that other creatures play. Central to Mino-Bimaadiziwin is accountability. The Anishinaabek understand that we owe duties to Anishinaabewaki, that to exercise dominion over the world is to harm, perhaps even destroy, the world.

The roles we play, the duties we possess, and the goals we hope to attain are embodied in our sacred teachings and stories. Anishinaabe elders have drawn numerous universal principles from the teachings, most notably the Nizhwaaswi Mishomis/Nokomis Kinoomaagewinawaan (Seven Grandfather/Grandmother Teachings): Nibwaakaawin (Wisdom), Zaagidwin (Love), Manaadjitiwaawin (Respect), Aakodewin (Bravery), Gwekowaadiziwin (Honesty), Dibaadendizowin (Humility), and Debwewin (Truth).[55] Anishinaabe people understand that each teaching helps Anishinaabe people to achieve Mino-Bimaadiziwin.

The Nizhwaaswi Kinoomaagewinawaan are akin in some respects to a bill of rights for Anishinaabe people, but much broader and more potent. **Nibwaakaawin** involves the search for knowledge.[56] Once one acknowledges and accepts the deep connection between Anishinaabewaki and the Anishinaabek, one will begin to acquire knowledge and wisdom.[57] It is the acceptance of the obligation that the Anishinaabek possess to work toward harmony and balance that opens the door to knowledge and wisdom. This knowledge is the for the "good of the people."[58] **Zaagidwin** is "mutual love," the love of all creation.[59] The love is mutual, meaning that if the Anishinaabek express love for Anishinaabewaki and all its creatures and gifts, then Anishinaabewaki will respond in kind. "To know love is to know peace."[60] Love is reciprocal. **Manaadjitiwaawin** is to internalize feelings of respect toward Anishinaabewaki and its creatures and fruits.[61] Respect grows as one's knowledge expands.[62] Respect is reciprocal. **Aakodewin** is bravery and courage, to live life with strength of heart.[63] Odemin, or heart, is a root of this word. Bravery means to do the right thing, no matter the consequences. "Bravery is to face the foe with integrity."[64] An Anishinaabe person who acts correctly, with integrity, and accepts accountability for their actions, epitomizes Aakodewin. **Gwekowaadiziwin**, or honesty, is directly related to Mino-Bimaadiziwin in that honesty is a necessary component of living life in a correct manner.[65] Honesty is closely related to Aakodewin and Dibaadendizowin.[66] **Dibaadendizowin**, or humility, is "utilized to express the understanding that an individual is a single part of creation and that they are dependent upon all of creation to survive."[67] Many Anishinaabe people understand that human beings came to Anishinaabewaki long after the rest of the creatures and other gifts of the world. Instead of assuming their arrival meant that they must be the most important creatures, the Anishinaabek understand themselves to be only modestly important.[68] A humble person is kind and generous.[69] Finally (though no more or less important than the other teachings), **Debwewin**, or truth, also derives from the root word for "heart," odemin.[70] The Anishinaabek seek truth in life, and to do so they must learn from humble and respectful listening and interacting with Anishinaabewaki. "Truth is to know all of these [teachings]."[71] Debwewin is a kind of culmination of the entirety of the Nizhwaaswi Kinoomaagewinawaan.

Anishinaabe belonging usually depended on doodem, or clan, membership and recognition.[72] There typically are seven doodemaag (clans) in Anishinaabe polities, and they also typically correspond to the Nizhwaaswi Kinoomaagewinawaan: Ajijaak (crane) is associated with Manaadjitiwaawin (respect); Maang (loon) is associated with Dibaadendizowin (humility); Waabizheshi (marten) is associated with Aakodewin (bravery); Mishiiki (snapping turtle) is associated with Nibwaakaawin (wisdom); Migizi (eagle) is associated with Debwewin (truth); Waawaashkesh (deer) is associated with Zaagidwin (love); and Mukwa (bear) is associated with Gwekowaadiziwin (honesty). Anishinaabe ogemaag (leaders) are drawn from each doodem, loosely akin to political parties, each of whom are obligated to advance arguments and positions consistent with their doodem's interests and personalities, as well as associated Kinoomaagewinawaan (teachings). Each doodem has equal power and prestige in political deliberations. Decisions are made with consensus, not majority vote. Deliberations continue until consensus is reached.

Balance. Harmony. Interconnectedness. Accountability. These are the keys to fulfilling Mino-Bimaadiziwin through the Nizhwaaswi Kinoomaagewinawaan.

It is no small step to impose the seven teachings on modern-day tribal governments. Tribal governments are not people, after all; they are legal, political, and economic entities, almost always operated from a corporate leadership structure. What we know from corporate theory is that the corporation has personhood, and it has very specific goals that its corporation and its officers are obligated to pursue. All Michigan tribes and almost all federally recognized tribes elsewhere are organized in a closely held corporate structure, with elected tribal officials serving as a board of directors with a firm grasp on the day-to-day operations of the broader government qua firm, which itself is organized in a hierarchical corporate structure beholden to the elected tribal officials. Tribal members are even akin to corporate shareholders. All of this was envisioned as the optimal tribal structure nearly a century ago by federal officials in the Department of the Interior who wished to help tribes reorganize into entities more likely to survive into the foreseeable future.[73]

For Michigan tribes (and likely most other tribes), the corporate structure comes with enormous benefits and severe consequences. Benefits include the reality that a corporate structure tends to allow for the efficient provision of tribal governmental services, tribal economic activity and regulation, and relations with the federal government. Consequences include the near eradication of traditional tribal governance. Critical to this essay's subject matter is the problem that corporations demand dividing lines between those who benefit from the corporation and those who do not. Additionally, the corporate structure requires corporate officials to determine the purpose of the corporation. For tribal governments, the purpose tends to involve providing governmental services and economic opportunities for tribal members in an environment where the tribal government usually has severely limited resources. To put it more bluntly, with tribal governments, there are those who benefit and those who do not.

Anishinaabe tribal leaders tend to act in accordance with Mino-Bimaadiziwin, providing and expanding opportunities to tribal citizens broadly to the greatest extent possible. But tribal leaders are elected in Michigan, and their electors are tribal citizens only. Nontribal citizens are intentionally excluded and occasionally demonized. Mino-Bimaadiziwin does not extend to nontribal citizens. This is exactly how the political philosophy of the United States operates.

The tragedy is that many Anishinaabe relatives are excluded. Blood quantum requirements, introduced initially by federal authorities and later adopted by tribal leadership, have divided the Anishinaabek into groups, allowing the exclusion of many from tribal governance benefits. To understand who is excluded from modern Anishinaabe tribal governance, it is useful to compare understandings of who was Anishinaabe before federal actions caused the organization of Anishinaabe polities into Indian tribal nations and now.

Consider the story of Leopold Pokagon, an ogema (leader) from a prominent Bodewadmi (or Potawatomi, one of the three Anishinaabe nations) family in what is now known as the St. Joseph River Valley in southwest Michigan and northern Indiana.[74] Pokagon is the individual for whom the Pokagon Band of Potawatomi Indians of Michigan and Indiana are named. Though his personal history is unclear, Pokagon was born in the northwest Lower Peninsula of Michigan, either to an Odawa or Ojibwe family in the Grand Traverse Band region. At some point in his early life, either in young childhood or as a young man, Pokagon moved south to Bodewadmi country and joined the family of Topinabee, who was leader of the Potawatomi at the time, eventually marrying in. Later, in the 1830s, he negotiated with the federal government during a period when the United States was obsessed with removing Indians to lands west of the Mississippi. Pokagon persuaded the government to allow his Band to remain in its homelands, where they remain to this day. In other words, the man for whom the Pokagon Potawatomi tribal nation is named likely was not Bodewadmi at all.

Now consider the people excluded from Anishinaabe tribal citizenship in the current era. GTB, for example, excludes anyone with less than one-eighth Michigan Odawa blood and anyone with less than one-quarter Indian blood.[75] In the *Menefee* case mentioned earlier, the GTB enrollment department denied enrollment of a tribal member's children for two reasons.[76] The first reason was that the children were enrolled in a Canadian Haudenosaunee First Nation, a fact that the enrollment office determined was a violation of the GTB prohibition on dual enrollment, a claim ultimately rejected by the tribal court.[77] The other reason was blood quantum: the petitioners had sufficient GTB blood (the requirement is one-eighth) but insufficient overall blood quantum (the requirement is one-quarter).[78] The petitioners wanted to count their blood quantum from their Haudenosaunee First Nation blood, but in Canada, one is either Indian or not, there is no blood quantum counting. So, the petitioners argued that their Canadian First Nations parent's blood quantum was four-quarters, which should have put them over the minimum requirement. The enrollment office claimed it could not verify Canadian Indian blood because of the lack of blood quantum data *and* that the United States opposed counting Canadian blood quantum. The tribe also claimed that if the GTB enrollment office counted Canadian blood, the Department of the Interior might choose to reconsider the tribe's federal recognition; Interior Department officials indeed had threatened to terminate the tribe (again) if the tribe did not adopt the membership criteria demanded by federal officials in the tribe's constitution. The tribal court agreed with the tribe and rejected the petitions. The Menefee family is one of the more prominent Native families in Michigan, well known at powwows all over the Great Lakes region, their children exceptionally gifted hockey players. Grand Traverse Band rejected these relatives because they did not possess sufficient blood quantum.

Consider my own family. My grandmother Laura was a descendant of both Leopold Pokagon, who was Bodewadmi, and Peter Marks, who was Odawa from the Grand Traverse region. My mother, my brother, and our children are all eligible for membership at GTB because we each have sufficient Odawa blood and overall Indian blood (counting the Potawatomi blood). We are also eligible for membership in at least two Bodewadmi nations (Pokagon and Match-E-Be-Nash-She-Wish), both of which are tribes that use lineal descendancy in their enrollment criteria. But we don't count our descendancy from Leopold Pokagon as GTB blood. Long ago, he married into the Bodewadmi community, so I guess that means he is Bodewadmi by ancestry, even though he was Odawa. A Pokagon descendant in the twenty-first century who married into the GTB community could never enroll at GTB because of the blood quantum requirement.[79] Much of this analysis is confusing and nonsensical.

GTB and the other blood quantum tribes defend their blood quantum requirements for a variety of reasons. Already discussed is the fear that the federal government will sniff out a liberalization of tribal enrollment practices and threaten to terminate the federal-tribal relationship. That being the case, when so many tribes employ lineal descendancy with no minimum blood quantum, seems unlikely. In litigation, tribes have claimed that liberalizing tribal blood quantum would bring too many people to these tribal nations seeking per capita gaming and judgment fund payments, jobs, government services, and so on, limiting the benefits available to current tribal members who meet the blood quantum minimum. Many tribal leaders and their tribal citizen constituents speak in the political language of exclusion, insisting that blood quantum is a solid proxy for excluding those who are undeserving—even our relatives, close and distant.

Mino-Bimaadiziwin and the Nizhwaaswi Kinoomaagewinawaan would seem to require more.

Moving Forward

Federal policies and tribal laws in the self-determination era are at loggerheads with Anishinaabe political philosophy. There are some relatively easy initiatives that Anishinaabe tribal nations could pursue to alleviate some of the harms associated with blood quantum, but not all of them, unfortunately. This section offers a few suggestions.

One initiative would be to reset the blood quantum of Anishinaabe tribal citizens as a matter of tribal law. It is well settled as a matter of law that tribal nations can decide their own membership criteria.[80] At least one Anishinaabe tribal nation has done exactly that (leaving one tribal citizen to walk out of the tribal meeting where the decision was finalized saying something like, "Funny, I don't feel any different"). Michigan Anishinaabe tribal nations, perhaps like numerous other tribal nations around the country, have already done exactly this—with federal participation—in the historic past. Consider the Durant Roll, the 1908/1910 federal census generated by federal officials to establish a list of eligible recipients for per capita distribution of a judgment award arising from a successful claim for treaty annuities.[81] Grand Traverse Anishinaabek listed themselves and their full-blood and half-blood relatives to receive a payment of $21.16 (the full share). The federal government's representative, Horace Durant, took the Anishinaabek at their word and recorded the census complete with blood quantum. This process was effectively a reset of Anishinaabe blood quantum. Some, but likely not all, of the full-blood Odawa signatories were actually full blood given the realities of, even by then, centuries of colonialism. As Minnesota Anishinaabe humorist Jim Northrup (and many other Native people) have pointed out, "I'm part white but I can't prove it." The Durant Roll is the base roll for the Anishinaabe tribal nations who are signatories to the 1836 Treaty of Washington, including BMIC, GTB, LRB, LTBB, and Sault Tribe. Anecdotally, I am aware of those within some of those tribal nations who wish to "audit" the Durant Roll for accuracy with an eye toward reducing the blood quantum of modern-day Anishinaabe tribal citizens. All this reconfirms that the Durant Roll may have been a blood quantum reset, at least for some people. If so, then there is precedent for Michigan Anishinaabe tribes to do so a century later. No written law prohibits it.

Consider next the decision of the Nottawaseppi Huron Band of the Potawatomi (NHBP) Supreme Court in *Wright v. Nottawaseppi Huron Band of the Potawatomi*.[82] NHBP is a lineal descendancy tribal nation in Michigan that recently amended its constitution to deny enrollment to any person born before January 1, 2019.[83] In other words, this Anishinaabe tribal nation has decided to close its enrollment to anyone except those who are very young. *Wright* involved an effort (still pending on remand at the time of this writing) by persons to enroll before the 2019 amendment passed, persons who claimed to be eligible before the amendment and who were denied an opportunity by the tribe to make their case to the enrollment office. The court reversed a trial court decision to dismiss the case on several grounds, notably sovereign immunity and laches.

The court focused its analysis on Mino-Bimaadiziwin and the Nizhwaaswi Kinoomaagewinawaan (using the Bodewadmi spellings of Mno-Bmadzewen and Noeg Kenomagewenen). Though this is not specifically a case about blood quantum, much of the analysis is transferable. For example, the court rejected the tribe's sovereign immunity defense, in part, based on the teaching of Debwewin (truth):

[T]he concept of Debwewin (truth), one of the Noeg Meshomsenanek Kenomagewenen (Seven Grandfather Teachings), strongly compels the judiciary to reach the merits. Debwewin asks us to seek the truth of the matter, which can be "detected through the beat of the heart and through the voice of the person and how the person speaks." . . . The Tribal Council's invocation of sovereign immunity is a demand to silence the Wright petitioners before they can speak on the merits of their claims. Silencing the petitioners prevents us from knowing who they are and, ultimately, prevents us from discovering the truth of this matter. While this court could not and would not override the plain language of the Constitution's authorization to sue the tribe or tribal officials, the plain language does not explicitly forbid this suit.[84]

The court agreed that the tribal constitution precluded a direct suit against the tribe;[85] the constitution allowed suits against tribal officials to enforce legal rights.[86] The tribe argued that the limited waiver of immunity for suits against tribal officials ran to the benefit of tribal citizens only. The court's holding allowed the petitioners, who were claiming to be eligible for tribal members and therefore Anishinaabe relatives, an opportunity to show their eligibility in a court proceeding.

The court additionally rejected the tribe's laches defense, relying on two of the Kinoomaagewinawaan:

In this case, the concepts of Kejitwawenindowen (respect) and Gwekwad-zewen (honesty), two of the Noeg Meshomsenanek Kenomagewenen, compels us to reject the Tribal Council's laches defense at this time. Kejitwawenindowen means "to act in a certain manner with thoughts of respect and honor upon it, to act in a certain manner with the perception of respectful thoughts upon it, and act in a certain manner with the feeling of respect in the mind." . . . Gwekwadzewen literally means "to live life in a correct manner, to live with a correct character, and to exhibit a correct nature."[87]

The petitioners attempted to file their enrollment petitions long before the 2019 amendment, but the enrollment office would not allow them to file their petition. In 2019, when the petitioners realized that the tribal citizenry would soon vote to amend the constitution, perhaps to bar persons in their situation, they brought suit against the tribe. The tribe argued that the failure of the petitioners to sue the tribe for their claims before the 2019 constitutional amendment was the fault of the petitioners, harming the tribe, which is the essence of the laches defense. The court disagreed because the petitioners showed that the tribe's enrollment office was closed to applications long before the 2019 amendment. The court also disagreed because the tribe made no factual showing of harm. The court worried that the tribe was not acting in accordance with the Kinoomaagewinawaan (teachings) of Manaadjitiwaawin (respect) and Gwekowaadiziwin (honesty). The tribal government's decision to close the enrollment office was authorized by the tribal constitution in certain circumstances,[88] but those circumstances were not addressed by the trial court. The appellate court remanded the matter.

* * *

Anishinaabe tribal nations in Michigan (and really everywhere) in their modern incarnations are relatively young, operating in a stage of experimentation and learning. These tribal nations have developed, with the assistance and occasional coercion of the federal colonizer, governmental structures and rules involving citizenship and dispute resolution. We know these structures and rules are satisfactory to the colonizer, but we also know these structures and rules are not consistent with our own culture and traditions.

For the last half century and longer, Anishinaabe tribal nations have been slow to draw from and incorporate Mino-Bimaadiziwin into our laws and justice systems. The negative consequences from copying the colonizer can be both obvious and insidious. But in recent years, tribal leaders and judges have more earnestly drawn from our culture in discrete areas and matters such as juvenile justice and environmental protection. Reconsideration of blood quantum rules and other restrictions on tribal membership is a necessary next step.

What if each citizen were valued
as someone who could and would make contributions
rather than someone who will drain resources?

Path Forward:
Indigenous Place In-Community

LOIS STEVENS

*"It is Place that holds our memories and the bones of our people . . .
this is the place that made us."*
—Gregory Cajete

Introduction

*I still remember the day I signed up for World Geography at Haskell Indian Nations
University. My parents taught me how to read a map at a young age. Growing up,
I would sometimes get to sit in the front seat of our family car during road trips, if
I could help my dad navigate the map while my mom and siblings slept in the back.
We were always going somewhere, at least that is how it felt. So, through my dad,
I learned to read a map efficiently; I learned the names of the towns, roads, and
landscapes, and the distances between it all. Memorizing places on a map was easy
to me, so I was confident that World Geography, even at the college level, would be
a breeze. Dr. Dan Wildcat changed that on the very first day when he talked about
the connection between people and the vast places on Mother Earth. I was in over
my head but completely fascinated. It opened my mind to what geography truly
represented. On those road trips, I wasn't just memorizing turns and distances; I
was developing connections with each place we passed. I was becoming a part of that
land's memory. How do I want the land to remember me?*

Indigenous Place brings an important perspective to the discipline
of Geography, helping academia understand the important link between
Indigenous Peoples and the land. The term "Geography" comes from an
ancient Greek word that sought to narrate the world; the translation
means "to write (graphein) a description of the earth (ge)."[1] It has been
acknowledged, however, that the act of making connections between

175

people and the world has long been practiced by communities around the world, long before the term was coined in Greece.[2] Indigenous Place brings with it ancestral knowledge of understanding our role as stewards within Mother Earth, bringing us into relationship within our communities and all that is human and nonhuman.[3] This connection continues to be vital to Indigenous movements across the country, as Indigenous communities fight for sovereign rights to protect the land, the resources, and the people for the next seven generations to come.

Geography has played a devastating role in the history of Indigenous Peoples because the science was not merely to explore the unknown—colonial society used geographic exploration as a method of expansion and control over Indigenous land.[4] By stripping Indigenous Peoples from their lands and their undeniable cultural identities tied to those places, colonization ushered Indigenous Peoples through generations of place-based traumas with resounding impacts on community and identity.

The constantly evolving impacts of colonization have limited our way of thinking and influenced how we apply cultural beliefs to modern aspects of decision-making within our communities. Indigenous communities are facing the realities of these impacts on multiple levels. At the forefront is our sovereign right to identify with our own people. The oppressive practice of blood quantum threatens the future of our tribal communities and the preservation of the lands we steward. Measuring tribal enrollment by blood quantum is not only a losing battle but also one that has created a hierarchy among tribal members, which mirrors that of our colonial oppressors. As we look to the possibilities beyond blood quantum, we have a chance to create an enrollment process that honors our ancestral lineage and our connection to Indigenous Place.

Geography and Indigeneity

While Indigenous Peoples lived in relationship with the land and understood that reciprocity benefited all, geography was used to separate the people from the land. Notable cultural geographer Bernard O. Nietschmann famously claimed, "More indigenous territory has been claimed by maps than by guns."[5] That is, while geographical exploration was not the cause of Indigenous deterritorialization, it was the most effective tool in removing Indigenous people from the places where our stories connect us to the land. Indigenous Peoples were pushed into villages and eventually onto reservations, destroying the ties to the relationships with land and place. These cultural ties were developed and nurtured by our ancestors, as they were passed down to each generation through story, song, artistry, agriculture, and ceremony. The relationships were severed, in some cases instantaneously, through genocidal tactics. Economic and political support drove the colonial agenda to bring order to what they perceived as chaotic or "savage" land management by Indigenous Peoples.

This act of bringing order to something that was deemed chaotic came yet again when the federal government sought to create order among unsettled peoples. The Dawes Act of 1887, or the General Allotment Act, forced a drastic geographic shift for Indigenous Peoples and introduced the idea of clean blood that has been a prominent act of racial hierarchy since the birth of limpieza de sangre (cleanliness of blood) in fifteenth-century Spain.[6] The attempt to control in the name of Geography was successful, as Indigenous Peoples across the United States experienced a roughly 65 percent land loss due to allotment and accompanying acts during that time period.[7] While blood quantum was not stated outright in the Dawes Act, blood played a much broader role in the attempted elimination of Indigenous Peoples by attacking their "history, identity, and geography."[8] It is by genocidal design that many tribes in the United States are still locked into blood quantum without a clear path out.

Today, most Indigenous land ownership has involved land purchased on the open market.[9] However, at some point, it will not matter how much land we buy back if we do not have a generation to pass it along to. So then, while Nietschmann states that more Indigenous territory has been claimed by maps than by guns, we now have a chance to rethink our understanding of those maps and revitalize our connection to Place.[10] We can strengthen our sovereignty and reclaim our territory. It is time to draw our own maps. We do this by reconfiguring our tribal enrollment processes so that greater importance is given to the quality of our commitment to Place and less on the quantity of blood in our veins.

Being of a Place

Geography has a long tradition of attempting to understand Place through complex relationships among processes and phenomena.[11] Understanding

Indigenous Geography, as a discipline, brings us deeper and closer to our identities because it tells us that "place is a way of knowing, experiencing, and relating with the world."[12] Indigenous Place is how we enact our relationship with geography. Indigenous authors and advocates for Indigenous knowledge in education Vine Deloria Jr. and Daniel Wildcat tell us that being Indigenous means "to be of a place."[13] They continue by saying Indigenous people "actively draw on the power of that place physically and spiritually."[14] It is something we are experiencing every day, but more than that, it is the experiences of our ancestors before us. We carry their stories and with them we carry a responsibility to continue telling those stories and passing them down to the next generation.

Because of the complexity of the traumatic events that brought most of us to our current geographic locations, each Indigenous community has a unique story to tell. With many communities displaced from their homelands, it is important to understand the stories of struggle that helped shape their current place in the world. Indigenous geographer Jay T. Johnson calls "being-in-place" a constant act of engaged learning.[15] Johnson and cultural geographer Soren Larsen add that when we are truly engaged with Place, we are retelling the stories that were written there, as an "act of remembrance."[16] However, Indigenous Place is not merely an act of remembrance or enthusiastic storytelling; it is constantly evolving because we are not only retelling our stories, but each one of us is also actively writing new stories in our communities every day, whether we realize it or not. Our stories are a heavy responsibility, not something that should be taken lightly. How do we fulfill our responsibility of carrying these stories forward, if the very identities of our next generations are in question due to an act of continued oppression?

Place as Community

When you are raised in-community,[17] you develop memories and connections with the community. Larsen and Johnson say that place challenges us to live together with human and nonhuman communities in our "shared predicaments of life, livelihood, and land."[18] Another prominent advocate for Indigenous knowledge in education, Gregory Cajete, adds to this by saying, "It is place that holds our memories and the bones of our people . . . this is the place that made us."[19] Whether a tribe resides on their ancestral lands or on lands forced upon them during multiple stages of removal, the stories of the people and the land are now woven together forever. Our very identities are tied to evolving landscapes, the human and nonhuman interactions that have taken place during and before our time here on earth. Every aspect of Indigenous Place becomes a part of our individual and communal story.

So what does this mean for how we identify? When you are raised *in-community*, all the shared predicaments and livelihoods interact to create who you are as a person, how you carry yourself in the world, and what values you model. These shared experiences connect you to that place until the end of time. When raised *in-community*, you will have the same memories of the quarry down the road. The same memories of the uncle who walks everywhere on the reservation or the auntie who makes the best corn soup. The same memories of your songs echoing through the hallways or blaring through the school bus speakers. The same memories of running around the powwow grounds, covered in dirt and sweat. The same memories of falling in the creek and being afraid of telling your mom because you weren't supposed to be down there in the first place. The same memories of running through corn fields, playing tag, and leaving the field with tiny scratches all over your legs and arms. The same muscle memory that gets your body moving when you step into the longhouse. We carry these memories of communal Place within ourselves, as part of our identity. And these memories cannot be defined by any percentage of blood.

Cajete tells us that these kinds of memories truly "make us" who we are, and that goes beyond blood quantum, goes beyond the Dawes Act, goes beyond the colonial idea of privilege.[20] When you are raised *in-community*, you share the responsibility of caring for the people, the land, and the future. This responsibility is born out of our spirit, that unseen power that connects us to each other and the earth. A friend once said that being Native, at its core, "is how you treat people and more importantly how you treat your community."[21] We were all born with gifts from the Creator, and it is our responsibility to use those gifts to give back to our communities. If we carry those gifts and choose not to share them, choose not to return to the land, choose not to care for the land, choose not to visit our relatives to show appreciation and compassion, we forfeit our ability to call ourselves members of that community.

Commitment to Community

By implementing blood quantum as a means to determine citizenship, we have put the future of our ancestral stories in the hands of many who are not fully equipped to care for them. This practice has narrowed our understanding of what it means to be a member of a tribal nation, so we have not required our tribal leadership to think about their responsibility to the community outside of that narrow mindset. Our current system has encouraged our leadership to think of tribal preservation in terms of colonial ideals of power, property, quantity, and commodity. Under the current model, our membership believes that simply being born with an ancestral lineage from a tribal nation gives them access to resources and automatically entitles them to an Indigenous voice. Traditionally, you earned those honors. This learned privilege is dangerous, as we rely on our enrolled citizens, regardless of their commitment to the community, to make compassionate decisions through a colonial government system.[22]

Additionally, in the age of social media, we witness a rise in individuals seeking to gain relevance through Indigenous identification. The term used is "influencer," and many abuse their blood quantum or physical appearance to cash in through social media platforms, providing content on Indigenous knowledge, practices, languages, artistry, and even ceremony. While claiming to be from a tribal nation or even enrolled in that nation, some of these individuals do not have any relationship with that tribal community; they do not give back to that community or contribute to the future of that community in any direct way, yet they accept money in the name of that tribe. This is a dangerous practice because these "influencers" are not always ill-intended individuals seeking followers and/or compensation; sometimes they are seeking the community their ancestral genes are craving. But with the rise of "pretendians," their cultural integrity may come into question, making it even harder for them to return.[23]

Protecting our community from those who seek to extract information without intentional contribution becomes a strong issue when our purpose on this earth is to continue our stories. How do we create an enrollment process that will safeguard the generations to come *and* protect our stories from those who may abuse the system to gain resources or relevance? Honoring Indigenous Place is a potential path toward intentional enrollment for sovereign tribal nations because it would allow people to celebrate their gifts by honoring how they contribute to the community. It would also call in[24] those who carry the stories in their blood but not yet in their spirits. Individuals may not have the memories of being raised in community, but that does not mean they cannot contribute. It doesn't mean they cannot come back. They still carry the stories of our ancestors; they should be allowed the space to continue their story by connecting themselves to their ancestral place and finding what they have to offer the community.

Conclusion

Most tribes are still operating under a colonial model of enrollment that was forced upon us. With continued use of the blood quantum construct as a measure of identity, we have perpetuated the idea that blood is enough. Not only is the notion of blood quantum proven false in its efficacy to measure identity, but it also quantifies Indigeneity in a way our ancestors would not understand. Haudenosaunee knowledge holder Bob Antone says that we need to unlearn "how we think, feel, and act in an oppressive environment to ensure that our oppression is not guiding our thinking."[25] In taking this journey away from the oppressed mind, we have to remember our purpose on Mother Earth. Indigenous architect Johnpaul Jones says, "The spirit of place is embedded deeply within us; we are connected to something larger than ourselves."[26] Indigenous Place reminds us to care for the land and its people. Carry on their stories. We cannot do that if we remain constricted to colonial ideals of hierarchy by blood.

Removing blood quantum is not the hard part; the question of "what next" is the hard part. While there is no single answer that will fulfill the needs of every tribe, each has the power to exercise sovereignty and draw their own community maps.[27] This call is for an intentional act to develop a multifaceted enrollment process that values connection to Place and commitment to the future of the community. Recognizing Indigenous Place as a potential path toward meaningful enrollment for sovereign tribal nations honors the stories of our ancestors, our relationships to all beings, and our responsibility to community.

Long after you are gone, this land will hold memories of you, and your community will carry the stories. How do you want them to remember you?

Two Truths

JOHN DANFORTH

In 2018 the Oneida Nation Trust Enrollment Department posted a job opening for a Project Specialist position. My immediate question to the hiring committee was "What projects will this position be working on?" It was explained to me that this position was intended to spend roughly 80 percent of their time working with the Sustain Oneida project.

Now, I had a vague idea of what Sustain Oneida was about. I knew it was targeted at discussing the effects of blood quantum on the Oneida Nation, and that's really about all the further I had invested time and energy into that problem. As I read over the explanation of the job description, I started to see the impact of the position and knew it was an opportunity I needed to pursue. Once hired, I became fully immersed in the bureaucracy of tribal governments and fully immersed in the depth of the blood quantum paradox.

I began running community meetings and presenting past, present, and future enrollment data projections to help paint a picture of the long-term outlook of continuing to use blood quantum. In these discussions I set out to simply let members of the Oneida Nation know that a blood quantum problem exists. I wasn't looking for answers on what to do next; I only aimed for participants to agree that blood quantum doesn't work. Naturally, the data speaks for itself. Oneidas have children with non-enrolled partners at a rate of 90 percent. If I lined up the most recent one hundred Oneida people who had a child, ninety of them will have had that child with a partner who isn't Oneida. If that lone Oneida parent isn't equal to or more than one-half Oneida, their child cannot enroll, and they have effectively reached the end of eligible lineage to become a member of the Nation.

People across developed countries, in general, are having fewer children than previous generations. For Oneida, couples are no longer having five to eleven kids like their grandparents' generation. They also aren't marrying the girl next door. We are having fewer children, but notably, we are having fewer eligible children. The Baby Boomer generation makes up about 26 percent of the enrolled population for the Oneida Nation today, and that generation birthed an echo boom of kids called Millennials. In the early 1990s, Oneida had more than five thousand members enrolled under the age of eighteen. Today the under-eighteen population is less than twenty-seven hundred kids, and 80 percent of this group is less than one-half Oneida. I could keep going on and on with statistics until I'm blue in the face, but we get it; blood quantum is not working to ensure the survival of the Oneida Nation.

I like the idea that two truths, sometimes completely opposite but covering the same topic, can exist at the same time. When it comes to blood quantum, the example of the Oneida Nation's long-term problem is parallel to many tribes across the United States. We have the same boilerplate constitution from the 1930s, and we found Class III gaming success in the 1990s. Today, we pay our people a nominal annual per capita payment if they have the minimum one-quarter Oneida Nation blood quantum required to enroll.

One time, my supervisor and I set out to talk to some tribal members at a local lunch event. I did my usual presentation on statistics to illustrate the problem, and then we mingled among the crowd to have those round-table discussions where community members express how they really feel. Unfiltered, one tribal member responded to our question of "What does it mean to be Oneida?" with, "It means we get money; that's what it means to be Oneida." I think a lot of enrolled members would scoff at that idea. My initial reaction was the same until I really sat back and thought about it.

A lot of new people showed up to enroll in the tribe after Class III gaming. When job opportunities became available as a result of the Oneida Casino expansion in 1993 and per capita payments began to be disbursed, new enrollments jumped almost 300 percent in the two years following. The tribe had a onetime per capita payment of $1,500 in 1999, and new enrollments for that year spiked again by nearly 300 percent. So, yeah, being Oneida means we get paid money. Without money or benefits, many eligible members may have continued to forgo enrolling. Herein lies our first truth: Being Oneida means you get money.

When you condition people to expect unearned funds on an annual basis, you can bet they're going to put up a fight to keep that benefit intact. That's the entire issue. Without money, changing enrollment criteria wouldn't be a conflict at all. So how far down the rabbit hole can blood quantum take a tribe? In my little bit of research, it can take a tribe very close to the point of no return. In 2014 the Secretary of the Interior was no longer needed to approve any amendments to the Oneida tribe's constitution. In short, each tribe can self-determine their own membership criteria without needing approval from Uncle Sam. Some tribes (without naming names) took that chance to immediately turn off their enrollments. What exactly does that mean? It means no new members, at all. None. Zero. These tribes become smaller and smaller, and the benefit-per-member ratio gets higher and higher. If a tribe goes from one thousand to eight hundred, that's two hundred fewer mouths to feed. That's two hundred fewer ways that they split the pot of gold from their casino. Wouldn't that tribe become extinct? If nothing else changes, yes, but their members would have passed away stinking rich. Herein lies the second truth: Most reasonable people don't want to see their tribe go extinct.

Now we find ourselves in the revolving door of the blood quantum paradox. Members don't want to give up their current benefits, and they also don't want the tribe to vanish. Grandparents want their grandchildren to be enrolled, but they also want to see them get support to go to college. Elders who rely on the annual distribution don't want to see those funds go away, because they need heat and food to get them through the winter. The list goes on and on.

What do we do next? Where do we go from here? Fortunately, the current enrolled membership of the Oneida Nation has taken measures, through our governing process, to promote and elevate the discussion of enrollment criteria. General Tribal Council, when in session, is the supreme governing body of the Oneida Nation. In short, a duly called meeting takes place when more than seventy-five enrolled members, over the age of eighteen, make quorum and accept a meeting agenda. During a recent General Tribal Council meeting, action was taken to create the On^yoteaka?ni?i Project Plan, which is intended to succeed the Sustain

Oneida Project and continue prioritizing community discussion. A decision as big as amending enrollment criteria is a constitutional amendment process that will take years for the current membership to deliberate and implement. Finding common ground among one another means being informed as much as possible on the issue.

While the discussion rages on, every year the Oneida Nation is declining in population. Since 2019, more tribal members have passed away than new members have been enrolled. This year is shaping up to be no different. Our population projections, courtesy of the Taylor Policy Group, predict that the rate of deaths per year will increase until 2050, simply because a large portion of the population is reaching the late stages of life. As part of their projections, the Taylor Policy Group also predicts that by the year 2070, if nothing changes for the Oneida Nation's enrollment criteria, the overall enrolled population will be approximately ten thousand, falling from its current seventeen thousand members. The enrolled minors will make up three hundred of that ten thousand. In the 1990s the Oneida Nation felt invincible. Gaming was a hit. There were thousands of enrolled kids. We couldn't get workers in the door fast enough to fuel the growth, and the future looked bright—until one day it didn't. If nothing changes, there will be fewer mouths to feed. Housing will no longer have a shortage but a surplus. The tribal school system will not have any students. Indian Preference will be used less to fill the organizational work needs. Those who remain will hold all the voting power and all the resources. Soon thereafter, met with empty seats, no applause or falling roses, the Oneida Nation's last member will take one last bow and let the curtain fall as they complete the Great Vanishing Act.

What will be our challenge in the future?

Osage Spring

JIM GRAY

After one hundred years of removal from our homelands in Missouri, Arkansas, and parts of two other states, the Osage Nation sold their lands in Kansas and purchased a reservation in Indian Territory in 1872.

In the summer of 1906, the US Congress passed and President Roosevelt signed into law the Osage Allotment Act. This law set in motion the introduction of Oklahoma as the forty-sixth state in the Union (1907), secured the Osage Nation subsurface as a Mineral Estate, and allotted all surface lands to the 2,229 members of the tribe. It also closed the membership rolls so each Osage man, woman, and child who received an allotment also received something akin to a corporate share in the development from mining, primarily oil and gas. Closing the rolls protected the value of each share in the Mineral Estate. This share was known as an Osage Headright.

Prior to the 1906 Osage Allotment Act, the Osage governed themselves under a constitutional form of government. Taking elements of their past clan and hereditary chief system of government that evolved over centuries and modernizing it to meet the current times, the 1881 Constitution established the Osage Nation in a governing document that set in motion their cultural, spiritual, and legal rebirth in these new lands. They also adopted the In-lon-ska ceremonial dances from their neighbors the Ponca and Kaw Tribes. After the Dawes Act was passed in the late 1880s, many tribes in Indian Territory accepted allotment, but the Osage Nation refused because they held their lands in fee title.

In 1901, the US Secretary of the Interior abolished the 1881 Osage Constitution, and it was not until the passage of the 1906 Osage Allotment Act that the Osage had a government. Section 9 of the Allotment Act designed the government of the Osage Nation. It created a tribal council consisting of a Chief, Assistant Chief, and eight members who were to be elected by only Osage men who were Headright owners. This new government had no power to make laws but rather was limited to simply passing resolutions. Their primary role was to approve allotments for the original allotees and approve leases for the oil companies. Resolutions passed by the Tribal Council carried no legal weight unless approved by the Bureau of Indian Affairs.

This unique land, the mineral estate structure, and the discovery of one of the largest oil fields in North America created a condition of an enormous amount of money concentrated in a small number of people. This brought some of the high profile and dark elements in society into the Osage Nation. By the early 1920s, Pawhuska, the capital of the Osage Nation, became a boomtown for the oil barons of the day (Phillips, Conoco, Sinclair, and others), who all made their fortunes drilling Osage oil. In 1923 alone, the Osage Nation was paid over $400 million in royalties adjusted for inflation.

Shocked by the amount of money the Osages were collecting, the federal government declared every Osage who was half-blood or more to be automatically declared "incompetent," and a local judge appointed white guardians over the financial affairs of individual Osages. Everything from clothing, cars, and funerals to materials for their homestead would often be ten times the cost that anyone else would pay. Being overcharged for every cost-of-living expense eventually put many Osages in debt to local merchants, which meant their allotment lands were ripe for the taking to clear the debt.

By then, Osages with Headrights started dying mysteriously (poison whisky, suicides, car wrecks, falling down a flight of steps), then, not so mysteriously because they were being murdered. At the time in the early 1920s, the killings caused the Osage Nation to offer a $20,000 reward to anyone who could bring these killers to justice. Since local law enforcement was simply ill equipped, lacked jurisdiction, or was, in some minds, complicit with their indifference to the deaths of Indians, little was done.

One of the FBI's first high-profile cases was the Osage murders. In time, they were able to charge and convict the mastermind of a series of killings centered around one Osage family. One of those victims included my great-grandfather, Henry Roan.

Some of this history is captured in David Grann's book *Killers of the Flower Moon* (2017), which was later made into a motion picture by Apple Films, directed by Martin Scorsese. The $200 million budget for this film makes this project the most expensive movie with a Native American theme ever made. The story centers on the series of killings investigated by the FBI and demonstrates how white men found ways to inherit a family's share of the Osage Mineral Estate by marrying into the family, then systematically killing off every member of the family till all their collective Osage Headrights would be inherited by the non-Osage spouse.

It is easy to see why federal policies such as assimilation, boarding schools, allotment, and the breakup of tribal governments left many tribes without the means to protect their members from exploitation. After the conviction of the killers depicted in the movie, the murders continued, as did the impacts of the loss of Osage lands and Headrights. Today, one-fourth of the original 2,229 Headrights belong to non-Osages, and the vast 1.4 million acres (about the area of Delaware) of surface land has been reduced to a small fraction of land that the Osage purchased in 1872.

In the years that followed the killings, things got quiet for the Osage Nation. The oil boom died down, and the big oil companies left and were replaced by medium-size companies who still paid a respectable sum of money to drill, but more changes were coming. Social movements were also in motion within the Nation. In the late 1940s, Osage women (who were Headright owners) were finally given the right to vote. A community group known as the Osage Nation Organization pushed for changes in voting rules from each Osage Headright owner to only vote the value of the fractionated share in tribal elections (for example, one-fourth of a Headright equaled one-fourth of a vote in tribal elections). This group advocated for a more democratic Osage government as well.

But not all change came from within the Osage Nation. In the 1950s, the US Congress introduced a bill to terminate tribes of their Trust status. The Nation was on the termination list because of their perceived economic success. It was believed the Osage did not need the protection of the United States any longer, even though Osages were still having white guardians appointed. This threat to the Trust Relationship between the United States and the Osage Nation caused the Osage Tribal Council to lobby Congress to take them off the bill by agreeing to pay for the continued presence of the Bureau of Indian Affairs (BIA) from their royalties collected from oil and gas leases.

In the 1970s, there was a growing concern about the legitimacy of the Osage Tribal Council to govern the entire population of Osages, even while there was a growing interest among Osages regardless of their Headright status to preserve their language and cultural affairs. By the 1980s, the Fletcher case was filed in federal court. The named plaintiff was William Fletcher, a full-blood Osage Headright owner. The suit was brought on behalf of other Headright owners and claimed among other things that the 1906 Osage Allotment Act violated the constitutional rights of Osages without a Headright by imposing on them a Tribal Council they could not vote for. By the 1980s, the demographics of the Nation had changed so much that half of all Osages had no right to vote in their own tribal elections.

In the 1990s, the Federal Court of the Northern District of Oklahoma ruled in favor of the plaintiffs and ordered the BIA to oversee a new government for the Osage and created a commission made up of the plaintiffs, members of the Osage Tribal Council, and representatives of the BIA. After conducting public meetings with Osages, the BIA wrote a constitution that was approved in 1994, expanding the Nation's rolls to include all Osages of lineal descent to be eligible for enrollment and voting rights in a new national council, with a president and vice president, while preserving the old Tribal Council now known as the Osage Minerals Council—which was only elected by Osage Headright owners to approve oil leases. On appeal, the Osage Tribal Council never waived their right to be sued, and the suit was overturned by the Tenth Circuit Court of Appeals. This decision resulted in restoring the Osage Tribal Council back to its original role and abolished the Osage National Council government.

By 2002, Osages without a political voice in their government vastly outnumbered Osages with Headrights, and even those with Osage Headrights felt it was time for a change. That year, the Osage Headrights owners voted the biggest wipeout in Osage election history since the 1906 Osage Allotment Act was passed, when nine out of ten elected incumbents were ousted by a wave of reform-minded candidates bent on restoring those elements of democracy that were taken away by the Tenth Circuit decision. In 2002, the leadership of the Osage Nation petitioned Congress to reaffirm the sovereign rights of the Osage people to (a) decide on who is an Osage, (b) determine what kind of government the Osage will have, and (c) ensure those Osages who receive an interest in the Osage Mineral Estate will not be impacted by this law. In December 2004 President Bush signed H.R. 2912 into Public Law 108-431.

In the two years that followed, another Osage Government Reform Commission was appointed by the Osage Tribal Council to go back to all the Osage people and seek input on what kind of government they wanted. This process yielded a three-branch government consisting of Executive, Legislative, and Judicial Branches, with the Osage Minerals Council existing as an independent agency within the Constitution.

While the idea of blood quantum as a criterion for membership came up in the public outreach by the Government Reform Commission, the Osages had more than one hundred years of coexistence with mixed-blood members under the Osage Headright system. They opted for lineal descendancy from the roll created by the 1906 Osage Allotment Act as a criterion for citizenship. Other mandates include the protection of the Osage culture and language as well as protection of our traditional districts and villages. On March 11, 2006, the Osage people voted for this Constitution with a two-thirds majority, and it was signed into law on May 5, 2006. March 11 is now a tribal holiday with events and activities celebrating Osage Sovereignty.

In the nineteen years since the establishment of a constitutional form of government for all the Osage people, the Osage Nation opened seven casinos and invested millions annually into tribal programs that help all Osages in health care, higher education scholarships, buying land back on our reservation, restoring bison herds, agricultural programs, cultural and language preservation, a free and independent press, and the beginnings of a K–12 immersion school—plus many more programs too numerous to include here.

The Constitution of the Osage Nation is recognized as a successor to the abolished constitution created in 1881. The recognition of every Osage expression of the inherent sovereignty of our past is present in our government today—best expressed by our preamble:

We the Wah-Zha-Zhe, known as the Osage People, having formed as Clans in the far distant past, have been a People and as People have walked this earth and enjoyed the blessings of Wah-kon-tah for more centuries than we truly know.

Having resolved to live in harmony, we now come together so that we may once unite as a Nation and as a People, calling upon the fundamental values that we hold sacred: Justice, Fairness, Compassion, Respect for and Protection of Child, Elder, All Fellow Beings, and Self.

Paying homage to generations of Osage leaders of the past and present, we give thanks for their wisdom and courage. Acknowledging our ancient tribal order as the foundation of our present government, first reformed in the 1881 Constitution of the Osage Nation, we continue our legacy by again reorganizing our government.

Aanikoobijigan: Intergenerational Connections as the Foundation of Contemporary Citizenship Requirements

JILL DOERFLER

One of the vital powers all nations have, including American Indian nations, is the regulation of citizenship. Citizenship is a much-debated topic in many countries with some currently questioning blood quantum citizenship requirements in the wake of political challenges. Who belongs? Who should have political recognition? The ongoing legacies of colonization make these questions especially difficult for American Indian nations. Yet American Indian nations are also evaluating their citizenship requirements, in some cases, as a part of overall constitutional reform and nation-building efforts. It's a significant challenge to envision what the best citizenship requirements are. There isn't a universal answer. There isn't a perfect answer. Yes, this is an opportunity for each nation to examine its history, teachings, and values and then leverage that knowledge to create the best possible future.

In the previous volume, *The Great Vanishing Act: Blood Quantum and the Future of Native Nations*, I wrote "'Making Ourselves Whole with Words': A Short History of White Earth Anishinaabeg Tribal Citizenship Criteria," which examined why the Minnesota Chippewa Tribe implemented a one-quarter Minnesota Chippewa Tribe[1] blood quantum requirement for enrollment/tribal citizenship in 1961, and the 2007–2015 effort for constitutional reform at White Earth. Elsewhere I've written in detail about both the history of blood quantum and how story, particularly the recreation story, connects to citizenship.[2] I was honored to be invited to write for the second volume in this series and excited that the focus is on what a future without blood quantum might look like.

In this piece, I explore how Anishinaabe/Ojibwe/Chippewa teachings and values might shape contemporary citizenship requirements, particularly within the Minnesota Chippewa Tribe as well as beyond. There have always been many independent Ojibwe political entities. Ojibwe scholar Anton Treuer notes that "the Ojibwe never functioned as one nation politically, economically, or even militarily but rather as a group of autonomous villages with many language and culture commonalities."[3] Ojibwe scholar Brenda Child notes that today, "the Ojibwe view their political organizations as small nations."[4] Some Anishinaabe/Ojibwe political entities in the United States and Canada have already moved beyond blood quantum, but a significant number have not.[5] I hope that all political bodies, Anishinaabe and otherwise, connect a cultural resurgence with enrollment/citizenship requirements. As we think about how to create enrollment/citizenship requirements that reflect and enact our teachings and values, I come back to family. Family has always been of central importance for Ojibwe people. Nishinaabe scholar Leanne Simpson has asserted, "The family is the microcosm of the nation."[6] In addition, a number of other scholars have long asserted that until the twentieth century, Native nations were groups of related/interrelated individuals. Drawing upon the critical work of Vine Deloria Jr., Lumbee scholar David E. Wilkins has argued, "tribal nations were and should become again sacred bodies of related kinfolk. This is the essence of what it means to be a tribal citizen within a First Nation."[7] When thinking about relationships in an Anishinaabe context, aanikoobijigan comes to mind. Aanikoobijigan means both "great-grandparent" and "great-grandchild." I'll discuss next how the continuous intergenerational connection of aanikoobijigan might serve as a foundation for citizenship.

Additionally, while extended family, clan, and community networks have always been key to the survival of Anishinaabe people, the individual independence required has often been overlooked. Another way of thinking about this is personal autonomy as personal sovereignty. Self-reliance and independence are classic hallmarks of Anishinaabe life. As renowned Anishinaabe scholar Basil Johnston explained:

> Yet despite the traditional communal spirit and mode of life, the
> Anishinaubae people championed and upheld the importance of

individuality and personal independence on the promise that the more self-reliant and free the individual, the stronger and better the well-being of the community. Both the individual and the community were best served by nurturing men and women who were resourceful, independent masters of their own time, space, and spirit, the equals of all other men and women in the community.[8]

When an individual is fully supported and empowered, they are better able to make valuable contributions to the family/clan, community, and nation. Reciprocity is another key Anishinaabe cultural practice that is perhaps best able to be carried out by individuals that are independent. Even though each person is dependent on the group, each person also makes contributions to the group.

Aanikoobijigan

I was born in 1979, the last of Generation X, and like most people in my generation, I did not grow up speaking the Ojibwe language at home, but I learned a few words here and there. I went to K–12 at Mahnomen Public School on the White Earth Reservation, and we had a few units that taught us Ojibwe words for common animals and colors. We learned that White Earth was Gaa-waabaabiganikaag and referenced the unique white clay in the area. As a graduate student I had the opportunity to take two full years of the language at the University of Minnesota, where I was privileged to learn from Pebaamibines (Dennis Jones) and James Vukelich Kaagegaabaw.[9] Of course, I am still learning. It's been exciting to see the results of half a century of Ojibwe language revitalization and proliferation of new technologies supporting this work.[10] We find deep and nuanced meanings embedded in language, which we can use to guide decision-making and the creation of law and policy in our nations today. This led me to ask: How might aanikoobijigan be useful in thinking about citizenship requirements for Ojibwe nations?

Aanikoobijigan is defined in the *Ojibwe People's Dictionary* as:

1. an ancestor
2. a great-grandparent
3. a great-grandchild[11]

The *Ojibwe People's Dictionary* notes that the stem of aanikoobijigan is aanikaw-, which is "the act of binding or joining things together."[12] A few examples of related words that use the same stem include:

- aanikoobidoon: "string it together, extend it by tying"[13]
- aanikoogwaadan: "sew another piece onto it (to make it bigger)[14]
- aanikoosidoon: "lay it joining something else"[15]

As I understand it, aanikoobijigan is fundamentally about intergenerational connections. A key element is that intergenerational connection is circular rather than linear. I've heard people talk about aanikoobijigan as a chain or set of links in a necklace. As I think about it more, and consider the root word, another way to think about it is what is commonly known as the daisy chain beading pattern—circles and circles of connections strung together in a beautiful web. For me, it also brings to mind the diverse and intricate beadwork patterns created with various stitching techniques on gashkibidaagans or bandolier bags.[16] Flowers, berries, branches, and leaves were created through thousands of beads and stitches. Each bead is distinct and beautiful on its own, yet when strung together they make an image that would be impossible without the collective. I see a balance of individual autonomy and collective, which are joined together.

Great-grandparents and great-grandchildren are inextricably linked even though we don't always get to have a personal relationship in this world. Two of my great-grandfathers lived to be over one hundred years old. By the time I was a child, their spouses, my great-grandmothers, had traveled on, and my great-grandfathers each lived in one-bedroom apartments in the Valley View Commons in Mahnomen. My memories of visiting them there are faint, but I know that Mother would take me to visit regularly. As they aged, they needed more care, and they moved across the street into the nursing home. I remember visiting them both there more clearly. They always asked questions about school and about our relatives who lived further away and couldn't visit regularly. My German American great-grandfather fought in WWI and then lost everything during the Great Depression. He moved to the western border of the White Earth Reservation, where he started over. He was able to get land and start a farm. The memories of war haunted him during his final years. My Ojibwe great-grandfather was sent to the Indian Industrial School in

Genoa, Nebraska,[17] when he was about three, after his mother died from childbirth complications. We don't know much about his time there. He returned to White Earth but never became the farmer that the US government wanted. He did have a love for horses and was known as a "snappy" dresser. He needed a degree of freedom and autonomy that I understand completely but that kept him at somewhat of a distance from his family. Yet we are forever linked. We are all linked to many relatives, some of which we had the honor of knowing and some of which we did not.

As I think about these intergenerational connections and about contemporary citizenship requirements, I go back to our teachings and time-honored traditions. I also see a connection between aanikoobijigan and the teachings about seven generations. This concept is often taught as looking seven generations into the future. A different way that I have been taught to think about seven generations is that we are always the fourth generation, and we should look back three generations as well as ahead three generations when making decisions. We should think: *What would be good for my ancestors?* AND *What would be good for my descendants?* This teaching has always resonated with me much more than the linear version. When we add aanikoobijigan, it evokes the intergenerational connections and the ways in which each of us is tied to the past, present, and future.

Blood quantum is not mentioned in any of these concepts and teachings, nor any others as far as I am aware. Furthermore, Ojibwe scholar Scott Lyons has argued, "There is nothing in the Ojibwe language that evokes biological notions like blood quantum or other essentialist traffickers of identity."[18] I don't think I am composed of one-half of the blood of each of my parents or one-fourth the blood of each of my grandparents or one-eighth of the blood of each of my great-grandparents. Our connection is not so easily quantifiable. In truth, it is not something that even I fully understand. Instead, blood quantum has served a tool of colonization, and as explained by sociologist Eva Garroutte: "The ultimate and explicit federal intention was to use the blood quantum standard as a means to liquidate tribal lands and to eliminate government trust responsibility to tribes, along with entitlement programs, treaty rights, and reservations."[19] A very direct example of this is the way in which the United States connected blood quantum and "competency" with regard to land sales at White Earth in the early 1900s.[20] As White Earth scholar David Beaulieu has asserted, "It is a rare moment in the historiography of the relationship between anthropology and the other social sciences to American Indians to find an example where the colonial nature and political purposes and the uses of academic enterprise seem so obvious and direct."[21]

Citizenship

Our teachings and traditions cannot be preserved and contained in boxes. That is of no use to us. We must continue to put our teachings into motion, into practice, in our everyday lives and also in our systems, our governments, all aspects of life. In my conversations and experiences, the primary obstacle to changing citizenship/enrollment to be more inclusive and reflective of our teachings and values are concerns about resources and entitlements. In some ways there will never be enough, and yet in another way there is always enough. All nations have to manage resources and entitlements and make tough decisions about priorities in a similar way that each of us do regarding our own budgets and expenses.[22] There is evidence that, in some cases, this way of thinking of connecting citizenship and resources connects back to colonization and the influence of the Bureau of Indian Affairs in the twentieth century. From the late 1930s through 1961, the elected officials of the Minnesota Chippewa Tribe (MCT) had intense discussions about enrollment. These discussions were at the behest of the Bureau of Indian Affairs, which strongly desired the MCT would impose enrollment criteria that would support population decline. For example, after five years of discussion, in 1941, the MCT easily passed a resolution that required lineal descent from the Act of January 14, 1889, for enrollment.[23] After the passage of the resolution, Superintendent Scott Shipp wrote to the Commissioner of Indian Affairs submitting the resolution along with his recommendation for approval to the Commissioner of Indian Affairs.[24] However, the resolution was rejected. In his response, Oscar Chapman, Assistant Secretary of the Department of the Interior, wrote:

> If the Minnesota Chippewa Indians desire to share their property with a large number of persons who are Indians neither by name, residence, or attachment but merely by the accident of a small portion of Indian blood . . . [t]he Minnesota Chippewa Tribe must realize that every new

name which they add to the membership roll will by that much decrease
the share every member now has in the limited assets of the Minnesota
Chippewa Tribe.[25]

While discussions of MCT leadership had centered on families and
kinship, Chapman made the focus on resources and tried to leverage a
model of scarcity and greed. I'm sure many MCT leaders had experienced
scarcity, but it did not stop them from welcoming new family members. It
was only after about two decades of additional pressure from the US government that MCT finally adopted a one-quarter Minnesota Chippewa
Tribe blood quantum minimum as the requirement for citizenship.[26]

In the more than half century that one-quarter Minnesota Chippewa Tribe blood has been a requirement for enrollment, the idea that
citizens are entitled to certain benefits has taken hold to a certain extent.
I've heard a number of people use the metaphor of a pie and assert that
we simply can't cut it any smaller, and others who assert that "there isn't
enough now." Someone once accused me of wanting to be enrolled so
that I could "get a house." I was a little taken aback and explained that
I have been paying my own mortgage for quite a few years and would
not expect a house from the Tribe if I were to be enrolled. Regardless of
where the mindset of people expecting to have the nation provide for all
their needs came from, I strongly believe that differentiating resources
and entitlements from citizenship today is both critical and aligned with
our long-standing traditions and practices. Historically, there were both
benefits and obligations that came with being a part of a family/clan, community, and nation.

Conclusion

I think we are overdue in evaluating how we can infuse tradition into
our citizenship requirements. I return to Johnston's assertions about the
value of individuals being "self-reliant and free." What if each citizen were
valued as someone who could and would make contributions rather than
someone who will drain resources? I think that if we embedded reciprocity
into services and programs, each person would be valued and empowered,
and we just might find the right stitch to continue to string generations
together in our political systems.

Seven Generations

Children play with full bellies
At the edge of the mating dance.
Beneath a sky thrown open
To the need of stars
To know themselves against the dark.
All night we dance the weave of joy and tears
All night we're lit with the sunrise of forever
Just ahead of us, through the trees
One generation after the other.

JOY HARJO

Afterword

I've been wrestling with some of these questions one-on-one, in conversation with families, and in our communities all my life. I dream that we are as resilient as our ancestors. That we might restore clan systems. That we might lean on our neighbors and learn from them. While one of us might not have the answer, together we will find a way beyond blood quantum. Together, we refuse to disappear.

May you continue to learn, grow, reflect, and hold steady in response to the existential questions facing us. I trust that long after I'm gone, we'll be still here.

NORBERT S. HILL JR.

Questions for Reflection

- What is our responsibility to address blood quantum—the policy and the ideology?
- What is our responsibility to our ancestors, ourselves, and our descendants?
- Who belongs? Who should have political recognition?
- What does it mean to be Indigenous? Who gets to decide?
- How can we encourage connection and belonging for our Native youth, so they grow up with strong identities?
- How do we honor our unique histories while also blending them with our current-day circumstances?
- How do we collectively go about gaining more insight into ways of being that carried our ancestors for thousands of years?
- What if each citizen were valued as someone who could and would make contributions rather than someone who will drain resources?
- What will be our challenge in the future?

Notes

Moving Past the Flawed Equations of Blood and Property

1. Martin Case, *The Relentless Business of Treaties: How Indigenous Land Became US Property* (St. Paul: Minnesota Historical Society, 2018).
2. Case, *Relentless Business of Treaties*, 6.
3. Case, *Relentless Business of Treaties*, 7.
4. See, for example, *The Great Vanishing Act: Blood Quantum and the Future of Native Nations*, ed. Kathleen Ratteree and Norbert Hill (Lakewood, CO: Fulcrum Publishing, 2017); Melissa L. Meyer, "American Indian Blood Quantum Requirements: Blood Is Thicker Than Family," in *Over the Edge: Remapping the American West*, ed. Valerie J. Matsumoto and Blake Allmendinger (Berkeley: University of California Press, 1999); Paul Spruhan, "A Legal History of Blood Quantum in Federal Indian Law to 1935," *South Dakota Law Review* 51 (2006); Kirsty Gover, *Tribal Constitutionalism: States, Tribes, and the Governance of Membership* (New York: Oxford University Press, 2010); Kim TallBear, *Native American DNA: Tribal Belonging and the False Promise of Genetic Science* (Minneapolis: University of Minnesota Press, 2013); Katherine Ellinghaus, *Blood Will Tell: Native America and Assimilation Policy* (Lincoln: University of Nebraska Press, 2017); Circe Sturm, *Blood Politics: Race, Culture, and Identity in the Cherokee Nation of Oklahoma* (Berkeley: University of California Press, 2002); and David E. Wilkins and Shelly Hulse Wilkins, *Dismembered: Native Disenrollment and the Battle for Human Rights* (Seattle: University of Washington Press, 2017).
5. See David E. Wilkins and Shelly Hulse Wilkins, "Blood Quantum: The Mathematics of Ethnocide" in Ratteree and Hill's *The Great Vanishing Act*, 210–27.
6. See Scott L. Malcomson, *One Drop of Blood: The American Misadventure of Race* (New York: Farrar, Straus and Giroux, 2000), 356.
7. Vine Deloria Jr., *Custer Died for Your Sins: An Indian Manifesto* (Norman: University of Oklahoma Press, (1969, 1988), 8.

8. See Cathy Corey's (a disenrolled Chukchansi) comments in Wilkins and Wilkins, *Dismembered*, 98, 154, where she graphically identifies the prominent role that money plays in many of the disenrollment decisions of her former nation.

9. Keith Grint, *Leadership: A Very Short Introduction* (New York: Oxford University Press, 2010), 16.

10. Grint, *Leadership*, 18.

11. Ella Deloria, *Speaking of Indians* (New York: Friendship Press, 1944), 27.

12. Malaak Khattab, "Red Lake Tribal Council Passes Resolution to Increase Blood Degree," Lakeland PBS, November 6, 2019, http://lptv.org/red-lake-tribal-council-passes-resolution-to-increase-blood-degree/.

13. Vine Deloria Jr., *A Better Day for Indians* (New York: Field Foundation, 1977).

14. Deloria, *Better Day*, 21.

15. Deloria, *Better Day*, 25.

The Federal Indian Blood Quantum Fiction

1. Vine Deloria Jr., *God Is Red: A Native View of Religion*, 30th Anniversary Edition (Lakewood, CO: Fulcrum Books, 2003), 244. Deloria spoke eloquently about many of the legal, political, and social aspects of blood quantum discussed in this essay, including "de-enrollment," during his last recorded interview in 2005, https://www.youtube.com/watch?v=YLI4srZuh5A.

2. C. Matthew Snipp, *American Indians: The First of This Land* (New York: Russell Sage Foundation, 1989), 30: "It was, and still is, impossible to designate a person as 3/4 blood quantum without knowing the blood types of his or her parents, grandparents, great-grandparents, and even earlier ancestors."; Kim TallBear, *Native American DNA: Tribal Belonging and the False Promise of Genetic Science* (Minneapolis: University of Minnesota Press, 2013), 54: "Blood fractions are not enumerated based on examinations with laboratory prostheses of blood the fluid or of the genetic material found in cells."; John H. Moore and Janis E. Campbell, "Blood Quantum and Ethnic Intermarriage in the Boas Data Set," *Human Biology* 67, no. 3 (June 1995): 499: "Blood quantum of course, is only loosely related to real genetic heritage and is based on the fiction that one inherits 'blood' equally from the male and female side."; Ryan W. Schmidt, "American Indian Identity and Blood Quantum in the 21st Century: A Critical Review," *Journal of*

Anthropology (January 15, 2012), https://doi.org/10.1155/2011/549521: "Using what today would be called pseudoscience to support a racial ideology established through 'scientific objectivity,' the physical anthropologists made claims of being able to accurately detect and separate mixed bloods from full bloods."

3. See Paul Spruhan, "A Legal History of Blood Quantum in Federal Indian Law to 1935," *South Dakota Law Review* 51, no. 1 (2006).

4. See Patricia Nelson Limerick, *The Legacy of Conquest: The Unbroken Past of the American West* (New York: W. W. Norton & Company, 1987), 338: "Set the blood quantum at one-quarter, hold to it as a rigid definition of Indians, let intermarriage proceed as it had for centuries, and eventually Indians will be defined out of existence. When that happens, the federal government will be freed of its persistent 'Indian problem.'"; Snipp, *American Indians*, 34: "Confronted by legal challenges, federal authorities were forced to concede that blood quantum definitions cannot be legally enforced for most purposes. Furthermore, the blood quantum information haphazardly collected in the early rolls is at best unsystematic, if not altogether unreliable."

5. Felix S. Cohen, *On the Drafting of Tribal Constitutions* (Norman: University of Oklahoma Press, 2006), 113; Kirsty Gover, *Tribal Constitutionalism: States, Tribes, and the Governance of Membership* (New York: Oxford University Press, 2010), 83.

6. See Snipp, *American Indians*, 34.

7. See Snipp, *American Indians*, 34.

8. See Snipp, *American Indians*. While this essay concerns nineteenth- and twentieth-century federal Indian blood quantum laws, Spruhan, "Legal History of Blood Quantum," 4, explains the colonial legal origins of blood quantum, dating back to at least 1705.

9. Joanne Barker, *Native Acts: Law, Recognition, and Cultural Authenticity* (Durham, NC: Duke University Press, 2011), 93–94; Sarah Krakoff, "Inextricably Political: Race, Membership, and Tribal Sovereignty," *Washington Law Review* 87, no. 4 (2012): 1041–132. As Sarah Krakoff notes, while the term "blood quantum" has become naturalized, it is necessarily a racialized term.

10. Lisa M. Poupart, "The Familiar Face of Genocide: Internalized Oppression among American Indians," *Hypatia* 18, no. 2 (Spring 2003): 86–100.

11. Cohen, *Drafting of Tribal Constitutions*, 113; David E. Wilkins and Shelly Hulse Wilkins, "Blood Quantum: The Mathematics of Ethnocide," *The Great*

Vanishing Act: Blood Quantum and the Future of Native Nations, ed. Kathleen Ratteree and Norbert Hill (Lakewood, CO: Fulcrum Publishing, 2017), 220.

12. Brackeen v. Haaland, 599 U. S. ___, No. 21-276 slip op. at 2 (2023) (Kavanaugh, J., concurring): "In my view, the equal protection issue is serious. Under the [Indian Child Welfare Act], a child in foster care or adoption proceedings may in some cases be denied a particular placement because of the child's race."; see also Adoptive Couple v. Baby Girl, 570 U.S. 637, 133 S. Ct. 2552 (2013): "This case is about a little girl (Baby Girl) who is classified as an Indian because she is 1.2% (3/256) Cherokee."

13. Gabriel S. Galanda, "In the Spirit of Vine Deloria, Jr.: Indigenous Kinship Renewal and Relational Sovereignty," SSRN Electronic Journal (January 2023): 10, https://ssrn.com/abstract=4338913.

14. In this essay the term "Indigenous" is used to hearken the People's original existence and place. See Deloria, *God Is Red*, 58: "The Indian is indigenous . . . to the land in the deep emotional sense of knowing that he or she belongs there."; consider Dr. Paulette Steeves' explanation of the term "Indigenous" as a paradigm that "turns a tool of oppression (cultural homogenization) into one of liberation (cultural unity) to support contemporary human rights struggles on a global scale.": Paulette F. C. Steeves, *The Indigenous Paleolithic of the Western Hemisphere* (Lincoln: University of Nebraska Press, 2021), 15; see Robert F. Berkhofer Jr., *The White Man's Indian: Images of American Indians from Columbus to the Present* (London: Vintage, 1968), 4: "Indian" is used as a colonial or federal construct; see Galanda, "In the Spirit of Vine Deloria, Jr.," 13: "Nation" or "tribe" is used to connote modern or neocolonial existence.

15. See, for example, Treaty with the Wyandot, Seneca, Delaware, Shawnee, Potawatomie, Ottawa, and Chippewa Sept. 29, 1817, Stat. 160, Art. 8.

16. See Treaty with the Wyandot.

17. See Treaty with the Wyandot.

18. See Galanda, "In the Spirit of Vine Deloria, Jr.," 12.

19. Melissa L. Meyer, "American Indian Blood Quantum Requirements: Blood Is Thicker Than Family," *Over the Edge: Remapping the American West*, ed. Valerie J. Matsumoto and Blake Allmendinger (Berkeley: University of California Press, 1999), 231, 235.

20. Sean S. Harvey, "Ideas of Race in Early America," *Oxford Research Encyclopedia of American History*, 2016, https://doi.org/10.1093/acrefore/9780199329175.013.262.

21. Harvey, "Ideas of Race."

22. Vine Deloria Jr., *Custer Died for Your Sins: An Indian Manifesto* (Norman: University of Oklahoma Press, (1969, 1988), 8.

23. Harvey, "Ideas of Race," 1: "American Indian, and African 'races' did not exist before colonization of the so-called New World."

24. Meyer, "American Indian Blood Quantum Requirements"; see also Robert A. Williams Jr., *The American Indian in Western Legal Thought: The Discourses of Conquest* (New York: Oxford University Press, 1990), 227.

25. TallBear, *Native American DNA*, 47.

26. Rennard Strickland, *Genocide-at-Law: An Historic and Contemporary View of the Native American Experience,* (Lawrence: University of Kansas Law Review, 1986), 713, 715.

27. Spruhan, "Legal History of Blood Quantum," 11; Gabriel S. Galanda and Ryan D. Dreveskracht, "Curing the Tribal Disenrollment Epidemic: In Search of a Remedy," *Arizona Law Review* 57, no. 2 (2015): 383.

28. Bethany R. Berger, "'Power Over This Unfortunate Race': Race, Politics and Indian Law in United States v. Rogers," *William and Mary Law Review* 45 (2004): 1957.

29. Jill Doerfler, *Those Who Belong: Identity, Family, Blood, and Citizenship among the White Earth Anishinaabeg* (East Lansing: Michigan State University Press, 2015): xxvi.

30. Moore and Campbell, "Blood Quantum and Ethnic Intermarriage," 499.

31. Snipp, *American Indians*, 34.

32. Snipp, *American Indians*, 34.

33. Doerfler, *Those Who Belong*, xxvi.

34. Doerfler, *Those Who Belong*, xxvi.

35. Galanda and Dreveskracht, "Curing the Tribal Disenrollment Epidemic," 396; Margaret D. Jacobs, "The Eastmans and the Luhans: Interracial Marriage between White Women and Native American Men, 1875–1935," *Frontiers: A Journal of Women's Studies* 23, no. 3 (2002): 29, 37; see also Meyer, "American Indian Blood Quantum Requirements," 239; Tommy Miller, "Beyond Blood Quantum: The Legal and Political Implications of Expanding Tribal Enrollment," *American Indian Law Journal* 3, no. 1 (2014): 323.

36. Moore and Campbell, "Blood Quantum and Ethnic Intermarriage," 4.

37. David E. Wilkins and Heidi Kiiwetinepinesiik Stark, *American Indian Politics and the American Political System* (Lanham, MD: Rowman & Littlefield, 2017), 30.

38. Spruhan, "Legal History of Blood Quantum," 4.

39. Spruhan, "Legal History of Blood Quantum," 4.

40. Spruhan, "Legal History of Blood Quantum," 4.

41. Meyer, "American Indian Blood Quantum Requirements" 239.

42. John Rockwell Snowden et. al., "American Indian Sovereignty and Naturalization: It's a Race Thing," *Nebraska Law Review* 80, no. 171 (2001): 193.

43. See, for example, Treaty with the Chippewa of the Mississippi 1847, Art. 4; see also Spruhan, "Legal History of Blood Quantum," 12: "The United States does acknowledge mixed-bloods explicitly as tribal members in a few treaties. Treaties with the Chippewa, Omaha, Pawnee, Ponca, and Winnebago each contain provisions recognizing mixed-bloods as tribal members."; David E. Wilkins and Shelly Hulse Wilkins, *Dismembered: Native Disenrollment and the Battle for Human Rights* (Seattle: University of Washington Press, 2017), 27: "[S]everal treaties . . . included language about blood . . . to identify a class of individuals who played important roles in treaty negotiations and were entitled to certain benefits, like land allotments and other treaty annuities."

44. Wilkins and Wilkins, *Dismembered*; Galanda and Dreveskracht, "Curing the Tribal Disenrollment Epidemic," 399: "[T]he seeds of blood quantum-based tribal membership requirements had been planted, through the sowing of Indian treaties—the supreme law of the land."

45. Kent Carter, The Dawes Commission and the Allotment of the Five Civilized Tribes, 1893–1914 (Ancestry, 1999), 106.

46. Cherokee Nation v. Nash, 267 F. Supp. 3d 86, 140 (D.D.C. 2017).

47. In re: Effect of Cherokee Nation v. Nash and Vann v. Zinke, Case No. SC-17-07, Final Order (Cherokee Sup. Ct. February 22, 2021, 8.

48. Jeremy M. Lazarus, "Blood Feud: Descendant Pushes to Be Recognized by Pamunkey Tribe despite Vestiges of 'Black Laws,'" *Richmond Free Press*, February 28, 2020.

49. See, for example, Galanda and Dreveskracht, "Curing the Tribal Disenrollment Epidemic," 430.

50. 25 U.S.C. § 677a(b).

51. Joseph G. Jorgensen, *The Sun Dance Religion: Power for the Powerless* (Chicago: University of Chicago Press, 1974), 152.

52. Wilkins and Wilkins, *Dismembered*, 59; Gabriel S. Galanda, "Tribal Neocolonialism: Disenrollment, Enrollment Moratoria, and Per-Capitalism,"

Critical Race Theory Summer School: Teaching Truth to Power, African American Policy Forum, July 21, 2022.

53. Galanda, "In the Spirit of Vine Deloria, Jr.," 2; see also Wilkins and Wilkins, *Dismembered*, 79.

54. Judith V. Royster, "The Legacy of Allotment," *Arizona State Law Journal* 27 (1995): 1, 9.

55. Frederick E. Hoxie, *A Final Promise: The Campaign to Assimilate the Indians, 1880–1920* (Lincoln, NE: Bison Books, 1984), 24.

56. 24 Stat. 388 (1887) (codified in part at 25 U.S.C. §§ 331–381 (2000)).

57. 25 U.S.C. § 348.

58. Nell Jessup Newton and Robert Anderson, *Cohen's Handbook of Federal Indian Law* (New York: LexisNexis, 2005), 16.03[a] (citing 25 U.S.C. § 348).

59. Hoxie, *Final Promise*, 24.

60. 25 U.S.C. § 349; see also Newton and Anderson, *Cohen's Handbook*, 1042.

61. 34 Stat. 182 (1906) (codified as amended at 25 U.S.C. §349 (1994)); Bacher v. Patencio, 232 F. Supp. 939, 942 (S.D. Cal. 1964), *aff'd*, 368 F.2d 1010 (9th Cir. 1966).

62. 25 U.S.C. § 348.

63. John P. LaVelle, "The General Allotment Act 'Eligibility' Hoax: Distortions of Law, Policy, and History in Derogation of Indian Tribes," *Wicazo Sa Review* 14 (1999): 251; Spruhan, "Legal History of Blood Quantum," 41; Francis Paul Prucha, *The Great Father: The United States Government and the American Indians* (Lincoln: University of Nebraska Press, 1986), 300–301.

64. Spruhan, "Legal History of Blood Quantum," 12 (citing Act of Apr. 26, 1906, ch. 1876, §§ 19, 22, 23, 34 Stat. 137, 144-45, Act of May 27, 1908, ch. 199, §1, 35 Stat. 312, 312); see also Newton and Anderson, *Cohen's Handbook*, 1049.

65. Spruhan, "Legal History of Blood Quantum," 12; Newton and Anderson, *Cohen's Handbook*, 1049.

66. Spruhan, "Legal History of Blood Quantum," 12; Newton and Anderson, *Cohen's Handbook*, 1049.

67. See Spruhan, "Legal History of Blood Quantum," 12; Newton and Anderson, *Cohen's Handbook*, 1049; LaVelle, *General Allotment Act*, 259.

68. Spruhan, "Legal History of Blood Quantum," 12; Newton and Anderson, *Cohen's Handbook*, 1049; LaVelle, *General Allotment Act*, 259; Hoxie, *Final Promise*, 181.

69. Newton and Anderson, *Cohen's Handbook*, 1049; LaVelle, *General Allotment Act*, 289; Spruhan, "Legal History of Blood Quantum," 44; Wilkins and Wilkins, "Blood Quantum," 217.

70. Spruhan, Legal History of Blood Quantum," 44.

71. Newton and Anderson, *Cohen's Handbook*, 1049; LaVelle, *The General Allotment Act*, 259.

72. Janet McDonnell, "Competency Commissions and Indian Land Policy, 1913–1920," *South Dakota History* 11, no. 1 (Winter 1980): 23.

73. Hoxie, *Final Promise*, 183.

74. Hoxie, *Final Promise*, 183; Prucha, *Great Father*, 298–99.

75. Angelique A. EagleWoman (Wambdi A. WasteWin), "Tribal Values of Taxation within the Tribalist Economic Theory," *Indigenous Nations Journal* 6, no. 1 (Spring 2008): 1, 7.

76. EagleWoman, "Tribal Values."

77. Snipp, *American Indians*, 34.

78. Snipp, *American Indians*, 34.

79. Alexandra Harmon, "Tribal Enrollment Councils: Lessons on Law and Indian Identity," *Western Historical Quarterly* 32, no. 2 (Summer 2001): 175, 185.

80. David E. Wilkins, *Documents of Native American Political Development: 1933 to Present* (New York: Oxford University Press, 2008), 4, 9.

81. Wilkins, *Documents.*

82. Harmon, "Tribal Enrollment Councils," 185.

83. Harmon, "Tribal Enrollment Councils," 185.

84. Harmon, "Tribal Enrollment Councils," 179.

85. See Galanda, "In the Spirit of Vine Deloria, Jr.," 11.

86. Act of June 30, 1919, 41 Stat. 9 (25 U.S.C. § 163).

87. Act of June 30, 1919.

88. Wilkins and Wilkins, "Blood Quantum," 218.

89. Simmons v. Eagle Seelatsee, 244 F. Supp. 808, 813 (E.D.Wash.S.D.1965): "The Act which authorizes the Secretary of the Interior generally to make up membership rolls of any Indian tribe directs that such rolls shall contain the ages and 'quantum of Indian blood' of those placed on the rolls." (citing Act of June 30, 1919, 41 Stat. 9, (25 U.S.C. § 163)), *aff'd*, 384 U.S. 209, 86 S. Ct. 1459, 16 L. Ed. 2d 480; see also Wilkins and Wilkins, "Blood Quantum," 218.

90. Simmons v. Eagle Seelatsee, 813.

91. Simmons v. Eagle Seelatsee, 813 (citations omitted; emphasis added).

92. See Simmons v. Eagle Seelatsee, 813; Galanda, "In the Spirit of Vine Deloria, Jr.," 3.

93. Simmons v. Eagle Seelatsee, 813.

94. Simmons v. Eagle Seelatsee, 813.

95. 25 U.S.C. §§ 461, 462, 465 (current version at §§ 5101, 5102, 5108 (2016)); see Felix Cohen, *Handbook of Federal Indian Law* § 4.04[3][a] at 252 n.362 (1982); Vine Deloria Jr. and Clifford M. Lytle, *American Indians, American Justice* (Austin: University of Texas Press, 1983), 14; Prucha, *Great Father*, 317.

96. 25 U.S.C. § 465 (current version at 25 U.S.C. § 5108 (2016)); see generally Carcieri v. Salazar, 555 U.S. 379 (2009).

97. 25 U.S.C. § 479 (current version at 25 U.S.C. § 5129 (2016)).

98. Vine Deloria Jr., ed., *The Indian Reorganization Act: Congresses and Bills* (Norman: University of Oklahoma Press, 2002).

99. Wilkins and Wilkins, "Blood Quantum," 219.

100. "To Grant to Indians Living under Federal Tutelage the Freedom to Organize for Purposes of Local Self-Government and Economic Enterprise: Hearing before the Committee on Indian Affairs United States Senate," 73rd Congress (1934): 263–64 (statement of Sen. Wheeler).

101. "To Grant to Indians."

102. "To Grant to Indians."

103. See 25 U.S.C. § 479; Spruhan, "Legal History of Blood Quantum," 47.

104. US Department of the Interior, Circular No. 3123 (Office of Indian Affairs, November 18, 1935).

105. US Department of the Interior, Circular No. 3123.

106. US Department of the Interior, Circular No. 3123.

107. Graham D. Taylor, *The New Deal and American Indian Tribalism: The Administration of the Indian Reorganization Act 1934–45* (Lincoln: University of Nebraska Press, 1980), 30.

108. Taylor, *New Deal*, 30.

109. Cohen, *On the Drafting of Tribal Constitutions*, xxiii; Elmer Rusco, "The Indian Reorganization Act and Self-Government," *American Indian Constitutional Reform and the Rebuilding of Native Nations*, ed. Eric D. Lemont (Austin: University of Texas Press, 2006), 55.

110. Cohen, *On the Drafting of Tribal Constitutions*, 113; Wilkins and Wilkins, "Blood Quantum," 220.

111. See Pauly Denetclaw, "Bloodlines," *Texas Observer*, July 19, 2021.

112. See Galanda, "Tribal Neocolonialism."

113. See Brackeen v. Haaland.

114. Jana Berger and Paula Fisher, "Navigating Tribal Membership Issues," *Emerging Issues in Tribal-State Relations* (2013), 61; Alan Parker, "Compare Paradigms: Tribal Citizenship v. Tribal Membership" (2020), 10 (on file with author).

115. Galanda, "In the Spirit of Vine Deloria, Jr.," 8.

116. See Barbara Anne Henderson, "Division by Blood: Examining a History of Political and Racial Clashes Underlying American Indian Identity," University of Montana, 2004; see, for example, Nicole Martin Rogers et al., "Red Lake Nation: Population Projections," (Wilder Research, 2022), 3, https://www.wilder.org/wilder-research/research-library/red-lake-nation-population-projections.

117. See generally *The Great Vanishing Act: Blood Quantum and the Future of Native Nations*, ed. Kathleen Ratteree and Norbert Hill (Lakewood, CO: Fulcrum Publishing, 2017); Galanda, "In the Spirit of Vine Deloria, Jr.," 14.

118. 25 U.S.C. § 355 note (2018); Caroline Halter, "Congress Strips Stigler Act of Blood Quantum Requirements," KGOU, December 21, 2018.

119. Parker, "Compare Paradigms," 10 (emphasis added).

120. Jennifer Scott, "Constitutional Amendment Changes Enrollment Criteria," *Nugguam*, October 2022; "MN Chippewa Tribe Votes to End Blood Requirement for Members," *U.S. News & World Report*, July 7, 2022; "St. Croix Tribe of Chippewa Votes to Remove 'Blood Quantum' Requirement, Update Constitution," *St. Croix 360*, November 27, 2023.

121. Angela Denning, "Blood Quantum Requirement Dropped for Sealaska Corporation Enrollment," KTOO, July 2, 2022.

122. See Galanda, "In the Spirit of Vine Deloria, Jr.," 10.

123. See Galanda, "In the Spirit of Vine Deloria, Jr.," 16.

Practicality:
Native American Tribal Adoption in Historical Perspective

1. See, for example, Ray Fogelson, "Perspectives on Native American Identity," *Studying Native America: Problems and Prospects*, ed. Russell Thornton (Madison: University of Wisconsin Press, 1998).

2. David E. Wilkins and Shelly Hulse Wilkins have called blood quantum

requirements "ethnocide," while Suzan Shown Harjo has referred to it as a "vampire policy" that needs to be quickly replaced: David E. Wilkins and Shelly Hulse Wilkins, "Blood Quantum: The Mathematics of Ethnocide," *The Great Vanishing Act: Blood Quantum and the Future of Native Nations*, ed. Kathleen Ratteree and Norbert Hill Jr. (Lakewood, CO; Fulcrum Press, 2017), 210–27; Suzan Shown Harjo, "Vampire Policy Is Bleeding Us Dry— Blood-Quantums, Be Gone!" *Indian Country Today*, February 14, 2001.

3. Matthew L.M. Fletcher, "Tribal Members and Indian Nationhood," *American Indian Law Review* 37, no. 1 (2017): 2.

4. David E. Wilkins and Shelly Hulse Wilkins, *Dismembered: Native Enrollment and the Battle for Human Rights* (Seattle: University of Washington Press, 2017), 142.

5. Ella Deloria, *Speaking of Indians* (New York: Friendship Press, 1944), 29.

6. Raymond J. DeMallie, "Kinship and Biology in Sioux Culture," *North American Indian Anthropology: Essays on Society and Culture*, ed. Raymond J. DeMallie and Alfonso Ortiz (Norman: University of Oklahoma Press, 1994), 133.

7. DeMallie, "Kinship and Biology in Sioux Culture," 131; Deloria, *Speaking of Indians,* 29–30.

8. William N. Fenton, *The Great Law and the Longhouse: A Political History of the Iroquois Confederacy* (Norman: University of Oklahoma Press, 1998), 31.

9. Christina Gish Hill, *Webs of Kinship: Family in Northern Cheyenne Nationhood* (Norman: University of Oklahoma Press, 2017), 67.

10. Numerous Seneca during my fieldwork since 1972 have proudly mentioned their ancestry to Mary Jemison: George H. J. Abrams, "Foreword," *A Narrative of the Life of Mrs. Mary Jemison,* James Seaver [1824] (Syracuse, NY: Syracuse University Press, 1990), xi.

11. Francis Jennings, *The Ambiguous Iroquois Empire* (New York: W. W. Norton, 1984), 5.

12. David Silverman has pointed out that the inclusion of Africans in tribal membership led to a reversal and more restrictive policies fearing white denial of Stockbridge "Indianness": *Red Brethren: The Brothertown and Stockbridge Indians and the Problem of Race in Early America* (Ithaca, NY: Cornell University Press, 2010). This fear was found in other Native American communities, especially in the South: Helen Rountree, "The Indians of Virginia: A Third Race in a Biracial State," *Southeastern Indians Since the Removal Era*, ed. Walter A. Williams (Athens: University of Georgia, 1979),

44–50. See also Mikaëla M. Adams, *Who Belongs? Race, Resources, and Tribal Citizenship in the Native South* (New York: Oxford University Press, 2016).

13. Daniel K. Richter, *The Ordeal of the Longhouse: The Peoples of the Iroquois League in the Era of European Colonization* (Chapel Hill: University of North Carolina Press, 1992), 136–37, 238–40. For the unique status of the Tuscaroras, see Barbara Graymont, "Editor's Introduction," *Fighting Tuscarora: The Autobiography of Chief Clinton Rickard*, ed. Barbara Graymont (Syracuse, NY: Syracuse University Press, 1973), xix.

14. See Joshua Piker, *Okfuskee: A Creek Indian Town in Colonial America* (Cambridge, MA: Harvard University Press, 2004); Andrew K. Frank, *Creeks and Southerners: Biculturalism on the Early American Frontier* (Lincoln: University of Nebraska Press, 2005).

15. See Colin Calloway, *White People, Indians, and Highlanders: Tribal People and Colonial Encounters in Scotland and America* (New York: Oxford University Press, 2010), 119, 155, 193–95, 204; Chief Alexander McGillivray, a descendant of these Scottish Highlanders, even sent his relative, David Moniac, to West Point: Laurence M. Hauptman and Heriberto Dixon, "Cadet David Moniac: A Creek Indian's Schooling at West Point, 1817–1822," *Proceedings of the American Philosophical Society* 152, no. 3 (September 2008): 322–48. Moniac became the first Native American graduate of West Point.

16. Christina Snyder, "Conquered Enemies, Adopted Kin, and Owned People: The Creek Indians and Their Captives," *Journal of Southern History* 73, no. 2 (May 2007): 257.

17. J. N. B. Hewitt, "Iroquois Cosmology, Part I," *Annual Report of the Bureau of American Ethnology for the Years 1899–1900* 21 (Washington, DC, 1903): 127–39; J. N. B. Hewitt, "Iroquois Cosmology, Part II," *Annual Report of the Bureau of American Ethnology for the Years 1925–1926* 43 (Washington, DC, 1928): 449–819. See also Fenton, *Great Law and the Longhouse*.

18. Arthur C. Parker, "Editorial Notes: The Kenjocketys," *The Life of General Ely S. Parker: Last Grand Sachem of the Iroquois and General Grant's Military Secretary* (Buffalo, NY: Buffalo Historical Society Publications, 1919), 313–16. For the Half-King (Tanaghrisson), see William A. Hunter, III, "Tanaghrisson," *Dictionary of Canadian Biography* (Toronto: University of Toronto Press, 1974), retrieved February 2, 2023 at https://www.biographi.ca/en/bio/tanaghrisson_3E.html. For Arthur C. Parker's adoption, see Joy Porter, *To Be an Indian: The Life of Iroquois-Seneca Arthur Caswell Parker* (Norman: University of

Oklahoma Press, 2001), 52–53. For William N. Fenton, see William N. Fenton, "He-Lost-a-Bet (Howanneyao) of the Seneca Hawk Clan," *Strangers to Relatives: The Adoption and Naming of Anthropologists in Native North America,* ed. Sergei Kan (Lincoln: University of Nebraska Press, 2001). Kevin White has called into question the authenticity of the Haudenosaunee adoption of anthropologists in the first half of the twentieth century: "Adoption, Incorporation, and a Sense of Citizenship and Belonging in Indigenous Nations and Culture: A Haudenosaunee Perspective," *AlterNative: An International Journal of Indigenous Peoples* 14 (November 2018), retrieved February 5, 2023, from https://doi .org/10.1177/1177180118808143. For Converse, see: "How I Became a Seneca Indian," Arthur C. Parker manuscript, Box 2, Folder 8, University of Rochester.

19. Laurence M. Hauptman interview with George Heron, former President of the Seneca Nation during the Kinzua Dam crisis, September 29, 1984, Allegany Indian Reservation.

20. Anthony F. C. Wallace, *The Death and Rebirth of the Seneca* (New York: Alfred A. Knopf, 1969), 45.

21. Wallace, *Death and Rebirth of the Seneca,* 103. For Chief Skenando(ah), see Laurence M. Hauptman, *Conspiracy of Interests: Iroquois Dispossession and the Rise of New York State* (Syracuse, NY: Syracuse University Press, 1999), 39–85.

22. Richter, *Ordeal of the Longhouse,* 32–38. Other war captives faced torture and were put to death. Two scholars suggest that some of the Hurons were enslaved. Ralph Watkins and William A. Starna, "Northern Iroquois Slavery: A Hypothesis," *Ethnohistory* 38, no. 1 (1991): 34–57.

23. Fenton, *Great Law and the Longhouse,* 178.

24. Northern Cheyenne constitution, originally adopted in 1935 and as amended in 1996, https://www.cheyennenation.com. Retrieved February 5, 2023.

25. John H. Moore, *Cheyenne Nation: A Social and Demographic History* (Lincoln: University of Nebraska Press, 1987), 9, 251–63.

26. Hill, *Webs of Kinship,* 66.

27. Hill, *Webs of Kinship,* 48–49, 66–78, 173–174; DeMallie, "Kinship and Biology in Sioux Culture," 130; Anne S. Straus, "Tell Your Sister Come to Eat," *Strangers to Relatives,* 175–84.

28. Leo K. Killsback, *A Sovereign People: Indigenous Nationhood, Traditional Law, and the Covenants of the Cheyenne Nation* (Lubbock: Texas Tech University Press, 2020), 107–108.

29. Jean-Baptiste Truteau, *A Fur Trader on the Upper Missouri: The Journal and*

Description of Jean-Baptiste Truteau, 1794–1796, eds. Ray DeMallie, Douglas R. Parks, and Robert Vézina (Lincoln: University of Nebraska Press, 2017), 317.

30. Hill, *Webs of Kinship*, 66–77; Joseph Jablow, *The Cheyenne in Plains Indian Trade Relations, 1795–1840* (Lincoln: University of Nebraska Press, 1994), 42.

31. Moore, *Cheyenne Nation*, 115.

32. Hill, *Webs of Kinship*, 66–77; Jablow, *Cheyenne in Plains Indian Trade Relations*.

33. Patricia C. Albers, "Symbiosis, Merger, and War: Contrasting Forms of Intertribal Relationship Among Historic Plains Indians," *The Political Economy of North American Indians*, ed. John H. Moore (Norman: University of Oklahoma, 1993), 127–8.

34. Jablow, *Cheyenne in Plains Indian Trade Relations*, 64.

35. *Constitution and Bylaws of the Crow Tribe of Indians* (2001).

36. Interview of Grant Bulltail, "Northern Plains History and Cultures: How Do Native People and Nations Experience Belonging?" Native Knowledge 360°, National Museum of the American Indian, retrieved February 8, 2023, https://americanindian.si.edu. Before his death, the remarkable Bulltail received the NEA Heritage Award.

37. Frank Rzeczkowski, *Uniting the Tribes: The Rise and Fall of the Pan-Indian Community on the Crow Reservation* (Lawrence: University Press of Kansas, 2012), 1–11.

38. Edwin Thompson Denig, *Five Indian Tribes of the Upper Missouri*, ed. John C. Ewers (Norman: University of Oklahoma Press, 1961), 195–200; James P. Beckwourth, *The Life and Adventures of James P. Beckwourth, Mountaineer, Scout, and Pioneer and Chief of the Crow Nation of Indians*, ed. Thomas D. Bonner (New York: Harper and Bros, 1856); Elinor Wilson, *Jim Beckwourth: Black Mountain Man and War Chief of the Crows* (Norman: University of Oklahoma Press, 1972); Robert M. Utley, *A Life Wild and Perilous: Mountain Men and the Paths to the Pacific* (New York: Macmillan, 1998).

39. Becky Shay, "Crow Tribe Adopts Candidate Obama in Historic Visit," *Billings Gazette*, May 20, 2008.

40. Robert H. Lowie, "The Tobacco Society of the Crow Indians," *Anthropological Papers of the American Museum of Natural History* 21, Part II (New York: Trustees of the American Museum of Natural History, 1919); Robert H. Lowie, *The Crow Indians* (New York: Farrar and Rinehart, 1935), 274–96; Max Big Man, "The Beaver Dance and Adoption Ceremony of

the Crow Indians," *Lifeways of Intermontane and Plains Indians in Honor of J. Verne Dusenberry*, ed. Leslie B. Davis, with notes by James S. Graham and C. Adrian Heidenreich (Bozeman: Montana State University, 1979). See also Fred W. Voget, *The Shoshoni-Crow Sun Dance* (Norman: University of Oklahoma Press, 1984), 63–73.

41. Lowie, "Tobacco Society"; Lowie, *Crow Indians*; Big Man, "Beaver Dance."
42. "Northern Plains History and Cultures."

In the Wake of Pretendians

1. Kim TallBear, "Genomic Articulations of Indigeneity," *Social Studies of Science* 43, no. 4 (2013): 509–33.
2. Jean Teillet, "Indigenization: How Genealogy and DNA Justify Race Shifting in Eastern Canada," *Canadian Issues* (2020), 40–43.
3. National Indigenous Identity Forum (NIIF), "Indigenous Voices on Indigenous Identity: What Was Heard Report" (2022), 4. Available at https://www.fnuniv.ca/wp-content/uploads/Indigenous-Voices-on-Indigenous-Identity_National-Indigenous-Identity-Forum_Report_March-22_June-22-FINAL.pdf. Retrieved May 27, 2023.
4. J. Kolopenuk, "The Pretendian Problem," *Canadian Journal of Political Science/Revue canadienne de science politique* (2022), 1–9.
5. J. Reardon and K. TallBear, "'Your DNA Is *Our* History': Genomics, Anthropology, and the Construction of Whiteness as Property," *Current Anthropology* 53, no. S5 (2012), S233–S245.
6. Jean Teillet, "There Is Nothing Innocent about the False Presumption of Indigenous Identity," The Globe and Mail, November 11, 2022. Available at https://www.theglobeandmail.com/opinion/article-there-is-nothing-innocent-about-the-false-presumption-of-indigenous/. Retrieved May 25, 2023.
7. Kathleen Ratteree, "Growing a Garden: An Educational Praxis of Allyship, Traditional Ecological Knowledge, and Western Science," 15, unpublished EdD dissertation, University of Wisconsin–Green Bay, 2023.
8. Ratteree, "Growing a Garden," 76.
9. Rebecca Nagle, "How 'Pretendians' Undermine the Rights of Indigenous People: We Must Guard against Harmful Public Discourse about Native Identity as Much as We Guard against Harmful Policy," *High Country News* (April 2, 2019), retrieved March 28, 2023, https://www.hcn.org/articles/tribal-affairs-how-pretendians-undermine-the-rights-of-indigenous-people.

10. Native American and Indigenous Studies Association (NAISA), "NAISA Council Statement on Indigenous Identity Fraud," September 15, 2015, https://naisa.org/about/documents-archive/previous-council-statements/naisa-council-statement-on-indigenous-identity-fraud/. Retrieved May 19, 2023.

11. Kolopenuk, "The Pretendian Problem."

12. C. M. Pascale, "Talking about Race: Shifting the Analytical Paradigm," *Qualitative Inquiry* 14, no. 5 (2008): 723–41.

The Explosion of the 2020 Census "Indian" Population and Its Implications for Tribal Policymaking

1. Ancestry.com, *United States Federal Census Schedule*, retrieved July 30, 2023.

2. Ancestry.com.

3. K. Zimmer, "Elizabeth Warren Has a Native American Ancestor. Does That Make Her Native American?" *The New York Times*, October 15, 2018, https://nyti.ms/3GoAqiQ.

4. R. Thornton, *American Indian Holocaust and Survival: A Population History Since 1492* (Norman: University of Oklahoma Press, 1987).

5. While common speech uses "intermarriage," we prefer "exogamy" for denoting childbirth with partners from outside the group (exo-), independent of marital status.

6. K. Eschbach and J. Taylor, "Some Challenges Demography Poses for Native Nation Building," New Horizons *Festschrift* in Honor of Stephen E. Cornell and Joseph P. Kalt, 2022, https://doi.org/10.61235/XVCE4701.

7. C. Sturm, *Becoming Indian: The Struggle over Cherokee Identity in the Twenty-First Century*, first ed. (School for Advanced Research Press, 2011).

8. OMB, "Statistical Directive 15: Revisions to the Standards for the Classification of Federal Data on Race and Ethnicity," *Federal Register* 62, no. 210 (1997): 58782–90.

9. US Census Bureau, "Additional Instructions for Respondents," Census.gov, https://www.census.gov/programs-surveys/decennial-census/technical-documentation/questionnaires/2020/response-guidance.html. Retrieved August 1, 2023.

10. R. Marks and M. Rios-Vargas, "Improvements to the 2020 Census Race and Hispanic Origin Question Designs, Data Processing, and Coding Procedures," August 3, 2021, https://www.census.gov/newsroom/blogs/

random-samplings/2021/08/improvements-to-2020-census-race-hispanic-origin-question-designs.html.

11. US Census Bureau, "Additional Instructions."

12. The Census Bureau tests questions thoroughly before changing the form. Testing showed that the new form used in the 2020 census would likely increase the number of people reporting themselves to be Indian. However, this was not a principal focus of evaluation. Instead, a principal concern was to assess the reliability of responses, that is, the probability that a respondent would answer the same way if asked the exact same question after an interval of time. The Bureau was also concerned to reduce the refusal of subjects to respond to the question, or to reject the race categories listed on the form—longstanding problems, particularly for Middle Eastern and Hispanic respondents. And the interest in these points of evaluation spanned all types of respondents, and not just Indians. The Bureau did note that different question wording and formats did seem to generate different response patterns for Indians but attributed this to small sample sizes of Indians in the different test panels: E. Compton, M. Bentley, S. Ennis, and S. Rastogi, "2010 Census Race and Hispanic Origin Alternative Questionnaire Experiment," US Census Bureau, 2013; K. Mathews, J. Phelan, N. A. Jones, S. Konya, R. Marks, B. M. Pratt, J. Coombs, and M. Bentley, *2015 National Content Test: Race and Ethnicity Analysis Report,* US Census Bureau, 2017.

13. US Census Bureau, "Decennial Census of Population and Housing Questionnaires & Instructions," Census.gov, 2020b, https://www.census .gov/programs-surveys/decennial-census/technical-documentation/ questionnaires.html.

14. For simplicity and consistency, the rest of this report will use the following abbreviations and terms for the following non-overlapping categories:

acronym	lay terms	designation herein
AI/AN	American Indian or Alaska Native	non-Hispanic, single-race AI/AN
H, AI/AN	Hispanic Indian	Hispanic, single-race AI/AN
AI/AN+C	multi-race Indian	non-Hispanic, multi-race AI/AN
H, AI/AN+C	Hispanic multi-race Indian	Hispanic, multi-race AI/AN

15. J. Nagel, *American Indian Ethic Renewal: Red Power and the Resurgence of Identity and Culture* (New York: Oxford University Press, 1997); Sturm, *Becoming Indian.*

16. J. S. Passel, "Provisional Evaluation of the 1970 Census Count of American Indians," *Demography* 13, no. 3 (1976): 397–409, https://doi.org/10.2307/2060536; J. S. Passel, "The Growing American Indian Population, 1960–1990: Beyond Demography," *Population Research and Policy Review* 16 (1997): 11–31.

17. E. C. Henson, M. R. Jorgensen, J. P. Kalt, and I. G. Leonaitis, "Assessing the U.S. Treasury Department's Allocations of Funding for Tribal Governments under the American Rescue Plan Act of 2020" (7; COVID-19 Response and Recovery Policy Briefs, 84), Harvard Project on American Indian Economic Development & Native Nations Institute, 2021, https://ash.harvard.edu/files/ash/files/assessing_the_u.s._treasury_departments_allocations_of_funding_for_tribal_governments.pdf?m=1635972521; US Department of Housing and Urban Development, *IHBG Final Allocation* [dataset], HUD, Public Indian Housing, https://www.hud.gov/sites/dfiles/PIH/documents/FY_2023_Final-Grant_Summary.pdf; Steven Manson, Jonathan Schroeder, David Van Riper, Tracy Kugler, and Steven Ruggles, National Historical Geographic Information System: Version 17.0 (17.0) [dataset], Minneapolis: IPUMS, 2022, https://doi.org/10.18128/D050.V17.0; Thornton, *American Indian Holocaust and Survival.*

18. C. A. Liebler, R. Bhaskar, and S. R. Porter (née Rastogi), "Joining, Leaving, and Staying in the American Indian/Alaska Native Race Category Between 2000 and 2010," *Demography* 53, no. 2 (2016): 507–40. https://doi.org/10.1007/s13524-016-0461-2; C. A. Liebler, S. R. Porter, L. E. Fernandez, J. M. Noon, and S. R. Ennis, "America's Churning Races: Race and Ethnicity Response Changes Between Census 2000 and the 2010 Census," *Demography* 54, no. 1 (2017): 259–84, https://doi.org/10.1007/s13524-016-0544-0.

19. US Department of Housing and Urban Development (HUD), IHBG Final Allocation [dataset], HUD, Public Indian Housing.

20. Native American Housing Assistance and Self-Determination Act, "Revisions to the Indian Housing Block Grant Program Formula Final Rule," *Federal Register* 81, no. 225 (2016): 83674–87.

21. Henson et al, "Assessing the U.S. Treasury Department's Allocations."

22. For example, the errors highlighted in HUD's case by a 2018 Inspector General Report entitled "HUD Did Not Have Adequate Controls to Ensure That Grantees Submitted Accurate Tribal Enrollment Numbers for Program Funding" (T. E. Shultze, Office of the Inspector General, HUD, 2018, https://www.hudoig.gov/sites/default/files/documents/2018-LA-0002.pdf). For an additional review of the issues in and implications of the HUD data, see A. Malinovskaya and E. Moreno, *American Indian Tribal Enrollment: What Can Be Learned from Over 20 Years of Data?* (forthcoming).

23. This is decidedly *not* to conclude any other equivalence between the two populations beyond magnitude.

24. Henson et al, "Assessing the U.S. Treasury Department's Allocations"; HUD, IHBG Final Allocation; US Census Bureau, Decennial Census [dataset], 2000, https://guides.lib.unc.edu/citedata/numeric#:~:text=The%20Census%20Bureau%20suggests%20the,%2Fstatistics%2Fdata%20release%5D; US Census Bureau, Decennial Census [dataset], 2010a, https://guides.lib.unc.edu/citedata/numeric#:~:text=The%20Census%20Bureau%20suggests%20the,%2Fstatistics%2Fdata%20release%5D; US Census Bureau, Decennial Census [dataset], 2020a, https://guides.lib.unc.edu/citedata/numeric#:~:text=The%20Census%20Bureau%20suggests%20the,%2Fstatistics%2Fdata%20release%5D.

25. Manson et al, National Historical Geographic Information System.

26. Manson et al, National Historical Geographic Information System.

27. Eschbach and Taylor, "Some Challenges Demography Poses."

28. S. Ruggles, S. Flood, R. Goeken, M. Schouweiler, and M. Sobek, IPUMS USA: Version 12.0 (12.0) [dataset], Minneapolis, MN: IPUMS, 2022, https://doi.org/10.18128/D010.V12.0.

29. Marks and Rios-Vargas, "Improvements to the 2020 Census Race."

30. Liebler et al, "Joining, Leaving, and Staying"; Liebler et al, "America's Churning Races."

"There's More at Stake Than Just My Love Life!"
Understanding Tribal Enrollment as a Reproductive Justice Issue

1. Pueblo is the Spanish word for "village." The term "Pueblo" can refer to a Native nation, a location, or a person. The nineteen New Mexico Pueblos are each distinct and separate Native nations; the village/reservation/land base each nation occupies is a Pueblo, and Native people who belong to

these communities are Pueblos. To me, Native nations, places, and people are all deserving of the distinction of a proper noun, so I always capitalize the word "Pueblo."

2. Kim TallBear, "The Political Economy of Tribal Citizenship in the US: Lessons for Canadian First Nations?" *Aboriginal Policy Studies* 1, no. 3 (2011).

3. I use the terms "Native" and "Indigenous" to broadly include those peoples with pre-existing sovereignty who were living together as a community prior to contact with settler populations. I specifically use "Native" when discussing communities on the North American continent and "Indigenous" when discussing a more global perspective. "American Indian" is used in the context of US federal policies.

4. P. Wolfe, "Settler Colonialism and the Elimination of the Native," *Journal of Genocide Research* 8, no. 4 (2006): 387–409.

5. A. Parker, "Conclusion: Journey Toward Asserting an Authentic Identity in the Twenty-First Century for American Indian Citizens and Their Tribal Nations," *American Indian Identity: Citizenship, Membership, and Blood*, ed. Se-ah-dom Edmo, Jessie Young, and Alan Parker (Santa Barbara, CA: Praeger, 2016): 154–5.

6. D. Rodriguez-Lonebear, "The Blood Line: Racialized Boundary Making and Citizenship among Native Nations," *Sociology of Race and Ethnicity* 7, no. 4 (2021): 527–42.

7. F. R. Skenandore, "Revisiting *Santa Clara Pueblo v. Martinez*: Feminist Perspectives on Tribal Sovereignty," *Wisconsin Women's Law Journal* 17 (2002): 356–7.

8. B. Klopotek, *Recognition Odysseys: Indigeneity, Race, and Federal Tribal Recognition Policy in Three Louisiana Indian Communities* (Durham, NC: Duke University Press, 2011).

9. E. P. Dozier, *The Pueblo Indians of North America* (Long Grove, IL: Waveland Press, 1970); J. S. Sando, *Pueblo Nations: Eight Centuries of Pueblo Indian History* (Santa Fe, NM: Clear Light Publishers, 1992); G. Valencia-Weber, "Santa Clara Pueblo v. Martinez: Twenty-Five Years of Disparate Cultural Visions: An Essay Introducing the Case for Re-argument before the American Indian Nations Supreme Court," *Kansas Journal of Law & Public Policy* 14, no. 1 (2004); M. Ebright, R. Hendricks, and R. W. Hughes, *Four Square Leagues: Pueblo Indian Land in New Mexico* (Albuquerque: University of New Mexico Press, 2014).

10. Valencia-Weber, "Santa Clara Pueblo v. Martinez."

11. "The Struggle to Belong under Kahnawake Community's 'Marry Out, Get Out' Rule," Canada Broadcasting Company Radio, June 29, 2016, https://www.cbc.ca/radio/outintheopen/pushed-out-1.3965254/ the-struggle-to-belong-under-kahnawake-community-s-marry-out-get-out-rule-1.3654368; "Kahnawake's Controversial 'Marry Out, Get Out' Policy Violates Charter, Judge Rules," Canada Broadcasting Company, May 1, 2018, https://www.cbc.ca/news/canada/montreal/kahnawake-membership-law-charter-1.4642770.

12. B. Theobald, *Reproduction on the Reservation: Pregnancy, Childbirth, and Colonialism in the Long Twentieth Century* (Chapel Hill: University of North Carolina Press Books, 2019).

13. "Benefits" refers to services that are provided to enrolled members of a federally recognized tribe. Some examples of benefits found in some Pueblos include health care through the Indian Health Service, housing support, and per capita payments (monetary payments made to enrolled tribal members from the tribal government based on business profits—often from casinos).

14. L. J. Udel, "Revision and Resistance: The Politics of Native Women's Motherwork," *Frontiers: A Journal of Women Studies* 22, no. 2 (2001): 43–62, https://doi.org/10.2307/3347054.

15. Udel, "Revision and Resistance"; R. Swentzell, "Testimony of a Santa Clara Woman," *Kansas Journal of Law & Public Policy* 14 (2004): 97.

16. L. Ross and R. Solinger, *Reproductive Justice: An Introduction*, vol. 1 (Berkeley: University of California Press, 2017).

17. M. Arvin, E. Tuck, and A. Morrill, "Decolonizing Feminism: Challenging Connections between Settler Colonialism and Heteropatriarchy," *Feminist Formations* (2013): 8–34; M. J. Guerrero, "'Patriarchal Colonialism' and Indigenism: Implications for Native Feminist Spirituality and Native Womanism," *Hypatia* 18, no. 2 (2003), 58–69.

18. Theobald, *Reproduction on the Reservation*.

19. University of Arizona Native Nations Institute, "What Is Native Nation Building?" https://nni.arizona.edu/what-native-nation-building.

20. S. Edmo, "The Problems of Modern Indian Identity: Intersectionality, the American Dream, the Myth of Scarcity, Disenrollment, and Belonging," *American Indian Identity: Citizenship, Membership, and Blood*, ed. Se-ah-dom Edmo, Jessie Young, and Alan Parker (Santa Barbara, CA: Praeger, 2016), 43.

Life at the Intersections:
A Black Oneida Perspective on Blood Quantum and Belonging

1. Circe Sturm, *Becoming Indian: The Struggle over Cherokee Identity in the Twenty-First Century* (Santa Fe, NM: School for Advanced Research Press, 2011).

2. Laurence M. Hauptman, *Seven Generations of Iroquois Leadership: The Six Nations Since 1800* (Syracuse, NY: Syracuse University Press, 2008).

3. Hauptman, *Seven Generations of Iroquois Leadership.*

4. Andrew Jolivétte, *Cultural Representation in Native America* (Lanham, MD: AltaMira Press, 2006).

5. Maria Root, *The Multiracial Experience: Racial Borders as the New Frontier* (Thousand Oaks, CA: Sage Publications, Inc., 1996).

6. Kim TallBear, "Genomic Articulations of Indigeneity," *Social Studies of Science* 43, no. 4 (May 30, 2013): 509–33.

7. Sturm, *Becoming Indian.*

8. Tina Norris, Paula L. Vines, and Elizabeth M. Hoeffel, "The American Indian and Alaska Native Population: 2010 Census Briefs," US Census Bureau, 2012, https://www.census.gov/library/publications/2012/dec/c2010br-10.html.

9. Susan Lobo and Kurt Peters, *American Indians and the Urban Experience* (Walnut Creek, CA: Altamira Press, 2001).

10. Jolivétte, *Cultural Representation in Native America.*

Learning Our Path into the Future

1. J. Archibald, *Indigenous Storywork: Educating the Heart, Mind, Body, and Spirit* (Vancouver: University of British Columbia Press, 2008).

2. K.T. Lomawaima and T. L. McCarty, *To Remain an Indian: Lessons in Democracy from a Century of Native American Education* (New York: Columbia Teachers College, 2006).

3. Lomawaima and McCarty, *To Remain an Indian,* 166.

4. Archibald, *Indigenous Storywork.*

5. L. B. Simpson, *Dancing on Our Turtle's Back: Stories of Nishnaabeg Recreation, Resurgence, and a New Emergence* (Winnipeg, MB: ARP Books, 2011).

6. Simpson, *Dancing on Our Turtle's Back,* 130.

7. Robert Antone, *Yukwalihowanahtu Yukwanosaunee Tsiniyukwaliho:t̂ As*

People of the Longhouse, We Honor Our Way of Life Tekaľhsaľ tsiniyukwaliho:ť Praise Our Way of Life (Buffalo, NY: ProQuest Dissertations Publishing), 2013.

8. Linda Smith, *Decolonizing Methodologies: Research and Indigenous Peoples* (London: Zed Books L.T.D., 2012).

Blood Quantum and the
Auto-Colonization of the Michigan Anishinaabek

1. Basil Johnston, *Ojibway Heritage* (Lincoln, NE: Bison Books, 1976, 1990), 109–18.

2. The histories of the Michigan Anishinaabe tribal nations presented here derive from numerous works: James A. Clifton, *The Pokagons, 1683–1983: Catholic Potawatomi Indians of the St. Joseph River Valley* (Lanham, MD: University Press of America, 1984); Charles E. Cleland, *The Place of the Pike (Gnoozhekaaning): A History of the Bay Mills Indian Community* (Ann Arbor: University of Michigan Regional, 2001); Matthew L.M. Fletcher, *The Eagle Returns: The Legal History of the Grand Traverse Band of Ottawa and Chippewa Indians* (East Lansing: Michigan State University Press, 2011); James M. McClurken, *Gah-Baeh-Jhagwah-Buk: The Way It Happened: A Visual Culture History of the Little Traverse Bay Bands of Odawa* (East Lansing: Michigan State University Museum, 1991); James M. McClurken, *Our People, Our Journey: The Little River Band of Ottawa Indians* (East Lansing: Michigan State University Press, 2009); *Diba Jimooyung—Telling Our Story: A History of the Saginaw Ojibwe Anishinabek*, ed. Charmaine M. Benz (Saginaw Chippewa Indian Tribe of Michigan, 2005).

3. Grand Traverse Band of Ottawa and Chippewa Indians v. Office of the United States Attorney for the Western District of Michigan, 369 F.3d 960, 962 (6th Cir. 2004): "In 1872, then-Secretary of the Interior, Columbus Delano, improperly severed the government-to-government relationship between the Band and the United States, ceasing to treat the Band as a federally recognized tribe. This occurred because the Secretary had misread the 1855 Treaty of Detroit, [11 Stat. 621]."

4. Bay Mills Indian Community Const. Art. III, § 2.

5. Grand Traverse Band of Ottawa and Chippewa Indians Const. Art. II, § 2(b)(2)(A).

6. Grand Traverse Band of Ottawa and Chippewa Indians Const. Art. II, § 3(a).

7. Grand Traverse Band of Ottawa and Chippewa Indians Const. Art. II, § 1(a)(2).

8. Hannahville Indian Community Const. Art. III, § 2(c).

9. Hannahville Indian Community Const. Art. III, § 2(a).

10. Hannahville Indian Community Const. Art. III, § 2(b).

11. Hannahville Indian Community Const. Art. III, § 3.

12. Keweenaw Bay Indian Community Const. Art. II, § 1(c).

13. Keweenaw Bay Indian Community Const. Art. II, § 1(b).

14. Keweenaw Bay Indian Community Const. Art. II, § 1(d).

15. Keweenaw Bay Indian Community Const. Art. II, § 3.

16. For example, Cash Martinez, "'It's Cultural Genocide': Native Americans Shine a Light on the Epidemic of Disenrollment," *El Tecolate*, April 6, 2023, https://eltecolote.org/content/en/its-cultural-genocide-native-americans-shine-a-light-on-the-epidemic-of-disenrollment/.

17. Little River Band of Ottawa Indians Const. Art. II, § 2.

18. Little River Band of Ottawa Indians Const. Art. II, § 1.

19. Little Traverse Bay Bands of Odawa Indians Const. Art. V, § A(3)(a).

20. Saginaw Chippewa Indian Tribe Const. Art. III, §§ 1(a)-(c).

21. Saginaw Chippewa Indian Tribe Const. Art. III, § 1(d).

22. Saginaw Chippewa Indian Tribe Const. Art. III, § 2.

23. Saginaw Chippewa Indian Tribe Const. Art. III, § 3(b).

24. For example, Snowden v. Saginaw Chippewa Indian Tribe, 32 Indian L. Rep. 6047 (Saginaw Chippewa Indian Tribe App. Ct. 2005); Gardner v. Cantu, No. 08-CA-1027 (Saginaw Chippewa Tribe App. Ct. 2008) (on file with author); Graverette v. Saginaw Chippewa Indian Tribe, Nos. 09-CA-1040, 09-CA-1041 (Saginaw Chippewa App. Ct. 2010), https://turtletalk.files.wordpress.com/2010/09/ayling-v-tribal-certifiers.pdf; Kequom v. Atwell, No. 12-CA-1051 (Saginaw Chippewa App. Ct. 2013) (on file with author); Alberts v. Saginaw Chippewa Indian Tribe of Michigan, No. 13-CA-1058 (Saginaw Chippewa Indian Tribe 2015) (on file with author).

25. 25 U.S.C. §§ 5123(a), (d).

26. 25 U.S.C. § 5123(d)(1).

27. 25 U.S.C. § 5123(a).

28. Snowden v. Saginaw Chippewa Indian Tribe, 6048.

29. Snowden v. Saginaw Chippewa Indian Tribe, 6048.

30. Snowden v. Saginaw Chippewa Indian Tribe, 6048.

31. Snowden v. Saginaw Chippewa Indian Tribe, 6049.

32. Cavazos v. Haaland, 579 F. Supp. 3d 141, 146 (D.D.C. 2022).

33. Cavazos v. Haaland, 146–7.

34. Cavazos v. Haaland, 146–7.

35. To Provide for the Use and Distribution of Funds Awarded to the Saginaw Chippewa Tribe of Michigan, Hearing before the Senate Committee on Indian Affairs, 99th Cong., 1st Sess. 34 (July 10, 1985) (Statement of Alvin Chamberlain).

36. Cavazos v. Haaland, 147.

37. Cavazos v. Haaland, 148.

38. Cavazos v. Haaland, 146.

39. Grand Traverse Band of Ottawa and Chippewa Indians v. Office of the United States Attorney for the Western District of Michigan, 198 F. Supp. 2d 920, 924 (W.D. Mich. 2002), aff'd, 369 F.3d 960 (6th Cir. 2004).

40. 45 Fed. Reg. 18322 (March 25, 1980).

41. Letter from Deputy Assistant Secretary, Indian Affairs (Operations), to Joseph C. Raphael, Chairman Grand Traverse Band of Ottawa and Chippewa Indians (November 4, 1983) (on file with author).

42. Letter from Acting Deputy Assistant Secretary, Indian Affairs, to Joseph Raphael, Chairman Grand Traverse Band of Ottawa and Chippewa Indians (March 18, 1985) (on file with author); Letter from Scott Keep, Assistant Solicitor, Tribal Government & Alaska Branch, to William Rastetter (July 2, 1985) (on file with author).

43. Grand Traverse Band of Ottawa and Chippewa Indians v. Bureau of Indian Affairs.

44. In re: Menefee, 2004 WL 5714978, at *5 (Grand Traverse Band Tribal Court 2004). Disclosure: the author served as GTB's counsel in this matter.

45. In re: Menefee, 2004 WL 5714978.

46. No. 2013-16-AP (Grand Traverse Band App. Ct. 2014), https://turtletalk.files. wordpress.com/2013/05/cholewka-v-gtb-tribal-council.pdf. Disclosure: the author served as an appellate judge and lead author of the opinion in this matter.

47. Cholekwa v. Grand Traverse Band of Ottawa and Chippewa Indians, No. 2019-31-AP (Grand Traverse Band App. Ct. 2020), https://turtletalk.files .wordpress.com/2021/06/ance-berry-v-gtb.pdf. Disclosure: the author served as appellate judge and wrote the opinion in this matter.

48. Cholekwa v. Grand Traverse Band, 3.

49. Cholekwa v. Grand Traverse Band, 4.

50. Cholekwa v. Grand Traverse Band, 4.

51. Cholekwa v. Grand Traverse Band, 4.

52. Cholekwa v. Grand Traverse Band, 5.

53. Cholewka v. Grand Traverse Band, 8 Am. Tribal Law 174, 181 (Grand Traverse Band Trial Ct., 2009).

54. Kekek Jason Stark, "Anishinaabe Inaakonigewin: Principles for the Intergenerational Preservation of Mino-Bimaadiziwin," *Montana Law Review* 82, no. 2 (Spring 2021): 293, 303, 305.

55. Karen Lynn Alexander, "Exploring the Use of Cultural Values in the Evaluation of Programs of Native American Tribes," 2023, 145–8 (PhD dissertation, on file with author). Keep in mind that many Anishinaabe people understand that these seven teachings are balanced out by equal and opposite negative teachings, though we will leave these understandings for another day.

56. Stark, "Anishinaabe Inaakonigewin," 306–7.

57. Leanne Betasamosake Simpson, "Land as Pedagogy: Nishnaabeg Intelligence and Rebellious Transformation," *Decolonization: Indigeneity, Education, and Society* 3, no. 3 (2014): 1, 12.

58. Edward Benton-Benai, *The Mishomis Book: The Voice of the Ojibwe* (Minneapolis: University of Minnesota Press, 1988).

59. Stark, "Anishinaabe Inaakonigewin," 309–10.

60. Benton-Benai, *The Mishomis Book.*

61. Stark, "Anishinaabe Inaakonigewin," 312–3.

62. Alexander, "Exploring the Use of Cultural Values," 146.

63. Stark, "Anishinaabe Inaakonigewin," 313–4.

64. Benton-Benai, *The Mishomis Book.*

65 Stark, "Anishinaabe Inaakonigewin," 314–5.

66. Alexander, "Exploring the Use of Cultural Values," 147.

67. Stark, "Anishinaabe Inaakonigewin," 316.

68. Stark, "Anishinaabe Inaakonigewin," 316.

69. Stark, "Anishinaabe Inaakonigewin," 316.

70. Stark, "Anishinaabe Inaakonigewin," 317–8.

71. Benton-Benai, *The Mishomis Book.*

72. Heidi Bohaker, *Doodem and Council Fire: Anishinaabe Governance through Alliance* (Toronto, ON: University of Toronto Press, 2020), 57.

73. See generally Valerie Lambert, *Native Agency: Indians in the Bureau of Indian Affairs* (St. Paul: Minnesota Historical Society Press, 2022), 24–26 discussing the white men who pushed for tribal self-determination in the 1930s).

74. See generally Clifton, *The Pokagons*. Disclosure: the author is a descendant of Pokagon.

75. GTB Const. Art. II, § 2(b)(2)(A).

76. In re: Menefee, 2004 WL 5714978.

77. In re: Menefee, 2004 WL 5714978, at *6-7.

78. In re: Menefee, 2004 WL 5714978, at *3-6.

79. One wonders if a Pokagon descendant from the Grand Traverse area would be able to enroll at Pokagon Potawatomi, but that's a question for another day.

80. See Santa Clara Pueblo v. Martinez, 436 U.S. 49, 72 n. 32 (1978); Restatement of the Law of American Indians § 18.

81. Memorandum from Acting Deputy Commissioner of Indian Affairs to Assistant Secretary of the Department of the Interior at 2-3 (October 3, 1979) (on file with author).

82. Wright v. Nottawaseppi Huron Band of the Potawatomi, No. 21-154-APP (Nottawaseppi Huron Band of the Potawatomi S. Ct. 2022), https://nhbp-nsn.gov/wp-content/uploads/2022/06/2022-6-3-Filed-NHBP-Supreme-Court-Opinion-Order-in-Wright-et-al-v-NHBP-et-al-21-154-APP.pdf. Disclosure: the author served as appellate judge and wrote the opinion in this matter.

83. Nottawaseppi Huron Band of the Potawatomi Const. Art. III, § 1(a)(3).

84. Wright v. Nottawaseppi Huron Band, 14 (quoting Mark F. Ruml, "The Indigenous Knowledge Documentation Project—Morrison Sessions: Gagige Inaakonige, The Eternal Natural Laws," *Religious Studies and Theology* 30, no. 2 (2011): 155, 164.

85. Wright v. Nottawaseppi Huron Band, 12–13 (citing NHBP Const. Art. X, § 1(a)).

86. Wright v. Nottawaseppi Huron Band, 12 (citing NHBP Const. Art. X, § 2(a)).

87. Wright v. Nottawaseppi Huron Band, 17–18 (quoting Stark, "Anishinaabe Inaakonigewin," 312, 314).

88. NHBP Const. Art. III, § 2(b).

Path Forward: Indigenous Place In-Community

1. Daniela Dueck, "The Geographical Narrative of Strabo Amasia," in *Geography and Ethnography: Perceptions of the World in Pre-Modern Societies* (Newark, UK: John Wiley & Sons, 2010), http://ebookcentral.proquest.com/lib/uwgb/detail.action?docID=477863.

2. Kurt A. Raaflaub and Richard J. A. Talbert, *Geography and Ethnography: Perceptions of the World in Pre-Modern Societies* (Newark, UK: John Wiley & Sons, 2009).

3. Soren C. Larsen and Jay T. Johnson, *Being Together in Place: Indigenous Coexistence in a More Than Human World*, first ed. (University of Minnesota Press, 2017).

4. Ron Johnston and James D. Sidaway, *Geography and Geographers: Anglo-American Human Geography since 1945* (Oxfordshire, UK: Routledge, 2015), https://doi.org/10.4324/9780203523056.

5. Bernard Nietschmann, "Defending the Miskito Reefs with Maps and GPS: Mapping with Sail, Scuba, and Satellite," *Cultural Survival Quarterly* 18, no. 4 (1995).

6. Katherine Ellinghaus, "Introduction: The Discourse of Blood in the Assimilation Period," in *Blood Will Tell: Native Americans and Assimilation Policy* (Lincoln: University of Nebraska Press, 2017), xi–xxxii, https://doi.org/10.2307/j.ctt1qv5ptw.4; Stephen Mayeaux, "Limpieza de Sangre: Legal Applications of the Spanish Doctrine of 'Blood Purity,'" In Custodia Legis webpage, The Library of Congress, September 10, 2021, blogs.loc.gov/law/2021/09/limpieza-de-sangre-legal-applications-of-the-spanish-doctrine-of-blood-purity.

7. Rebecca M. Webster, "This Land Can Sustain Us: Cooperative Land Use Planning on the Oneida Reservation," *Planning Theory & Practice* 17, no. 1 (February 10, 2016), https://www.tandfonline.com/doi/abs/10.1080/14649357.2015.1135250.

8. Ellinghaus, "Introduction."

9. Webster, "This Land Can Sustain Us."

10. Nietschmann, "Defending the Miskito Reefs with Maps and GPS."

11. Glen Coulthard, "Place against Empire: Understanding Indigenous Anti-Colonialism," *Affinities: A Journal of Radical Theory, Culture, and Action* 4, no. 2 (Fall 2010): 79–83.

12. Coulthard, "Place against Empire."

13. Vine Deloria and Daniel Wildcat, *Power and Place: Indian Education in America* (Lakewood, CO: Fulcrum Publishing, 2001).

14. Deloria and Wildcat, *Power and Place*.

15. Jay T. Johnson, "Place-Based Learning and Knowing: Critical Pedagogies Grounded in Indigeneity," *GeoJournal* 77, no. 6 (December 1, 2012): 829–36, https://doi.org/10.1007/s10708-010-9379-1.

16. Jay T. Johnson and Soren C. Larsen, *Deeper Sense of Place: Stories and Journeys of Indigenous-Academic Collaboration* (Corvallis: Oregon State University Press, 2013), http://ebookcentral.proquest.com/lib/ku/detail.action?docID=3384221.

17. The term "in-community" is used here to include all who grew up in an Indigenous community. It is meant to be inclusive, as communities are made up of many backgrounds, religions, languages, privileges, and so on. It is used to celebrate the differences by acknowledging our communal identities.

18. Larsen and Johnson, *Being Together in Place*.

19. Gregory Cajete, *Look to the Mountain: An Ecology of Indigenous Education*, 1st ed. (Durango, CO: Kivakí Press, 1994).

20. Cajete, *Look to the Mountain*.

21. Anonymous, personal communication, December 12, 2023. Community member chose to remain anonymous.

22. See L. Stevens and B. Yellowbird-Stevens, "Operations Management Roles and Responsibilities: Providing a Space for Haudenosaunee Decision-Making," *Tribal Administration Handbook: A Guide for Native Nations in the United States*, ed. Joseph Bauerkemper and Rebecca M. Webster (East Lansing: Michigan State University Press, 2022), muse.jhu.edu/book/100882.

23. See Jessica Kolopenuk, "The Pretendian Problem," *Canadian Journal of Political Science* 56, no. 2 (June 2023): 468–73, https://doi.org/10.1017/S0008423923000239.

24. Rather than call out, the term "call-in" is used to encourage positive community engagement that involves conversation, compassion, and context. See Jessica Bennett, "What If Instead of Calling People Out, We Called Them In?" *New York Times*, November 19, 2020, https://www.nytimes.com/2020/11/19/style/loretta-ross-smith-college-cancel-culture.html; see also "Call Out & Call In Racism," *Creative Equity Toolkit*, accessed January 25,

2024. https://creativeequitytoolkit.org/topic/anti-racism/call-out-call-in-racism/.

25. Robert Antone, "Yukwalihowanahtu Yukwanosaunee Tsiniyukwaliho:T^ As People of the Longhouse, We Honor Our Way of Life Tekal^hsal^ Tsiniyukwaliho:T^ Praise Our Way of Life," ProQuest, 2013, https://www.proquest.com/openview/8af104b852eb1a8a6d2de286679c6e5f/1.pdf?pq-origsite=gscholar&cbl=18750.

26. Duane Blue Spruce, Tanya Thrasher, and National Museum of the American Indian, *The Land Has Memory: Indigenous Knowledge, Native Landscapes, and the National Museum of the American Indian*, 1st ed., ed. Duane Blue Spruce and Tanya Thrasher (Chapel Hill: University of North Carolina Press in association with the National Museum of the American Indian, Smithsonian Institution, 2008).

27. Nietschmann, "Defending the Miskito Reefs with Maps and GPS." Refer back to Nietschmann's ideas of using maps to retell our stories and honor connections to land as we make our own maps.

Aanikoobijigan: Intergenerational Connections as the Foundation of Contemporary Citizenship Requirements

1. After the passage of the Indian Reorganization Act (IRA) in 1934, six Anishinaabe reservations/bands/nations in Minnesota (White Earth, Leech Lake, Grand Portage, Fond du Lac, Bois Forte, and Mille Lacs) joined together to create the Minnesota Chippewa Tribe (MCT) in 1936. *Constitution and By-Laws of the Minnesota Chippewa Tribe*, Minnesota Chippewa Tribe, official website, accessed May 30, 2023, https://www.mnchippewatribe.org/constitution.html.

2. Jill Doerfler, *Those Who Belong: Identity, Family, Blood, and Citizenship among the White Earth Anishinaabeg* (East Lansing: Michigan State University Press, 2015).

3. Anton Treuer, *Ojibwe in Minnesota*, The People of Minnesota series (St. Paul: Minnesota Historical Society Press, 2010), 5.

4. Brenda J. Child, *Holding Our World Together: Ojibwe Women and the Survival of Community* (New York: Viking Penguin, 2012), xvi.

5. For additional information and analysis on the number of American Indian nations in the United States that continue to use blood quantum as a requirement for citizenship, see Desi Rodriguez-Lonebear, "The

Blood Line: Racialized Boundary Making and Citizenship among Native Nations," *Sociology of Race and Ethnicity* 7, no. 4 (2021): 527–42.

6. Leanne Simpson, *Dancing on Our Turtle's Back: Stories of Nishinaabeg Re-Creation, Resurgence and a New Emergence* (Winnipeg, MB: Arbeiter Ring Publishing, 2010), 145.

7. David Wilkins, "Self-Determination or Self-Decimation? Banishment and Disenrollment in Indian Country," *Indian Country Today*, August 31, 2006, updated September 12, 2018, accessed June 9, 2023, https://ictnews.org/archive/self-determination-or-self-decimation-banishment-and-disen-rollment-in-indian-country.

8. Basil Johnston, *The Manitous: The Spiritual World of the Ojibway* (St. Paul: Minnesota Historical Society Press, 2001), xix.

9. James Vukelich Kaagegaabaw website, accessed May 29, 2023, https://www.jamesvukelich.com/.

10. *The Ojibwe People's Dictionary*, https://ojibwe.lib.umn.edu.

11. *Ojibwe People's Dictionary*.

12. *Ojibwe People's Dictionary*.

13. *Ojibwe People's Dictionary*.

14. *Ojibwe People's Dictionary*.

15. *Ojibwe People's Dictionary*.

16. For an excellent history of the Ojibwe bandolier bag, see Marcia G. Anderson, *A Bag Worth a Pony: The Art of the Ojibwe Bandolier Bag* (St. Paul: Minnesota Historical Society Press, 2017).

17. "The Indian Industrial School at Genoa was the fourth largest non-reservation boarding school established by the United States Office of Indian Affairs. The village of Genoa, Nebraska was selected because the U.S. federal government already owned the former Pawnee Reservation property there. The facility opened on February 20, 1884, and, like other federal Indian boarding schools, its mission was to educate Native American children in order to assimilate them into American society. The students that came to the Genoa Indian School were from more than ten states and over 40 different tribal nations. In time, the school grew from the original 74 students to an enrollment of 599 in a single year and encompassed over 30 buildings on 640 acres. The school was in operation from 1884 through 1934." Genoa US Indian School Foundation Museum, accessed May 29, 2023, https://genoaindianschoolmuseum.org/.

18. Scott Richard Lyons, *X-Marks: Native Signatures of Assent* (Minneapolis: University of Minnesota Press, 2010), 56.

19. Eva Marie Garroutte, *Real Indians: Identity and the Survival of Native America* (Berkley: University of California Press, 2003), 42.

20. Doerfler, *Those Who Belong*, 1–30.

21. David Beaulieu, "Curly Hair and Big Feet: Physical Anthropology and the Implementation of Land Allotment on the White Earth Chippewa Reservation," *American Indian Quarterly* 8, no. 4 (Autumn 1984): 282.

22. As noted by the author, more analysis is needed, but her initial research results showed that "Native nations with gaming operations are more likely to use blood quantum than Native nations without gambling." Rodriguez-Lonebear, "The Blood Line," 538. Also see Gabriel S. Galanda and Ryan D. Dreveskracht, "Curing the Tribal Disenrollment Epidemic: In Search of a Remedy," *Arizona Law Review* 57, no. 2: 383–474, and David E. Wilkins and Shelly Hulse Wilkins, *Dismembered: Native Disenrollment and the Battle for Human Rights* (Seattle: University of Washington Press, 2017).

23. The resolution passed unanimously among the Tribal Executive Committee and thirty-five to twelve among the Tribal Delegates. Resolution No. IV, Rules Governing the Qualifications for Enrollment in the Minnesota Chippewa Tribe, July 26, 1941, NARA-DC, RG 75, CCF, Consolidated Chippewa, File 32610-1941, 053.

24. F. J. Scott to Commissioner of Indian Affairs, August 5, 1941, NARA-DC, RG 75, CCF, Consolidated Chippewa, File 32610-1941, 053.

25. Oscar L. Chapman to Ed. M. Wilson, December 23, 1942, NARA-DC, RG 75, CCF, Consolidated Chippewa, File 32610-1941, 053.

26. Doerfler, *Those Who Belong*, 41–54.

Contributors

Kenzie Allen

Kenzie Allen is a poet and multimodal artist, and she is a first-generation descendant of the Oneida Nation of Wisconsin. The author of *Cloud Missives* (Tin House, 2024), Allen has been awarded the James Welch Prize for Indigenous Poets, a 92NY Discovery Prize, the 49th Parallel Award in Poetry, and fellowships from Vermont Studio Center, Aspen Words, Hedgebrook, and In-Na-Po (Indigenous Nation Poets). Her poetry can be found in *Poetry Magazine, Narrative, The Iowa Review, Boston Review, Best New Poets*, and other venues.

Marena Bridges

Marena Bridges is an adjunct instructor and ABD doctoral candidate in Leadership and Change at Antioch University. Her research delves into the intricate world of Oneida mourning rituals, matriarchal structures, and the layers of intergenerational trauma. With a unique perspective as a Black Oneida woman transitioning as a child from city life to reservation living, Bridges's work shines a light on the nuanced debates around community membership and challenges traditional notions of identity beyond blood quantum. Her scholarship has been recognized with accolades such as the Toni A. Gregory Conference Award for Interdisciplinary Scholarship and the Graduate College Dean's Fellowship. When not immersed in academia, Bridges finds joy in beading, exploring YouTube, caring for her dog, and supporting her older brother as a full-time caregiver.

John Danforth

John Danforth has worked for the Oneida Nation since 2017 and currently serves as the interim Director of the Trust Enrollment Department. Danforth completed an associate of applied business degree from the Golf Academy of America–San Diego, a bachelor of business administration degree from University of Wisconsin–Green Bay, and a master of business administration degree from St. Norbert College. Along with his wife,

Catrina, the Danforths own and operate a small business in Oneida, Hidden Valley Driving Range. Together, Danforth, Catrina, two daughters Nyah and Vera, and a son, Tyolahkwisu, are enrolled members of the Oneida Nation residing on the Oneida Nation Reservation.

Philip J. Deloria

Philip J. Deloria (Dakota descendant) is the Leverett Saltonstall Professor of History at Harvard University, where his research and teaching focus on the social, cultural, and political histories of the relations among American Indian peoples and the United States. He is the author of several books, including *Playing Indian* (Yale University Press, 1998), *Indians in Unexpected Places* (University Press of Kansas, 2004), *American Studies: A User's Guide* (University of California Press, 2017) with Alexander Olson, and *Becoming Mary Sully: Toward an American Indian Abstract* (University of Washington Press, 2019), and has co-edited two books and numerous articles and chapters. Deloria received a PhD in American Studies from Yale University in 1994, taught at the University of Colorado, and then, from 2001 to 2017, taught at the University of Michigan before joining the faculty at Harvard in January 2018. Deloria was a long-serving trustee of the Smithsonian Institution's National Museum of the American Indian. He is former president of the American Studies Association, the Organization of American Historians, and the Society for American History; an elected member of the American Philosophical Society and the American Academy of Arts and Sciences; and the recipient of numerous prizes and recognitions.

Jill Doerfler

Dr. Jill Doerfler grew up on the White Earth Reservation in northern Minnesota and is the daughter of an enrollee of the White Earth Nation. She is a professor and department head of American Indian Studies at the University of Minnesota Duluth. She has lectured and published widely on the topics of citizenship, blood quantum, and constitutional reform. Her book *Those Who Belong: Identity, Family, Blood, and Citizenship among the White Earth Anishinaabeg* (Michigan State University Press, 2015), examines staunch Anishinaabe resistance to racialization and the complex issues surrounding tribal citizenship and identity. She co-authored *The White Earth Nation: Ratification of a Native Democratic Constitution* (University of Nebraska Press, 2012) with Gerald Vizenor and co-edited *Centering Anishinaabeg Studies: Understanding the World Through Stories*

(Michigan State University Press, 2013) with Niigaanwewidam James Sinclair and Heidi Kiiwetinepinesiik Stark.

Richard G. Elm-Hill Jr.

Richard "Lotni" Elm-Hill is an enrolled member of the Oneida Nation of Wisconsin. Lotni is the author of *Bellingham: The City of Some Dude's Excitement* and has been featured in *Yukhika-latuhse Wisconsin's Indigenous People's Voice in Arts and Culture*. He was awarded an Oneida Fellowship Award in 2019 from the Oneida Nation Arts Program and the Wisconsin Arts Board. For nearly a decade, he studied poetry and story at the Great Mother and New Father Conference. He earned a master of science in Applied Leadership for Teaching & Learning from the University of Wisconsin–Green Bay and is an Associate Director at First Nations Development Institute. He is also the co-founder of Three Track Mind and Storywell, and a member of Ohe·láku (Among the Cornstalks).

Karl Eschbach

Karl Eschbach is an adjunct professor in the School of Public and Population Health at the University of Texas Medical Branch (UTMB) in Galveston, Texas. A demographer and sociologist, his research has focused especially on understanding the mechanisms producing economic and health disparities among racial and ethnic populations, with particular focus on Indigenous peoples and persons of Mexican birth or descendancy in the United States. Dr. Eschbach has been a professor at the University of Houston and the University of Texas-San Antonio and was a Senior Fellow at the Sealy Center on Aging at UTMB. He served a term as the State Demographer of Texas, with the responsibility to produce estimates and projections for the state, and to advise members of the legislative and executive branches of state government about the impacts of population trends on service needs and resources. He has published in leading academic journals including *Demography, American Journal of Epidemiology, Archives of Internal Medicine*, and *American Journal of Public Health*.

Matthew L.M. Fletcher

Matthew L.M. Fletcher, '97, is the Harry Burns Hutchins Collegiate Professor of Law at Michigan Law. He sits as the chief justice of the Pokagon Band of Potawatomi Indians, the Poarch Band of Creek Indians, and the Grand Traverse Band of Ottawa and Chippewa Indians. Fletcher also sits as an appellate judge for the Cabazon Band of Mission Indians, the Colorado River Indian Tribes, the Hoopa Valley Tribe, the Lower Elwha Klallam Tribe, the Mashpee Wampanoag Tribe, the Match-E-Be-Nash-She-Wish Band of Pottawatomi Indians, the Nottawaseppi Huron Band of Potawatomi Indians, the Rincon Band of Luiseño Indians, the Santee Sioux Tribe of Nebraska, and the Tulalip Tribes. He is a member of the Grand Traverse Band.

He previously taught at Michigan State University College of Law and the University of North Dakota School of Law. He has been a visiting professor at the law schools at the University of Arizona; the University of California, Hastings; the University of Michigan; the University of Montana; and Stanford University. He is a frequent instructor at the Pre-Law Summer Institute for American Indian students.

He was lead reporter for the American Law Institute's *Restatement of the Law of American Indians*. He has published articles in the *California Law Review, Michigan Law Review, Northwestern University Law Review*, and many others. His hornbook, *Federal Indian Law* (West Academic Publishing), was published in 2016 and his concise hornbook, *Principles of Federal Indian Law* (West Academic Publishing), in 2017. Fletcher co-authored the sixth and seventh editions of *Cases and Materials on Federal Indian Law* (West Academic Publishing, 2011 and 2017) and both editions of *American Indian Tribal Law* (Aspen, 2011 and 2020), the only casebook for law students on tribal law. He also authored *Ghost Road: Anishinaabe Responses to Indian-Hating* (Fulcrum Publishing, 2020); *The Eagle Returns: The Legal History of the Grand Traverse Band of Ottawa and Chippewa Indians* (Michigan State University Press, 2012); and *American Indian Education: Counternarratives in Racism, Struggle, and the Law* (Routledge, 2008). He co-edited *The Indian Civil Rights Act at Forty* with Kristen A. Carpenter and Angela R. Riley (UCLA American Indian Studies Press, 2012) and *Facing the Future: The Indian Child Welfare Act at 30* with Wenona T. Singel and Kathryn E. Fort (Michigan State University Press, 2009).

Fletcher worked as a staff attorney for four Indian Tribes: the Pascua Yaqui Tribe, the Hoopa Valley Tribe, the Suquamish Tribe, and the Grand Traverse Band. He previously sat on the judiciaries of the Lac du Flambeau Band of Lake Superior Chippewa Indians, the Little River Band of Ottawa Indians, and the Turtle Mountain Band of Chippewa Indians; he also served as a consultant to the Seneca Nation of Indians Court of Appeals.

He is married to Wenona Singel, a member of the Little Traverse Bay Bands of Odawa Indians, and they have two sons, Owen and Emmett.

Gabriel S. Galanda

Gabriel S. Galanda is an Indigenous human rights attorney and the managing lawyer at Galanda Broadman, PLLC, an Indigenous rights firm in Seattle, Washington. Galanda sues federal, state, local, and tribal government actors and others who violate Indigenous human rights.

Galanda has been named to *Best Lawyers in America* from 2007 to 2024 and dubbed a Super Lawyer by his peers from 2013 to 2024. The American Bar Association awarded him the Spirit of Excellence Award in 2022 and named him a Difference Maker in 2012. The Washington State Bar Association honored Galanda with the Excellence in Diversity Award for his "significant contribution to diversity in the legal profession" in 2014. For his staunch advocacy against tribal disenrollment practices, the University of Arizona College of Law awarded him the Professional Achievement Award, and Western Washington University named him a Distinguished Alumnus in 2018. The University of Arizona College of Law named Galanda its 2022–2023 Alumnus of the Year. He has also received the Native Justice Award from the Northwest Indian Bar Association.

Among Galanda's many scholarly writings on Indigenous rights issues, he published "Curing the Disenrollment Epidemic: In Search of a Remedy" in *Arizona Law Review* in 2015, and "In the Spirit of Vine Deloria, Jr.: Indigenous Kinship Renewal and Relational Sovereignty" in the book *Of Living Stone: Perspectives on Continuous Knowledge and the Work of Vine Deloria, Jr.* in 2024. He has also lectured on those issues at Harvard, Yale, Cornell, University of California Berkeley and Irvine, and Arizona law schools and has testified before the United Nations Office of the High Commissioner on Human Rights in Geneva, Switzerland.

Galanda belongs to the Round Valley Indian Tribes of California, descending from the Nomlaki and Concow Peoples.

Jim Gray

James (Jim) Roan Gray is the former principal Chief of the Osage Nation (2002–2010). He was the youngest chief in the history of the Osage Nation. During his term, Chief Gray led the Osage Nation through a comprehensive restoration of Osage sovereignty—the right to determine their own citizens and form their own government. This led to enrollment of thousands of Osages who had been left off the rolls for nearly one hundred years and a referendum vote that adopted a constitutional form of government for the first time in generations. This effort gave all Osages over age eighteen the right to vote in tribal elections.

Before his term in office, Gray was the publisher of the *Native American Times* based in Oklahoma, covering statewide and national issues facing Indian country in business, arts, culture, music, entertainment, politics, and legal affairs.

After his terms in office, Gray was a tribal administrator for the Cherokee Nation, Sac and Fox Nation, and Pawnee Nation. He also served as executive director of the Native American Contractors Association. In more recent years, he has been a consultant working in Indian Country on energy, government reform, and government relations. Today, as a direct descendent of one of the victims, he has been a sought-out spokesman on the topic of the Osage murders that occurred during the 1920s, made into a major Hollywood motion picture *Killers of the Flower Moon*.

Today, he resides in Skiatook, on the Osage Reservation in Oklahoma, with his wife, Olivia, and their children, Mary, Henry, Sarah, Olivia, James, Naomi, and Nettie. He also enjoys time with his four grandchildren, Bravery, Mina, Essabelle, and Honor.

Laurence M. Hauptman

Laurence M. Hauptman is the SUNY Distinguished Professor Emeritus of History at State University of New York at New Paltz, where he taught courses on Native American history, New York history, and Civil War history for forty years. He is the author, co-author, or co-editor of numerous books and articles on Native American history. In addition, he has been a frequent contributor of articles to *New York Archives* magazine published by the New York State Department of Education and *American Indian*, the magazine for the general reader published by the Smithsonian's National Museum of the American Indian. Over the past four decades, Hauptman has been honored for his research and writings by the New York State Board of Regents, the Pennsylvania Historical Association, the Wisconsin Historical Society, the New York State Historical Association, and the New York Academy of History. On October 25, 2011, Dr. John B. King Jr., then New York State Commissioner of Education, who later became the United States Commissioner of Education, awarded Hauptman the State Archives Lifetime Achievement Award for his research and publications on the Empire State.

Hauptman has testified as an expert witness before committees of both houses of Congress and in the federal courts and has served as a historical consultant for the Oneida Nation of Wisconsin, the Cayuga, the Mashantucket Pequot, and the Seneca. In 1987 and again in 1998, he was the recipient of the Peter Doctor Memorial Indian Scholarship Foundation Award from the Six Nations for his writings and applied work on behalf of Native Americans in eastern North America. On August 10–11, 2012, Dr. Hauptman was honored by the Seneca Nation of Indians who bestowed on him the name Haiwadogêsta', meaning "interpreter" or "he straightens or explains the words."

Joy Harjo

Joy Harjo is an internationally renowned poet, performer, and writer of the Muscogee (Creek) Nation. She served three terms as the twenty-third Poet Laureate of the United States, was the Board of Directors Chair of the Native Arts & Cultures Foundation, and is a Chancellor of the Academy of American Poets. Harjo is the author of ten books of poetry, several plays, prose collections, children's books, and two memoirs; she has also produced seven award-winning music albums and edited several anthologies. Her many honors include Yale's 2023 Bollingen Prize for American Poetry, the National Book Critics Circle Ivan Sandrof Lifetime Achievement Award, the Ruth Lilly Poetry Prize for Lifetime Achievement from the Poetry Foundation, the Academy of American Poets Wallace Stevens Award, and a Guggenheim Fellowship. She lives in Tulsa, Oklahoma, where she is the inaugural Artist-in-Residence for the Bob Dylan Center.

Suzan Shown Harjo

Suzan Shown Harjo is an enrolled Cheyenne citizen of the Cheyenne and Arapaho Tribes, and is Hotvlkvlke Mvskokvlke, Nuyakv. She is founding president of The Morning Star Institute (1984–), which is dedicated to Native cultural and traditional rights, research, and stereotype-busting. A founding trustee of the National Museum of the American Indian—Smithsonian (NMAI), her coalition work that began in 1967 led to NMAI, repatriation laws, and nationwide museum reforms, and she edited and curated NMAI's award-winning book and exhibition on treaties (2014–2027), *Nation to Nation*.

In awarding her a 2014 Presidential Medal of Freedom, the United States's highest civilian honor, President Barack Obama called her "one of the most effective advocates for Native American rights," saying she has "fought all her life for human, civil, and treaty rights of Native peoples. . . . With bold resolve, Suzan Shown Harjo pushes us to always seek justice in our time."

In 2023, Princeton University awarded Harjo an honorary doctorate in humane letters, with this citation: "A tireless advocate at the center of almost every Native American legislative, legal, and cultural issue, her work has led to the protection of rights, cultures, and sacred places, and the return of more than one million acres of Indigenous lands. She is an activist, poet, journalist, curator, playwright, and more—and the force behind the decades-long effort to remove sports team names and mascots that promote stereotypes of Native Peoples from high schools to the National Football League."

After a career in New York City in broadcasting, arts and letters, and Native rights work, she began work in Washington, DC, as the news director at the American Indian Press Association. Her columns, poetry, and other writings have been widely published and anthologized, including in every version of *Indian Country Today*. Selected for an Oklahoma Journalism Hall of Fame Lifetime Achievement Award (2024), she was also inducted into the National Native American Hall of Fame in the category Advocacy (2022).

The first Vine Deloria Jr. Distinguished Indigenous Scholar (Arizona, 2008), Harjo was the first to receive back-to-back residencies at the School of Advanced Research (2004 poetry fellow and summer scholar) and the first woman awarded the honorary doctorate of humanities (2011) from the Institute of American Indian Arts. The first Native woman Montgomery Fellow (Dartmouth, 1992), she was also the first Native woman elected to both of the two oldest learned societies in the United States: the American Academy of Arts and Sciences, 1780 (2020), and the American Philosophical Society, 1743 (2022).

Desirae Louise Hill

Desirae Louise Hill (she/her) is the co-founder and managing creative director at Three Track Mind—a design studio and consultancy supporting small businesses, and nonprofits doing purposeful work. She earned a BA in Business Administration with a concentration in marketing while also studying literature at Western Washington University. Hill holds a technical degree in Visual Communications and is a candidate for a MSM and MBA at the University of Illinois–Urbana Champaign.

Megan Minoka Hill

Megan Hill (First Generation Oneida Descendant) is the senior director of the Project on Indigenous Governance and Development and the director of the Honoring Nations program at the Harvard Kennedy School. The core mission of the project is to arm Indigenous people with the tools needed to (re)build their nations and govern effectively through research, teaching, leadership development, policy analysis, and pro bono advising for and with Native nations and communities. Its flagship program, Honoring Nations, is a national awards program that identifies, celebrates, and shares outstanding examples of tribal governance. Founded in 1998, the awards program spotlights tribal government programs and initiatives that are especially effective in addressing critical concerns and challenges facing the more than 570 Indian nations and their citizens.

Hill currently serves on the boards of the Native Governance Center and the Dr. Rosa Minoka Hill Fund. She is active within the Harvard community and is a member of the NAGPRA Advisory Committee for the Peabody Museum. Previously, she worked as Director of Development at both the University of New Mexico and Arizona State University and as a Senior Program Officer for the Institute of American Indian Arts. Megan graduated from the University of Chicago with a master of arts degree in the social sciences and earned a bachelor of arts in International Affairs and Economics from the University of Colorado, Boulder.

Norbert S. Hill Jr.

Norbert Hill, Oneida, is the former Area Director of Education and training for the Oneida Nation of Wisconsin. Hill's previous appointment was vice president of the College of Menominee Nation for the Green Bay campus. Hill served as the executive director of the American Indian Graduate Center (AIGC) in New Mexico, a nonprofit organization providing funding for American Indians and Alaska Natives to pursue graduate and professional degrees. Previous positions include executive director of the American Indian Science and Engineering Society, assistant dean of students at the University of Wisconsin–Green Bay, and director of the American Indian *Winds of Change* and *The American Indian Graduate*, magazine publications of the American Indian Science and Engineering Society (AISES) and the American Indian Graduate Center (AIGC), respectively. Hill holds an honorary doctorate from both Clarkson University (1996) and Cumberland College (1994). Past board appointments include Environmental Defense

Fund, chair and board member of the Smithsonian Museum of the American Indian, and the Wisconsin Historical Society. In 1989, Hill was awarded the Lifetime Achievement Award from the National Action Council for Minorities in Engineering.

Jennifer Hill-Kelley

Jennifer Hill-Kelley, Oneida, Kiowa, and Comanche, currently resides in Oneida, Wisconsin. Her Oneida name is Yothale, meaning "she speaks," and her Kiowa name is Gootah heen dahgn kah, meaning "main bird sound."

Hill-Kelley serves her community as the elected chair of the Oneida Trust and Enrollment Committee and serves on the board of directors for two Oneida Nation corporations. Previously, she has served as an Oneida Appellate Court Judge and on many other Oneida Nation committees, including the Oneida Nation Arts Board, the Oneida Youth Leadership Institute, Oneida Seven Generations Corporation, and the Utilities Commission. Her leadership is rooted in her experience with the Americans for Indian Opportunity Ambassadors Program, which is an indigenous values-based leadership program. She has also participated in Wisconsin Women in Government 2011, Leadership Green Bay 2010, and the Environmental Leadership Program Fellow 2000–2003.

Her broad professional experience includes working as a manager and consultant with tribal governments and tribal and nonprofit organizations. Her expertise is leading teams in pursuit of improving organizational alignment, improving institutional efficiencies, and delivering outcomes through restructuring, strategic planning, project management, systems thinking, data collection, and program evaluation. She has more than twenty years of experience as a program administrator and a grant writer for education, social service, and environmental programs, and for multi-year grant projects. She has also served as a policy and legislative analyst. She is a facilitator and trainer of a range of topics including supervision and leadership, program planning, program evaluation, and equity. Hill-Kelley holds a MS in Environmental Science and Policy from University of Wisconsin–Green Bay and a BS in microbiology from the University of Oklahoma.

Toni House

Toni House is Wolf Clan from the Oneida Nation. Her professional priorities have focused on Indigenous language learning and cultural preservation. This has taken her through various fields of work, such as midwifery, human services, continuous improvement consulting, homeschooling, and academia. She is currently a full professor for the Human Services Leadership Department at the University of Wisconsin–Oshkosh and does nonprofit work in the areas of Indigenous arts, seed saving, and agriculture. Her writing has been featured in *Tribal Administration Handbook* (Michigan State University Press, 2022), *Administrative Theory & Praxis* (Special Issue, 2022), the *Journal of American Indian Education* (2021), *Contemporary Justice Review: Issues in Criminal, Social, and Restorative Justice* (2012), *Human Services Today* (2010), and the *Journal of Humanistic Education and Development* (1995).

House believes the Indigenous way of life aligns perfectly with human services leadership. In relationship to her leadership, she has done a lot of learning, sharing, and promoting of Indigenous knowledge and its impact on the development of leadership principles and positive personal and community change. The principles of leadership according to the Oneida are those of peace of mind, peaceful actions, and power. Through her personal healing and professional growth, she has prioritized revitalizing Indigenous knowledge and leadership principles in a way that promotes positive change within her personal life, family, community, Indigenous Nations, and the University system.

Sadie Kelley

Sadie Kelley, Yewelahawi, She Brings the Wind in Oneida, comes from the people of the Oneida, Kiowa, Comanche, Muskogee Creek, Shoshone and Paiute Nations, Cherokee, and Absentee Shawnee.

A senior at Colorado Mesa University, studying political science and sports management, Kelley served as the head coordinator of the CMU Native American Student Association and was the co-captain of the CMU women's golf team. She also served on the Student Athlete Advisory Council as the women's golf team representative and vice chair. In these roles, Kelley provided leadership and was the social media coordinator for both the women's and men's golf teams. She has also been named to the Rocky Mountain Athletic Conference Academic Honor Roll.

Kelley's professional experience includes serving as Pro Shop Assistant at Thornberry Creek at Oneida Golf Course and in an LPGA tournament internship. She also worked as a student volunteer for the Tehatiw^nakhwa? Language Nest in the Oneida Head Start Language

Immersion program after completing six years of Oneida language classes. Kelley was a participant in the Native Americans in Philanthropy Native Youth Grantmakers program, an Indigenous values-based leadership program, to build networking skills and to advocate for tribal communities within the philanthropic sector. She also completed the University of Wisconsin–Madison Information Technology Academy, a three-year pre-college program focused on hands-on technology coursework, college preparatory academics, and personal wellness development. Kelley was recognized by the Wisconsin Indian Education Association as the High School Student of the Year in 2020. She enjoys traveling, golfing, concerts, sewing, and attending powwows and ceremonies.

Doug Kiel

Doug Kiel (PhD, University of Wisconsin–Madison, 2012) is a citizen of the Oneida Nation and studies Native American history, with particular interest in the Great Lakes region and twentieth-century Indigenous nation rebuilding. He is working on a book manuscript entitled *Unsettling Territory: Oneida Indian Resurgence and Anti-Sovereignty Backlash*. Prior to joining the Northwestern University faculty, he taught at Williams College, Columbia University, the University of Pennsylvania, and Middlebury College. He is the recipient of grants and fellowships from the Ford Foundation, the Woodrow Wilson National Fellowship Foundation, the Lyndon Baines Johnson Foundation, the American Philosophical Society, the Newberry Library, and the School for Advanced Research (SAR) in Santa Fe, New Mexico, among others. Beyond the university, Kiel has worked in several museums, testified as an expert witness regarding Indigenous land rights, and in 2008 was an Indigenous Fellow at the United Nations Office of the High Commissioner for Human Rights (OHCHR) in Geneva, Switzerland. He currently serves on the advisory committee for the renovation of the Field Museum's exhibition on Native North America.

Danielle Lucero

Danielle Lucero is a PhD candidate in the Justice and Social Inquiry program in the School of Social Transformation at Arizona State University. She holds an EdM from the Harvard University Graduate School of Education in Learning and Teaching and a BA in Anthropology and Ethnic Studies from Columbia University. Lucero is an enrolled member of the Pueblo of

Isleta located in central New Mexico as well as Chicana with connections to the northeastern New Mexican town of Santa Rosa. Lucero's research seeks to investigate the relationships between tribal enrollment, examine Pueblo women's experiences with reproductive and social labor, and explore the connections between identity, belonging, place, and tribal membership. Her research is prompted by questions and statements like "How many babies are born because of blood quantum rather than love?" and "I want an enrolled child, so I can't leave him." Her research utilizes critical Indigenous research methodologies, ethnography, and a reproductive justice framework.

Kadin Mills

Kadin Mills is a 2024 graduate of the Medill School of Journalism at Northwestern University. He is a first-generation descendant of the Keweenaw Bay Indian Community of Lake Superior Ojibwe. He is also of German and Irish descent. Mills worked closely with Dr. Patty Loew as a research assistant on the 2022 Tribal Youth Media Workshop, taking part in community building efforts in Indigenous communities across the country.

Mills has written for *The Daily Northwestern*, where he served as both Opinion editor and In Focus editor. He has also contributed to WBEZ's Curious City, reporting on local Indigenous history in Chicago. Mills is the recipient of a 2021 award from the Kaplan Institute for his unpublished writing on Indigenous resistance in northern Minnesota. He was also a 2022 Udall Scholar in Tribal Public Policy and a recipient of a 2022 Fletcher Award from the Northwestern University Office of Under-graduate Research for his work with Dr. Loew.

Daniel Ramirez

Born in 1953, Daniel Ramirez is a certified descendant of the Saginaw Chippewa Tribe of Michigan. His mother, a full-blood Saginaw Swan Creek Black River Chippewa, was born in 1917 and served as his lifelong inspiration. Drawing from her influence, Ramirez earned both his bachelor of fine arts and master of fine arts degrees from the University of Michigan Art School.

Over the past thirty years, he has built a thriving career in retail and art consulting, earning numerous awards at prestigious art competitions across the country. Renowned for his expertise in watercolors, acrylics, charcoal, and pastel drawings, Ramirez's works have been featured in the permanent collections of several museums. His art is also sold in over seventy art stores, museum gift shops, and galleries spanning from New York City to Los Angeles.

With a dedicated base of collectors who continue to support his work, Ramirez regularly exhibits at Native American art shows, national conferences, academic programs, trade shows, and prominent art fairs across the United States.

Artley M. Skenandore

Artley M. Skenandore is a member of the Turtle Clan, Oneida Nation, and a lifelong resident in Oneida, Wisconsin. His learning journey includes an undergraduate degree in education from St. Norbert College, De Pere, Wisconsin, and a master of science degree in administration from University of Wisconsin–Milwaukee. His most recent achievement is a doctorate in First Nation Studies from University of Wisconsin–Green Bay.

Skenandore's current professional role is Oneida Nation High School principal for the Oneida Nation School System. He has also served as an Oneida culture and language instructor, elementary vice principal, and principal. He has served the Oneida Nation in the professional capacity of Director of Economic Development and general manager. His experience journey has provided the opportunity to work with Tribal Nations across Turtle Island in nation-building projects in the areas of education, economic development, housing, and cultural revitalization. His dedication to the seventh generation of our Indigenous Nations is best served by encouraging everyone to make a personal commitment to have influence every day with good words and a good mind. Traditional roles and responsibilities as a citizen of the Oneida Nation are embedded in him as he raises his family with the guidance of our original knowledge, according to our ceremonial calendar, and within our clan families.

Skenandore offers his gratitude to the many citizens of the Oneida Nation who continue to learn the language and cultural ways that fortify and renew our identity and the future of the Oneida Nation. He offers heartfelt gratitude that his learning pathway across Turtle Island has provided the opportunity to encourage young students from Indigenous nations to make a positive contribution toward the future. He shares with you all his personal mission to have influence today for the seventh generation tomorrow, ensuring clean air, clean water, sovereign foods, and care for our families.

Amber Starks

Amber Starks (aka Melanin Mvskoke, she/her) is an Afro-Indigenous (African American and Native American) advocate, organizer, cultural critic, decolonial theorist, and budding abolitionist. She is an enrolled citizen of the Muscogee (Creek) Nation and is also of Shawnee, Yuchi, Quapaw, and Cherokee descent. Her passion is the intersection of Black and Native American identity. Her activism seeks to normalize, affirm, and uplift the multidimensional identities of Black and Native peoples through discourse and advocacy around anti-Blackness, abolishing blood quantum, Black liberation, and Indigenous sovereignty.

Starks hopes to encourage Black and Indigenous peoples to prioritize one another and divest from compartmentalizing struggles. She ultimately believes the partnerships between Black and Indigenous peoples (and all People of Color) will aid in the dismantling of anti-blackness, white supremacy, and settler colonialism globally. She earned a bachelor of science degree in general science (with an emphasis in biology and anthropology) from the University of Oregon.

Lois Stevens

Lois Stevens is a mother, teacher, researcher, geographer, and member of the Oneida Nation in Wisconsin. She is an assistant professor of First Nations Studies and the First Nations Education Doctoral Program at the University of Wisconsin–Green Bay. She received her PhD from the University of Kansas in geography. Growing up on the Oneida Reservation, she developed a deep appreciation for ancestral knowledge, community relationship, and an understanding of her impact on Mother Earth. As a researcher and geographer, her research interests involve the effects of environmental and climatic change on Indigenous food systems and Place-based adaptation within Indigenous communities. She is also invested in empowering Indigenous voices in academia by fostering a love for collaborative research and writing.

Jonathan Taylor

Jonathan Taylor is an economist with expertise in natural resources, gaming, and American Indian development. He provides counsel to Native nations in the United States and Canada consisting of public policy analysis, strategic advice, and economic research. He has offered expert testimony in litigation and public proceedings for a number of Native

American groups. Taylor has assessed the economic impacts of tribal enterprises (including casinos), assessed tribal tax regimes, assisted in tribal institutional reform, provided public policy analysis and negotiation support for resource development, valued nonmarket attributes of natural resources, helped to project population, and educated tribal executives. Taylor is president of the Taylor Policy Group, an economics and public policy consultancy; a research affiliate at the Harvard Project on Indigenous Governance and Development at the Kennedy School; and a program associate of the Native Nations Institute, Udall Center for Studies in Public Policy, University of Arizona, Tucson.

Burton W. Warrington

Kcheyonkote Burton W. Warrington—Menominee, Prairie Band Potawatomi, and Ho-Chunk—was raised on the Menominee Reservation and currently splits time between Wisconsin Rapids and the Menominee Reservation with his wife and four children. Professionally, he dedicates his time in service to a variety of local and national initiatives. In his home community, he serves as the president, executive director, and co-founder of Menomini yoU, Inc., a community-level 501(c)3 with the mission of revitalizing the Menominee language. Nationally, he splits time as the president of Indian Ave Group LLC—a collection of family-owned businesses—and co-director of Indigenous Peoples initiatives with a social impact organization.

Warrington's career has included a unique mix of legal, business, management, and policy experience. As an attorney, he has provided both legal and strategic advisory services to clients across the country. As the president and CEO of a large economic development company, he developed and managed economic holdings in both operating companies and private equity transactions. As a counselor to the Assistant Secretary of Indian Affairs, US Department of Interior, he was involved in a variety of national issues including Indian gaming, economic and energy development, fee-to-trust issues, and natural resource and cultural rights protection. He has also served in a variety of advisory roles across the country.

Warrington graduated from Menominee Indian High School, holds a bachelor of science in Business Administration—Tribal Management from Haskell Indian Nations University, and holds a Juris Doctor degree from the University of Kansas School of Law.

KanyΛhtakelu (Snow scattered here and there), Rebecca M. Webster

Rebecca M. Webster is an enrolled citizen of the Oneida Nation in Wisconsin. She is an assistant professor at the University of Minnesota Duluth in the American Indian Studies department. She teaches undergraduate and graduate courses in Tribal Administration and Governance programs. Prior to joining UMD, she served the Oneida Nation as an attorney for thirteen years. In addition to her academic interests, she grows heirloom traditional foods with her family on their ten-acre farmstead Ukwakhwa: Tsinu NiyukwayayΛthoslu (Our foods: Where we plant things) and with Ohe·láku (Among the Cornstalks), a co-op of Oneida families that grow Iroquois white corn together. She received her BA, MPA, and JD degrees from the University of Wisconsin–Madison and her PhD in Public Policy and Administration from Walden University.

YakoyΛtehtauhi (She is continually going along learning), Amelia M. Webster

Amelia Webster is an enrolled citizen of the Oneida Nation. She is currently a junior in high school studying at the College of Menominee Nation. She has a passion for research and writing, especially on topics related to her experiences. While she is still exploring career paths, she enjoys working with nature and animals. Amelia and her sister started a business as part of a homeschool project in 2019 that serves the Oneida community.

David E. Wilkins

David E. Wilkins is a citizen of the Lumbee Nation and is the E. Claiborne Robins Distinguished Professor of Leadership Studies at the University of Richmond. He is a professor emeritus at the University of Minnesota, where he held the McKnight Presidential Professorship in American Indian Studies. He earned his PhD in political science from the University of North Carolina–Chapel Hill in December 1990.

Wilkins is the author or editor of a number of books, including *Documents of Native American Political Development: 1933 to Present* (Oxford, 2019); *Red Prophet: The Punishing Intellectualism of Vine Deloria, Jr.* (Fulcrum, 2018); *Dismembered: Native Disenrollment and the Battle for Human Rights* with Shelly Hulse Wilkins (Fulcrum, 2017); *Hollow Justice:*

Indigenous Claims in the United States (Yale, 2013); *The Navajo Political Experience*, 4th ed. (Rowman & Littlefield, 2013); *The Hank Adams Reader* (University of Washington Press, 2011), and *The Legal Universe* with Vine Deloria Jr. (Fulcrum, 2011). His articles have appeared in a range of social science, political science, law, history, American Indian studies, and ethnic studies journals.

Index

—A—

Please note page numbers with *f* indicate figures; page numbers with *n* indicate endnotes.

Aakodewin, 165–166
Aanikoobijigan, 195–201
abbreviations, 225*n*14
abortions, 24
Abrams, George H. J., 44, 219*n*10
acronyms, 225*n*14
adoption, 31, 43–51, 50, 91, 126, 159, 163
Adoptive Couple v. Baby Girl, 212*n*12
Africa, 126
African Americans, 6, 16–17, 24, 50
Africans, 6, 22, 23, 45–46, 66, 219*n*12
Agard, Nadema, 84
Ajijaak, 166
Alaska, 75
Alaska Native corporations, 40
Alaska Natives, 67, 69, 70, 79–82, 225*n*14
Albers, Patricia C., 49
Alexander, Karen Lynn, 234*n*55
Allen, Kenzie, 55, 94
allotment: blood quantum and, 7, 16; as
    disastrous, xv; distribution of, 14;
    exploitation and, 191; factionalism
    and, 5; fee patent for, 34–35; land
    loss and, xvii, 177; M'Collock and,
    30; Osage and, 189–190; Saginaw
    Chippewa and, 161–162; Wheeler-
    Howard Act and, 37
American Community Survey, 78
American Indian: acronym for, 69, 225*n*14;
    census for, 70, 82; defined, 69;
    population of, 67, 71, 73, 77, 79; race,
    70, 73
American Indian nations, 151, 195, 238*n*5
American Rescue Plan Act (ARPA), 74
*Ance-Berry v. Grand Traverse Band of Ottawa
    and Chippewa Indians,* 163
ancestry: adoption and, 47, 49; blood
    and, 31; decoding, 126–127; for

membership, 123; mixed, 70; from
    multiple tribes, 115; population
    growth and, 77; Seneca and, 219*n*10
Ancestry.com, 66, 79
Anishinaabe Inaakonigewin Tribe,
    164–170
Anishinaabe Tribe: blood quantum rules
    for, 158–164; on citizenship, 164–170;
    history of, 231*n*2; introduction to,
    157–158; MCT and, 238*n*1; Michigan,
    157–173, 231*n*2; Mills on, 109–113;
    moving forward for, 170–173; Red
    Lake Nation of, 8; teachings of,
    234*n*55
anti-Black racism, 16, 123, 125–126
Antone, Robert, 181
Apalachee Tribe, 45
Apple Films, 191
Arapaho Tribe, 48–49, 248
Archibald, Jo-Ann, 150–151
Arikara Tribe, 48
Arizona, 81
Arkansas, 189
ARPA. *see* American Rescue Plan Act
    (ARPA)
artisan: defined, 87
Asians, 23
assimilation: by blood, 30–33; exploitation
    and, 191; as federal law, 33–34;
    identity and, 57
Assiniboine Tribe, 49
Australia, 21, 23
Australian Labor Party, 23
auto-colonization, 157–173
Automated Election Services, 9

—B—

Baby Girl, Adoptive Couple v., 212*n*12
Barrus, Tim, 85
Bay Mills Indian Community (BMIC),
    158–159, 171
Beaulieu, David, 200
Beaver Dance Ceremony, 50

Beckwourth, James P., 50
belonging: Anishinaabe Tribe and,
    158; blood quantum and, 123–130;
    citizenship and, 13, 17, 37, 158; food
    and, 131–138; identity and, 57; race
    and, 30; sovereignty and, 131–138
benefits: defined, 229n13
Bennett, Jessica, 237n24
Bent, William, 49
Bentley, M., 225n12
Benz, Charmaine M., 231n2
Berkhofer, Robert F., Jr., 212n14
"Better Day for Indians, A" (Deloria, Jr.), 8
Blacks, 6, 16–17, 25, 69, 70, 123–129
blood: assimilation by, 30–33; in blood
    quantum, 96; color of, 21–27;
    defined, 31; degree of Indian, 13–19,
    163–164; Nazis and, 25; purity of, 22;
    quantizing of, xviii; race and, 21–27,
    31; as racial, 90
blood quantum: as authenticity, 14; auto-
    colonization and, 157–173; belonging
    and, 123–130; BIA and, xviii;
    colonialism and, 14; community and,
    180; de-enrollment in, 210n1; defined,
    13, 57, 96; as degree of Indian blood,
    13–19; as divisive, 112; as economic
    tool, 6; eliminating, 10; factionalism
    and, 5; genetics vs., 126–127; of GTB,
    162–164, 169, 170; Indigenous Place
    and, 176, 177; in IRA, xviii–xix; Kaw,
    65; Michigan Anishinaabe and, 157–
    173; Nazi history and, 25; one-drop
    rule and, 17, 19; Oneida and, 183–186;
    Osage and, 193; as racial term, 211n9;
    reconfiguring, 6; for Red Lake, 8;
    reliance on, 7; reproductive choices
    and, 96–99; sexual relations and, 103;
    significance of, 5–6; solutions to, 7;
    white supremacy and, 26
blood quantum fiction, 29–40
blood quantum laws, 26, 30, 37–39, 211n8
blood quantum policies, 19, 25–27, 97, 120
blood quantum requirements, 112, 118–120,
    127, 145, 157, 158, 162–163, 168, 170,
    195, 218n2
blood quantum rules, 5, 47, 77, 158–164,
    173
blood symbolism, 31
BMIC. see Bay Mills Indian Community
    (BMIC)
boarding school era, 141, 143
boarding schools, xvii, 4–5, 13, 112, 191

Bois Forte Tribe, 238n1
Brackeen v. Haaland, 212n12
Bridges, Marena, 123
Bulltail, Grant, 49, 50, 222n36
Bureau of Indian Affairs (BIA): blood
    quantum in, xviii, 5, 33, 38; Cheyenne
    and, 47; GTB and, 162–163; IRA and,
    161; MCT and, 200; Osage and, 190,
    192; reproductive choices and, 99;
    Saginaw Chippewa and, 161
Bureau of Indian Affairs (BIA) Pawnee
    Agency, 65
Bush, George W., 193

—C—

Cajete, Gregory, 175, 178–179
California, 6, 76, 131
call-in: defined, 237n24
Campbell, Janis E., 210n2
Canada, 26, 98, 169, 196
Canadian First Nations, 163, 169
Canadian Haudenosaunee First Nation, 169
capitalism, 7, 16–17, 19, 40
Carter, Asa Earl, 84
Carter, Forrest, 84
Case, Martin, 3, 4
Catawba Tribe, 45
Cayuga Nation, 133
Census Bureau, 65, 66, 68–70, 73, 76–82,
    225n12
census Indian populations, 69, 72f5, 75f6,
    77f8
census race question, 71f4
ceremonies, 3, 48, 50, 99, 152f13
Certificate of Degree of Indian Blood
    (CDIB), 110
Chapman, Oscar, 200–201
Cherokee Nation, 32, 39, 45, 49, 84–85
Cheyenne Adoption Pipe Ceremony, 48
Cheyenne River Sioux Tribe, 81
Cheyenne Tribe, 47–49
Chickasaw Tribe, 45
Child, Brenda, 196
Chippewa Tribe, 30, 36, 40, 49, 109, 160,
    196
Choctaw Tribe, 45
Cholewka v. Grand Traverse Band of Ottawa
    and Chippewa Indians Tribal Council,
    163
Christianity, 5, 7
Christjohn, Louisa, 134
Christjohn, Moses, 134
Chukchansi Tribe, 6, 210n8

Churchill, Ward, 84
citizenship: Anishinaabe, 164–170, 173;
   belonging and, 13, 17, 37, 158; blood
   quantum for, 38, 77, 180, 238n5;
   Cherokee, 32; children and, 115;
   colonization and, 200; descent vs.,
   xviii; exclusion from, 39; GTB,
   164; identity and, 70; of Indian
   populations, 72f5, 73, 75n6; Jews
   and, 24; Native nations determining,
   79; Osage Allotment Act for, 193;
   policies for, 10; quantum vs., xviii;
   South Africans and, 25
citizenship criteria, 30, 83, 120
citizenship decisions, 83
citizenship policies, 67, 120
citizenship requirements, 195–201
citizenship rules, 39
citizenship standards, 91
civil rights, 6, 10
Civil War, 32
clan mothers, 134
clan structure, 43
Class III gaming, 184
Cleland, Charles E., 231n2
Clifton, James A., 231n2
climate crisis, 4
Cody, Iron Eyes, 84
Collier, John, xvii, 37, 38
colonialism: Blacks and, 16, 129; blood
   quantum and, 17–19, 112, 119,
   171; Case and, 3; Deloria, Jr. and,
   xv; effects of, 3; eliminating, 27;
   expanding, 27; IRA and, xv, xvii;
   legacy of, 22; Lytle and, xv; racial
   purity laws and, 22; sex and, 104;
   shifting of, xvi
colonial rule, 83
colonization: belonging and, 57; blood
   quantum and, 199; citizenship and,
   200; identity and, 57, 113, 176; legacy
   of, 195; race and, 31
community: defined, 237n17; eligibility
   and, 120; identity and, 8, 57, 98, 123;
   Indigenous Place in, 175–181
community membership, 129
Compton, E., 225n12
Congress: Anishinaabe Tribe and, 157;
   blood metric in, 38; Burke Act in, 34;
   Census Bureau and, 79; colonialism
   in, xvi; constitutions and, 160;
   Eastern Oklahoma Tribal allottees
   and, 34; exercising oversight, 90;

General Allotment Act in, 33; IACA
   and, 87, 89; Native identity in,
   90; Northern Ute and, 33; Osage
   Allotment Act in, 189; Osage and,
   191, 192; Pamunkey and, 33; passing
   IRA, 37; passing 25 U.S.C. 163, 36;
   Saginaw Chippewa and, 161; self-
   determination in, 157; Stigler Act
   in, 39
Conoy Tribe, 45
consultants: hiring, 9
Converse, Harriet Maxwell, 46
Corey, Cathy, 210n8
corn, 131–138
Corpus, Chris, 86
Coushatta Tribe, 45
Creating Stronger Nations, Inc., 9
Creek Tribe, 45
Crow Nation, 49–50, 99
Crow Reservation, 49
Crow Tobacco Society, 50
cultural knowledge, 123, 128
cultures: as birthright, 18; eradication of, 129
Curtis, Annie E., 65
Curtis, Charles, 65–66, 65f1, 66f2, 68, 80
Custer Died for Your Sins (Deloria, Jr.), 6

—D—

Dakota Tribe, 44, 48
Danforth, John, 181
Darwin, Charles, 22–23
Darwinism, 21–25, 27
Dawes Act, 16, 29, 34, 177, 179, 189
Debwewin, 165, 166, 171
Decolonizing Methodologies (Smith), 154
degree of Indian blood (DIB), 13–19,
   163–164
Delaware Tribe, 30
Deloria, Ella, 7, 8, 44
Deloria, Vine, Jr., xv, 6, 8–10, 29, 31, 178,
   196, 210n1, 212n14
DeMallie, Raymond, 44
Department of Housing and Urban
   Development (HUD), 73–74, 75f6
descendancy dynamics, 67, 68f3, 76, 77, 79
descent: quantum vs., xviii
Dibaadendizowin, 165, 166
Dietz, William, 85
discrimination, 24, 25, 27
disenrollments, 33, 160, 161–163, 210n8
Dismembered: Native Disenrollment and the
   Battle for Human Rights (Wilkins and
   Wilkins), 43

DNA analysis, 66, 126
DNA testing, 6, 7, 57, 126
Doerfler, Jill, xviii, 31, 195
doodem, 166
Dunbar-Ortiz, Roxanne, 84
Durant, Horace, 171
Durant Roll, 170, 171
Durham, Jimmie, 84

—E—

Eagle Seelatsee, Simmons v., 216n89
Eastern Band Cherokee, 84
Edmo, Se-ah-dom, 104
education: of American Indians, 151;
    blood quantum and, 7; factionalism
    and, 5; identity and, 115; Indigenous
    knowledge in, 178; Oneida Nation
    and, 149
1836 Treaty of Washington, 171
1828 Carey Mission Treaty, 107
emancipation, 6
England, xvi
Ennis, S., 225n12
enrollment: of Anishinaabe, 164, 196;
    blood quantum and, xix, 8, 9, 15, 19,
    35, 38, 43, 96–99, 119, 145, 157, 158,
    176, 181; Class III gaming and, 184;
    Collier and, 38; Congress and, 36;
    of Curtis, 66; as fluid, 51; of GTB,
    161–164, 168–170; identity and, 6,
    96, 115, 118, 119, 120; of MCT, 195,
    200, 201; of NHBP, 171; of Osage,
    192; of Pamunkey, 33; of past, 51;
    reproductive choices and, 96–99;
    in reproductive justice, 95–105;
    reproductive justice and, 101–104;
    of Saginaw Chippewa, 161; shadow
    systems on, 99–101; switching, 116; in
    United States, 37, 115
enrollment councils, 35, 36
enrollment criteria, 163, 185–186
enrollment laws, 30
enrollment policies, 7
enrollment process, 120, 177, 180
Enätesen, 143
Eschbach, Karl, 65
ethnocide: defined, 218n2
ethnology, 31
eugenics, 15, 21, 22, 24–27, 25, 31, 34
euthanasia, 24
exogamy: centuries of, 68; defined, 67;
    descendancy dynamics and, 68f3, 79;

distribution of, 78f9; evidence of,
    77–78; intermarriage *vs.,* 224n5
exogamy laws, 98

—F—

factionalism, 5
Falmouth Institute, 9
family: identity and, 57, 143–146, 149, 150
family identity, 143–145
federally recognized tribe, xvii, 158, 159,
    167
Federal Trade Commission (FTC), 88
Fenton, William N., 44, 46
Fifteenth Amendment, 6
First Nations, 26
Five Nations, 45
Flandreau Indian School, 111
Fletcher, Matthew L. M., 43, 157, 231n2
Fond du Lac Chippewa Tribe, 80, 238n1
food, 131–138
Fourteenth Amendment, 6
French and Indian War, 46
full bloods, xix, 8, 14, 31, 33, 44, 96, 171

—G—

Galanda, Gabriel S., 29
gaming, 6, 33, 91, 170, 184, 186
Gardeau Reservation, 44
Garroutte, Eva, 199
gender roles, 102
genealogy: descendancy dynamics and, 79;
    eugenics, 31
General Allotment Act, 177
General Tribal Council (GTC), 137
genetics, 126–127, 145
genocide, 13–15, 17–18, 24, 137, 143
geography, 175–178
Germany, 21, 24
Gish Hill, Christina, 47–48
global warming, 7
God Is Red (Deloria, Jr.), 29
Goodman, Effie, 85
Grand Portage Reservation, 238n1
*Grand Traverse Band of Ottawa and Chippewa
    Indians, Ance-Berry v.,* 163
Grand Traverse Band of Ottawa and
    Chippewa Indians (GTB), 158–159,
    161–164, 168–171
*Grand Traverse Band of Ottawa and Chippewa
    Indians Tribal Council, Cholewka v.,* 163
*Grand Traverse Band of Ottawa and Chippewa
    Indians v. Office of the United States*

Attorney for the Western District of Michigan, 231*n*3
Grann, David, 191
Gray, Jim, 189
Graymont, Barbara, 220*n*13
Great Depression, 47, 198
Great Law of Peace, 134
Great Vanishing Act, The (Doerfler), 39, 195
Greece, 175
Green, Rayna, 85
Grint, Keith, 7
Gros Ventre Tribe, 50
Gun Lake Tribe, 159
Gwekowaadiziwin, 165, 166

—H—

Haaland, Brackeen v., 212*n*12
half blood, 5, 37, 47, 171, 190
Half-King (Chief), 46
Hannahville Indian Community, 158, 159
Harjo, Joy, 203
Harjo, Suzan Shown, 83, 218*n*2
Hart, J. C., 65
Haskell Indian Nations University, 175
Haudenosaunee Confederacy, 116
Haudenosaunee Tribe, 44, 47, 137, 149, 151, 152*f*13, 153, 181, 221*n*18
Hauptman, Laurence M., 43, 221*n*19
Heron, George, 221*n*19
heteronormativity, 104
Hidatsa Tribe, 48
Highwater, Jamake Mamake, 85
Hill, Norbert, xix
Hill-Kelley, Jennifer, 115, 116–118
Hispanic American Indians, 67, 72, 73, 76
Hispanic Indian, 72–74, 76, 225*n*14
Hispanic multi-race Indian, 225*n*14
Hispanics, 72, 73, 76
history: of American Indian education, 151; identity and, 141–142; oral, 143
Hitchiti Tribe, 45
Hitler's American Model (Whitman), 24
holism, 150
Holocaust, 24
Hoover, Herbert, 66
House, Toni, 131
"How to Be a Real Indian" (Allen), 53–55
human rights, 6, 10, 22, 23, 25, 26, 101

—I—

identity: assimilation and, 58; of Blacks, 16–17; blood quantum and, 5, 6, 14, 18, 96, 98, 126–127; census race

and, 69; in community, 237*n*17; defined, 43, 57–58; Deloria, Jr. and, 8; enrollment and, 6, 96, 115, 118, 119, 120; false, 88 (*see also* pretendians; Pseudo-Indians); family, 143–145; as inclusive, 123; Indigenous, **57**, 68–72, 128, 129; individual, 143–145; language and, 117; membership and, 128; multiracial Indigenous, 123–127; multi-tribal Native, 115–120; Nuremberg Laws and, 27; of Oneida, 149, 150; place and, 179; questions, 90; racial classification of, 69; racism and, 16; in reproductive justice, 96; social, 143–145; time and, 141–146
identity negation, 125–126
Immigration Restriction Act of 1901, 23
immigration restrictions, 24
inclusion, 50
inclusivity, 129
in-community: defined, 237*n*17
Indian: defined, xv, xviii, 37, 39, 69, 83, 87, 212*n*14; multi-race, 74–81, 78–79, 225*n*14; number in US, 66
Indiana, 168
Indian Arts and Crafts Act (IACA), 87–88, 89
Indian Child Welfare Act (ICWA), 91
Indian Health Service, 26, 229*n*13
Indian Housing Block Grant Program (IHBG), 73–74
Indian population: census Indians and tribal citizens in, 73–74; evidence of exogamy in, 77–78; growth in, 74–77; implications for Native Nations in, 78–82; introduction to, 65–68; low point of, 67; in 1950, 68; seven decades of census Indians in, 68–73
Indian Reorganization Act (IRA): blood in, xv; blood quantum and, xix, 29, 37–39, 145; Cheyenne and, 47; constitutions and, 160; Crow and, 49; federally recognized tribes and, 158; GTB and, 162; identity and, 141; MCT and, 238*n*1; membership in, xvii; organization of, xv; parts of, xv; passage of, 141; Pseudo-Indian Act and, 89; Saginaw Chippewa and, 161
Indigenous: defined, 212*n*14, 228*n*3
Indigenous identity, 57–63, 68–73, 128, 129
Indigenous Place, 175–181
Indigenous Storywork (Archibald), 150
individual identity, 143–145

inequality, 22
inheritance: shadow systems on, 99–101
In re Menefee, 163, 168–169
intermarriage, 24, 43, 46, 49, 78, 97, 126,
    224n5
Inuit, 26
Iroquois Confederacy, 44, 45, 46, 47
Isleta Pueblo, 95

—J—
J. Dalton Institute, 9
Jefferson, Thomas, 17
Jemison, Mary, 44, 46, 219n10
Jennings, Francis, 44
Jews, 24
Jim Crow legislation, 6, 23–24, 27
Johnson, Jay T., 178
Johnston, Basil, 157, 196, 201
Jones, Dennis, 197
Jones, Johnpaul, 181
Judeo-Christian history, 4

—K—
Kaehkānawapahtam, 143
Kaliwiyo, 153
Kanehatunksla, 153
Kanehelatuksla, 151–152
Kansas, 65, 66f2, 189
Kaw Census, 65f1
Kaw Indians, 65, 66, 80, 189
Kayeniyoliwake, 153
Kayenlakowa, 153
Kayēs Mamāceqtawak, 142
Kelley, Sadie, 115, 118–120
Kenjockety, 46
Keweenaw Bay Indian Community
    (KBIC), 107, 113, 158–160
Kiel, Doug, 21
Killers of the Flower Moon (Grann), 191
Killsback, Leo K., 48
Kimball, Yeffe, 85
kinship: belonging and, 30, 40; blood
    quantum and, 14, 18, 33–37, 40, 98;
    Case on, 4; in Cheyenne, 48, 49;
    in Dakota, 44; defined, 4; identity
    and, 43, 57; Indigenous, 33–37, 39;
    in Lakota, 44; membership and, 51;
    property and, 4, 6–7
kinship systems/societies, 3, 29, 31, 40
Kiowa Gourd Clan, 117
Kiowa Tribe, 48
knowledge: for Anishinaabe, 165; in
    learning, 151, 154, 155; for Oneida, 149

knowledge sources, 152f13
Krakoff, Sarah, 211n9

—L—
Lac Vieux Desert Band of Lake Superior
    Chippewa Indians, 158–159
Lake Superior Ojibwe, 107
Lakota Tribe, 44, 48
land: Pueblo, 99
language: in community, 237n17; identity
    and, 43, 117, 143–146; in Immigration
    Restriction Act, 23; knowing and,
    153; speaking original, 152
Larsen, Soren, 178
learning: to be, 150–152, 154; defined, 151;
    to do, 151, 154–155; identity and, 149,
    150; to learn, 151, 152, 153–154
Leech Lake Reservation, 238n1
Letchworth State Park, 44
Lightfeather, Melody, 85
Limerick, Patricia Nelson, 211n4
lineal descent, 96
Littlefeather, Sacheen, 85
Little River Band of Ottawa Indians (LRB),
    159, 160, 171
Little Traverse Bay Bands of Odawa
    Indians (LTBB), 159–160, 171
Locke, John, 4
Loew, Patty, 112, 113
Lomawaima, T. S., 151
LOTNI, 1, 139
LRB. *see* Little River Band of Ottawa
    Indians (LRB)
LTBB. *see* Little Traverse Bay Bands of
    Odawa Indians (LTBB)
Lucero, Danielle, 95
Lyons, Oren, 116
Lyons, Scott, 199
Lytle, Clifford, xv

—M—
Maang, 166
Mahnomen Public School, 197
"Making Ourselves Whole with Words"
    (Doerfler), xviii
Manaadjitiwaawin, 165–166
Mandan Tribe, 48
Marks, Peter, 169
marriage, 32, 78, 98
marry out, get out policies, 98
Massachusetts, 45
Match-E-Be-Nash-She-Wish Band of
    Pottawatomi Indians, 159

matrilineal descent, 123, 128
McCarty, T. L., 151
McClurken, James M., 231*n*2
McGillivray, Alexander, 220*n*15
McGirt v. Oklahoma, xix
M'Collock, William, 30
Mein Kampf (Hitler), 25
membership: for Africans, 219*n*12; blood lines for, 43; blood quantum for, xviii, 83, 97, 123; Cheyenne, 47–48; for children, 97; community, 129; Creek, 46; Crow, 49; defined, xvii; Deloria, Jr. views on, 8–9; incorporating, 51; Interior Secretary and, 37; intermarriage and, 97; LRB, 160; marry out, get out policies and, 98; new, 3; for newborns, 38; Northern Ute, 33; Oneida, 127; Osage, 193; Pueblo, 100; Red Lake, 8; rewriting rules for, 129; self-determination and, 97; shadow systems and, 100; sovereignty and, 97
membership criteria/requirements, 103, 123, 128, 161, 162, 163
membership laws/policies/rules, 38, 43, 97, 98, 104, 162
membership rolls, 189
membership threshold, 83
men: adopted by Cheyenne, 49; adopted by Crow, 50; clan structure for, 43; enrollment and, 98–99
Menefee, In re, 163, 168–169
Menominee Tribe, 142, 146
Menomini yoU, Inc., 146
Métis Tribe, 26
Michigan, 107
Michigan Anishinaabe Tribe, 157–173, 231*n*2
Migizi, 166
Mille Lacs Tribe, 238*n*1
Mills, Kadin, 107
Mineral Estate, 189, 191, 193
Minnesota, 8, 40, 238*n*1
Minnesota Chippewa Tribe (MCT), 196, 200–201, 238*n*1
Mino-Bimaadiziwin, 158, 164, 165, 167, 168, 170, 171, 173
minorities, 21, 24, 25, 72–73
Mishiiki, 166
mixed bloods, 31–34
mixed race, 5, 69, 71, 76, 123, 126
Mohawk Council of Kahnawake, 98
Moniac, David, 220*n*15

Montana, 37
Moore, John H., 47, 210*n*2
motherhood, 102
muilticultural Indigenous nations, 44–46
Mukwa, 166
multi-race Indian, 74–81, 78–79, 225*n*14
multi-tribal Native identity, 115–120
Munsee Tribe, 45
Muscogee (Creek) Tribe, 45

—N—

Nagle, Rebecca, 62
Nanticoke Tribe, 45
Nasdijj (writer), 85
Natchez Tribe, 45
National Congress of American Indians, 89
nationalism, 22
Native: defined, 228*n*3
Native American and Indigenous Studies Association, 62
Native American Housing Assistance and Self-Determination Act (NAHASDA), 74
Nazis, 24, 25, 27
Nebraska, 199
Nevada, 119
New Deal legislation, xvii
New Mexico, 96, 100, 101, 227*n*1
New York, 46, 126, 133
New York Times, 66
Nibwaakaawin, 165
Nietschmann, Bernard O., 176
1930 Census, 66
Nizhwaaswi Mishomis/Nokomis Kinoomaagewinaawaan, 158, 164, 165, 166, 167, 170, 171, 172
Nēmat, 145–146
nobility: defined, 31
non-Hispanic American Indians, 67, 73, 77, 80
Northern Cheyenne Tribe, 44, 47, 49, 221*n*24
Northern Ute Tribe, 33
Northrup, Jim, 171
Northwestern University, 110
Nottawaseppi Huron Band of the Potawatomi, Wright v., 171
Nottawaseppi Huron Band of the Potawatomi (NHBP), 159, 171
Nuremberg Laws of 1935, 24, 27

—O—

Obama, Barack, 50

ogemaag, 158, 166
Oglala Lakota Tribe, 80
Ohkay Owingeh Tribe, 69
Ojibwe People's Dictionary, 198
Ojibwe Tribe, 107, 196
Oklahoma, 116, 118, 119, 189
Oklahoma, McGirt v., xix
Omāēqnomenēw Ahkēw, 142
Omāēqnomenēweqnesen, 142
one-drop rule, xviii, 6, 16–19
Oneida Nation, xix, 47, 60, 116–120, 123–
    129, 132, 134, 149–151, 183–186
Oneida National School System, 128
Oneida Nation Elementary School, 123, 149
Oneida Nation Trust Enrollment
    Department, 183
Oneida Reservation, 131
Oneida Trust and Enrollment Committee,
    xix
oral history, 143
Osage Allotment Act, 189, 193
Osage Constitution, 189
Osage Headright, 189
Osage Nation, 189–194
outmarriage, xviii, 8

—P—
Pacific Islanders, 23
Pacific Island Labourers Act, 23
Paiute Sun Dance, 117
Pamunkey Black Law, 32
Pamunkey Indian Tribe, 32–33
Parker, Alan, 39, 97
Parker, Arthur C., 46
Parker, Ely S., 46
patriarchy, 102
Piegan Tribe, 49
place: being of a, 177–178; as community,
    178–179; connection to, 181; identity
    through, 43
Plains Indians, 49–50
Plecker, Walter, 17
Pokagon, Leopold, 168, 169
Pokagon Band of Potawatomi Indians,
    159, 168
Ponca Tribe, 189
population control, 21
Potawatomie Tribe, 30
Poupart, Lisa, 30
power: of racial purity laws, 21–27
powwows, 117
pretendians, 57–63
privilege, 97, 108, 179, 180, 237n17

Proclamation Line of 1763, xvi
property: blood quantum and, 5; Case on,
    4; kinship and, 4, 6–7; privatization
    of, 4; value of, 6
property relationship, 4
property rights, 9, 100
Pseudo-Indian Act, 89–90
Pseudo-Indians, 84–90
Pueblo: defined, 227n1
Pueblo Tribe, 69, 95–96, 99–102

—Q—
quantum: descent *vs.,* xviii
Quebec Superior Court, 98
Quinault Indian Nation, 40

—R—
race: belonging and, 30; in blood quantum,
    96; in census, 70, 71f4, 74–76,
    78–79, 78f9, 81; colonization and, 31;
    defined, 31; Indigeneity and, 127; in
    Indigenous societies, 31; mixed, 5, 69,
    71, 76, 123, 126; power and, 21–27;
    racial purity laws and, 21–27
racial capitalism, 17
racial characteristics, 31
racial hierarchies, 22, 25, 27, 125, 177
Racial Integrity Act, 17
racial purity, 127
racial purity laws, 21–27
racism, 16, 19, 21, 22, 27, 31, 32, 40, 123,
    125–126
Rastogi, S., 225n12
Ratteree, Kathleen, xix, 59
Red Lake Nation of Anishinaabe, 8
Relentless Business of Treaties (Case), 3
religion, 5, 144, 237n17
removal, 7, 13, 57, 179, 189
Reproduction on the Reservation (Theobald),
    99
reproductive choices, 96–101
reproductive decisions/matters, 102–105
reproductive justice, 95–105
reproductive nation building, 96, 104–105
reproductive politics, 105
residency requirement, 43, 161
Resistance at Standing Rock, 141
Returned & Services League, 23
Revolutionary War, 137
Rhoades, Bernadine, 117
Richter, Daniel, 47, 220n13, 221n22
rights: blood quantum and, 43; civil, 6, 10;
    deprivation of, 9, 21; human, 6, 10,

22, 23, 25, 26, 101; intermarriage and, 43; property, 9, 100; of tribal citizens, 91; voting, 25; women's, 26
Roan, Henry, 190
Rodriguez-Lonebear, Desi, 238n5
Romero, Joanelle, 86
Roosevelt, Theodore, 189
Rose, Ed, 50
Rose, Princess Pale Moon, 85
Rusco, Elmer, 38

—S—

Saginaw Chippewa Indian Tribe, 158, 160–162, 164
Santa Clara Pueblo, 83
Saponi Tribe, 45
Sault Ste. Marie Tribe of Chippewa Indians, 159, 171
Schmidt, Ryan W., 210n2
Scorsese, Martin, 191
Sealaska Corporation, 40
segmentation, 5
segregation, 24–25
self-determination, 13, 15, 62, 97, 101, 105, 145, 151, 154, 157, 170, 235n73
self-government, 80
self-identification, 57, 69, 80, 81, 96
Seneca Nation, 30, 44, 46–47, 48, 219n10, 221n19
shadow systems, 97–98, 99–101
Shawnee Tribe, 30, 45
Shipp, Scott, 200
Silas, Pam, 110
Silverman, David, 219n12
Simmons v. Eagle Seelatsee, 216n89
Simpson, Leanne, 151, 196
Skenandoa(h), (Chief), 47
Skenandore, Artley M., 149
slave trade, 22
Smith, Andrea, 85
Smith, Linda Tuhiwai, 154
Smith, Paul Chaat, 117
Snipp, C. Matthew, 210n2, 211nn4,8
social control, 21–22
social experimentation, 4
social identity, 143–145
social media, 59, 60, 62, 63, 86, 119, 180
South Africa, 21, 25, 27
South Dakota, 80, 111
Sovereign Educational Framework, 150f12
sovereignty: belonging and, 131–138; blood quantum and, 13, 15, 18, 19, 30, 112, 181; blood quantum fiction and, 30;

British rule and, 23; Census Bureau and, 78; educational, 151; enrollment and, 120; food and, 131–138; IACA and, 87; IRA and, xvii; membership and, 97; personal, 196; pre-existing, 228n3; reproductive decisions and, 96–97, 104–105; rights and, 9–10; strengthening, 177
Spain, 22, 177
Spanish Empire, 100
Speaking of Indians (Deloria), 44
Spotted Eagle, Chris, 86
Spruhan, Paul, 32, 37, 214n43
St. Croix Chippewa Tribe, 40
Standing Rock Sioux, 84
Stark, Kekek, 165
Starks, Amber, 13
Starna, William A., 221n22
Steeves, Paulette, 212n14
sterilizations, 24, 26
Stevens, Lois, 175
Stigler, Act, 39
Stockbridge-Munsee Mohican Tribe, 45, 219n12
Storm, Arthur Charles, 85
Storm, Hyemeyohsts, 85
sui-colonialism, 38, 40
Sullivan Campaign, 137
Sustain Oneida project, 183, 185–186

—T—

TallBear, Kim, 31, 96, 210n2
Taylor, Jonathan, 65
Taylor Policy Group, 186
Teillet, Jean, 58
Tennessee, 75
Tewa Tribe, 69
Theobald, Brianna, 99
Thirteenth Amendment, 6
time: identity and, 141–146
Tonawanda Seneca Nation, 46
treaties: blood quantum and, 5, 30–33; Case examines, 3; colonialism and, 3; gaming and, 91; in Michigan, 158; nineteenth-century, 29; with United States, 158
Treaty with the Syandot, Seneca, Delaware, Shawnee, Potawatomie, Ottawa, and Chippewa Tribes of 1817, 30
Treuer, Anton, 196
tribal nations: number of US, 43
tribal policy making: census Indians and

tribal citizens in, 73–74; evidence of
exogamy in, 77–78; growth in, 74–77;
implications for Native Nations in,
78–82; introduction to, 65–68; seven
decades of census Indians in, 68–73
Truteau, Jean-Baptiste, 48
Tuscarora Tribe, 45, 220n13
Tutelo Tribe, 45
2020 Census: census Indians and tribal
citizens in, 73–74; evidence of
exogamy in, 77–78; growth in, 74–77;
implications for Native Nations in,
78–82; introduction to, 65–68; seven
decades of census Indians in, 68–73

—U—
United Keetoowah Band of Cherokee
Indians, 84
United States: American Indian nations in,
238n5; Anishinaabe in, 157, 159, 196;
blood quantum in, 29, 30–33, 39, 43,
183; Canadian blood quantum and,
169; citizenship in, 79; Darwinism
in, 23; enrollment in, 96, 115;
eugenics in, 24, 26; founding of, 141;
geography in, 177; growth in, 4; GTB
in, 162; health coverage in, 7; Indian
population in, 68; IRA in, xvi–xvii;
Jim Crow laws in, 24; marry out, get
out policies in, 98; Ojibwe in, 196;
Osage in, 191; political statuses in, 97;
property system in, 4; racial purity
laws in, 21; removal in, 168; Saginaw
Chippewa in, 161; sterilizations in,
26; treaties with, 158
United States Census, 66f2
University of Arizona Native Nations
Institute, 104
University of Minnesota Duluth, 59
US Civil War, 6
US Constitution, 6
US Supreme Court, 83, 91
US Treasury, 74, 75f6

—V—
Virginia, 32
voting rights, 25
Vukelich Kaagegaabaw, James, 197

—W—
Waabizheshi, 166
Waawaashkesh, 166
Wallace, Anthony F. C., 47

Warren, Elizabeth, 66, 80
Warrington, Kcheyonkote Burton W.,
241, 257
Warwick University, 7
Washington, George, 137
Watkins, Ralph, 221n22
Webster, Amelia M., 57, 61–62
Webster, Rebecca M., 57, 59–61
West Point, 220n15
Wheeler, Burton, 37
Wheeler-Howard Act, 37. see also Indian
Reorganization Act (IRA)
White, Kevin, 221n18
White, Randy Lee, 86
White Australia policy, 23, 27
White Earth constitution, xviii
White Earth Reservation, 197, 238n1
Whitehorse, Randy, 86
White Mountain Apache Tribe, 80–81
whites, 24, 25, 58, 69, 70, 72, 235n73
white supremacy, 16, 17, 26, 256
Whitman, James Q., 24
Wildcat, Daniel, 175, 178
Wilkins, David E., 3, 32, 43–44, 196, 210n8,
214nn43,44, 216n89, 218n2
Wilkins, Shelly Hulse, 43–44, 210n8,
214nn43,44, 216n89, 218n2
Wisconsin, 80, 116, 117, 126, 131
women: adopted by Cheyenne, 49; adopted
by Crow, 50; clan structure for,
43; enrollment and, 98–99; food
and, 133–134; Osage, 191; Pueblo,
95, 96, 100, 101–102; reproductive
empowerment of, 101; reproductive
matters for, 104; rights of, 26;
sovereignty and, 105; sterilizations
of, 26
World War II, 25
Wright v. Nottawaseppi Huron Band of the
Potawatomi, 171
WWI, 198
Wyandot Tribe, 30
Wyoming, 75

—Y—
Yankton Tribe, 49
Yount Man Afraid of His Horses, (Lakota
warrior), 49
Yuchi Tribe, 45
Yukwatsistay^, 154, 155

—Z—
Zaagidwin, 165